And What Do YOU Mean by Learning?

Seymour B. Sarason

Heinemann
Portsmouth, NH

Heinemann

361 Hanover Street
Portsmouth, NH 03801–3912
www.heinemann.com

Offices and agents throughout the world

Library of Congress Cataloging-in-Publication Data

Sarason, Seymour Bernard, 1919–
   And what do you mean by learning? / Seymour B. Sarason
      p. cm.
Includes bibliographical references.
  ISBN 0-325-00639-3 (alk. paper)
1. Learning. 2. Educational change—United States. I. Title.
  LB1060.S27 2004
  370.15'23—dc22   2003021258

Editor: Lois Bridges
Production editor: Sonja S. Chapman
Cover design: Night & Day Design
Author photo: Zach Fried
Typesetter: Valerie Levy/Drawing Board Studios
Manufacturing: Steve Bernier

Printed in the United States of America on acid-free paper
T & C Digital

To Nathaniel Feuerstein

with his grandfather's love.

Contents

Preface

This book is centered around two assertions. The first is that the word or concept of learning is not only lacking in substance but also has the characteristics of an inkblot; in addition, the relationship of those characteristics to actions is illogical, confusing, and self-defeating. The second assertion is that unless and until research provides a credible basis for distinguishing between contexts of productive and unproductive learning in the classroom, educational reform will be fruitless. I know that together the two assertions will elicit surprise in some people, disbelief in others, if only because people unreflectively assume that what they mean by learning is obviously clear, right, natural, and proper, and not in need of scrutiny. I do not claim to have done justice to either assertion but I do claim that there is evidence that both assertions cannot and must not be dismissed out of hand.

Learning is not a thing. Learning is a process that occurs in an interpersonal and group context, and it is always composed of an interaction of factors to which we append labels such as *motivation, cognition, emotion* or *affect,* and *attitude.* Neither singly nor in their interactions is the strength of these factors ever zero. Direct observation of the learner can give us a limited, albeit important, picture of the factors always part of the learning process. How we intuit or deduce the role of the factors depends on the psychological-conceptual sophistication of the teacher. For example, parents of preschoolers are always trying to make sense of the relation between what they directly see and what may be in the minds of their youngsters. That is why in the pages of this book I contrast the parent-as-teacher with the classroom teacher. For example, when a nine-month-old child unexpectedly begins to display marked anxiety when strangers come near, parents may become puzzled, especially when the child has never displayed such behavior. The parent may ask, Why this "new" behavior, what does it mean, what does it portend, what should or can I do, what is going on in that little head? In a classroom of twenty to twenty-five children the teacher is almost daily asking and trying to answer similar questions she has about students. Teacher and parent feel compelled to do something, but at the same time neither feels secure about what is going on in the child's mind.

Teachers, like parents, get concerned when a child cannot do something children of that age should be able to do. Both seek answers because both have to act. If you peruse any of the widely used books by parents on infant and child care, containing as they do instances of puzzling or difficult behavior a parent seeks to repair or prevent, you will see that the advice given in the book is based on the author's implicit or explicit conception of learning. And over the decades different authors have differed widely (even wildly) in their conceptions, as Hurlbert's (2003) recent book has so clearly demonstrated.

Your conception of the learning process not only has enormous implications for classroom learning contexts but also goes a long way to explaining why I have long predicted that educational reforms, resting as they do on a superficial conception of learning, will continue to be disappointing. This book was written not only for educators, but also for a general public puzzled by how little the reform movement has to show despite the fact that since World War II several billions of dollars have been poured into the reform movement by federal, state, and local governments, as well as foundations. In fact, the failures of the educational reform movement should have alerted us a long time ago to the possibility that our conception of learning and its contexts is part of the problem. For example, it is now the conventional wisdom to proclaim mantra-like that schooling will not improve unless there is a partnership between teachers and parents, that they need each other and the child needs both of them if he or she is to benefit from the partnership. But what do we ordinarily mean by and about partnerships? If we know anything about partnerships, marital or business, it is that they are not interpersonal beds of roses. That has long been the case in the relationship between teachers and parents. That should not be surprising for many reasons, but let me mention a few here which would explain why this book contains what it does. First, both before and after a child starts school, parents know and experience their child in ways teachers do not and cannot. Similarly, teachers know that child in ways that parents do not and cannot. What teachers and parents know may vary from being similar to being widely discrepant. Second, partnership requires—it certainly implies—that each partner knows what the other one is thinking, doing, and why. Each should feel safe expressing their point of view because they have the same goal: maximizing the quantity and quality of what the child learns. When, as is so often the case, issues of turf, temperament, and power enter the picture, the exchange of knowledge about and experience with the child plummets and the goal of the partnerships is negatively affected. Partnership becomes a label, not a reality; the partners do not learn with or from each other. Third, aside from the fact that teachers receive no training whatsoever in how they should talk and relate to parents, the culture of schools in no way makes up for that mission in training. What are schools for? The universal answer is that they are places where children learn. No one, educators or otherwise, has ever said that schools are places where teachers learn. I have long regarded it as a glimpse of the obvious that teachers cannot be expected to create and sustain a context of productive learning for children if such a context does not exist for teachers. And such a context hardly exists for teachers. In many schools it exists not at all; the poor quality of parent-teacher relationships is but one instance of it. Fourth, parents, indeed people generally, are ignorant of how a teacher is embedded in a school system in which he or she is at the bottom of an organization chart with layers of administrators above her in power and responsibility but who provide little or no direct help with the learning of teachers and students, let alone of parents.

So we have at least three school learning contexts: teacher and students, teacher and administrators, teacher and parents. None of these contexts is independent of each other and all of them are under increasing critical scrutiny because of puzzled dissatisfaction with the level of quality of student learning. It is not surprising that public frustration leads to blame assignment and scapegoating, a reaction that is understandable but in my opinion will continue to be without positive consequences. It is quite understandable to me that a parent with a child in school is most concerned with who is her child's teacher this year, who may be the child's teacher next year, etc. And I say "concern" advisedly because parents know that their year will be a good or bad year depending on who their child's teacher is. It is the rare parent who has not had bad years. It is, I suppose, too much to expect of parents that they understand that teachers are victims of training programs that ill equipped them for the awesome, demanding, sensitive role of teacher, and that school systems do little or nothing to help. In my experience there is one group of teachers who will agree with what I have said: these are teachers whose children are in school and who for one or another reason have reservations about how their children are being taught or treated, meet with the teacher, and end up resentful because they have been made to feel unjustly critical, subjective, or demanding. Someone should do a study of such encounters between teachers. I predict that the results will be similar to what is described in books written by physicians who became hospital patients.

Learning is not a thing, it is a process. This book is an elaboration of that assertion. There is learning and there is learning. I try on

these pages to distinguish between contexts of productive and unproductive learning. And by *productive* I mean that the learning process is one which engenders and reinforces wanting to learn more.
Absent wanting to learn, the learning context is unproductive or
counterproductive. *Is it not noteworthy that the word or concept of* learning *probably has the highest of all word counts in the diverse literatures in
education and yet when people are asked what they mean by learning they
are taken aback, stammer or stutter, and come up with a sentence or two
which they admit is vague and unsatisfactory?*

Teachers, like parents and everyone else, have far from complete
control over the context in which they carry out their assigned roles.
The mother and father may not see eye to eye on how to rear their
child, the father may not be around much and the mother feels over-
burdened and alone, if there is more than one child the mother and/
or the father may feel they are not giving each the quality and quantity of the attention the parents think each child needs, financial resources constrict what parents would like to have for their children,
etc. It is no different in the case of teachers, a fact parents tend not to
recognize and appreciate. I have written about educational reform in
previous books and in this book I had no intention to go over or even
summarize what I have written. The one exception has to do with the
nature of the relationship between the classroom teacher and those in
the administrative hierarchy whose responsibility it is to insure or
monitor the degree to which contexts of classroom learning are appropriate and effective. If the relationship between the teacher and administrators is superficial and infrequent, as is now the case, changes
and improvement in student learning cannot occur. In this book I devote only one chapter to this issue because it will give readers, especially if they are not educators, some understanding of why in the
school culture the concept of learning is not discussed, challenged, or
changed. "And what do you mean by learning?" Is it not strange that
that question is hardly discussed in schools? Would you not find it
strange if in churches and synagogues there was hardly any discussion
of the essential feature of religion: faith?

It took the better part of the twentieth century for mental health
professionals to begin to recognize that troubled children and parents
can be helped beyond a small degree by treating any or all of the family not in a one-on-one way but rather literally as a family. Every family is a system of relationships in which each member affects all other
members in small or large ways. The task of understanding and altering the family's system is never easy. We blithely acknowledge that
classrooms and schools are part of a school "system," and then proceed to deal with the major problems by riveting on part X, then on

part Y, and so on, as if each part in no way bears the imprimatur of a larger system. In theory and practice, it is a confirmation of Mencken's caveat that for every major problem there is a simple answer that is wrong. It is like the way we use the concept of learning where we are not aware we are missing the trees for the forest. In my experience, parents have a working understanding about their family as a system, although it tends not to prevent them from reacting only to its parts. That is far less the case with school personnel for whom the concept of system is as murky and superficial as their concept of learning.

What were the features of the learning contexts that were productive for you? If readers ponder that question, they will have no difficulty following my argument, and, I predict, they will agree with me, especially those who are parents.

I can assure the reader that I do not mean I believe that I have said the last word on learning. I shall be more than content if this book stirs discussion on what is meant by learning. And my cup of content will overflow if it persuades readers that noncosmetic educational reform will be impossible unless it rests on a conception of learning radically different from the contentless one about which it can be securely said that it has been neither practical nor helpful.

As always, it is with the deepest gratitude that I acknowledge my thanks to Lisa Pagliaro for the many practical ways she is helpful to me.

—Seymour B. Sarason
Stratford, Connecticut

Chapter One

The Major Themes

This book was written for those, in or out of the education community, who are puzzled by or disillusioned with decades of efforts to improve schooling and its outcomes. Beginning in 1965 I predicted the current state of affairs primarily on the basis that reform policies were being implemented in obviously self-defeating ways and I had no reason to believe that it would be different in the future. My emphasis on the mistakes of implementation diverted me from giving weight to another reason I did not clearly develop, or from which I did not pursue some obvious conclusions. As I look back on those early years, I think it was a case of not wanting to pursue that line of thought because if I did, issues of implementation would have to be regarded as of secondary importance to the substance and direction of that second reason. In subsequent writings I did pursue that second reason because, being involved in schools as intensively as I was, that reason became for me a glimpse of the obvious. Although intellectually satisfying—I knew what the basic problem was—it made the prospect for reform galactically more difficult.

That second reason can be put succinctly: *Unless, and until, on the basis of careful studies and credible evidence we gain clarity and consensus of the distinguishing features of classroom contexts of productive and unproductive learning, the improvement of schooling and its outcomes is doomed.* The history of reform efforts is testimony to the recognition that the bulk of American classrooms are contexts of unproductive learning, and the diverse efforts of reform had to have the goal of making them productive. They failed because they were not clear about what they

1

meant by *productive, unproductive,* and *learning.* I ask the reader to respond to a question I have in recent years asked scores of teachers, teachers of teachers, school administrators, school reformers: What do you mean by learning? In light of the fact that the word *learning* is at or near the top of the most frequently appearing words in the educational literature, you would expect that answers would not take long to give, that people would not by facial expression and body language appear puzzled or surprised, that it would not be an unrevealing one- or two-sentence reply, that you would consider their answers to be discernibly similar. What I have gotten is a potpourri of answers that defies categorization. It took me too long to recognize that my own experiences in learning contexts were far more complex than is indicated by conventional definitions of learning. That disconnect between the personal experience of learning and how the word *learning* is used to shape and justify practice goes a long way to explaining the ineffectiveness of reform. That is what this book is about.

If I am right about what the basic problem is, which must be clarified and its validity established by credible evidence in practical applications, it will mean that a radical change will be required in the selection and preparation of all educators at all levels of practice. The most difficult change will be in the political system, because to take seriously the features of classroom contexts of productive learning means that teachers will be using their time in ways that make the concept of respect for individuality other than empty rhetoric and pious sloganeering. Making class size smaller will be necessary but not sufficient; it will require teachers selected and trained very differently than they are now. The political system, and initially the general public, will not take kindly to increasing school budgets. Politicians, a word I do not use pejoratively, do not know the history of educational reform except that it has not been successful. They have latched on in the past to one nostrum after another, prayerfully approving each as a silver bullet. Today we hear much about holding schools accountable for getting their students to meet standards. I have listened to legislators (and the President) wax enthusiastic about "finally" passing laws requiring schools be held accountable. By the same data and logic politicians "finally" should be held responsible for approving past reform efforts for which credible data justifying them never existed. That is why in this book I emphasize that no educational reform intended to have an impact on all schools should be supported before its claims have been studied, analyzed, and evaluated in a small number of pilot studies. Is that asking too much? Do we allow drugs to be marketed without requiring proponents to present data to the Federal

Drug Administration demonstrating that its positive effects far out-weigh its negative side effects?

In Chapters 7 and 8 I take up the criticism that I am impractical, not wrong but impractical in regard to the world as we know it. The words *practical* and *impractical,* like the word *learning,* are used as if we know what criteria we do or should employ in judging a person, an idea, a course of action, a gadget, as practical or impractical. None of these changes is inherently practical or impractical. It is only when we practice with them, when we have a before and after measure that we can judge them as practical or impractical. All but a few people on this earth believed that a machine could or would be invented that would fly in the air and carry a person. It was the stuff of millennia-old dreams and hopes. Only obsessed, impractical dreamers would devote their lives to the quest. If the Wright brothers' demonstration settled the question, let us not ignore the fact that much of the world refused to believe it.

The argument I present in this book derives from three consider-ations:

1. There have been attempts before I came on the scene which have taken seriously the features and significances of a context of pro-ductive learning. Each attempt was a reaction to what was con-ventional and unproductive.

2. There were three attempts, not conceived and implemented by me, which were serious attempts resting on follow-up data con-firming expectations of positive results.[1]

3. In each study the students came from very poor, ethnic, or racial backgrounds in which the level of parental education was low, the kind of children for whom the term "at risk" is clearly appropriate.

I chose to refer only to these three studies because I came to know them very well over the years preceding publications of their findings. I do not claim that these studies were exemplary in design and analysis,

---

1. Two of the studies are by Levine (2001) and Bensman (2000). The third study is by Heckman et al. (1995) and is an initial report which will be followed by a more com-prehensive one in a year or so. I include reference to his seven-year project because I had many opportunities to visit and observe what was being done over those years. To-gether the three studies stimulated me to write this book. I am sure there are other similar studies but—like that of Aiken (1942)—which I had no opportunity to visit and observe. There are thorny problems in writing up these kinds of studies and I discuss them in some detail in my 2002 book, *Educational Reform. A Self-Scrutinizing Memoir.*

that there is no need for more rigorous replications. But I do claim that what they have reported will be impressive to those who read their publications. In one of the two studies which dealt with high school students all but one of the students at its beginning were black, with a previous record of poor or low achievement and troublesome behavior. By the third year white, middle-class parents sought to enroll their children in that school.

Six decades ago two German physicists (one male, one female) demonstrated on the basis of previous research and theory the release of energy by the splitting of one atom by another atom of the same chemical element. No physicist doubted that that one experiment literally opened vistas of a future of an endless supply of energy. It would take at least a century or so, probably more, to approximate or reach that goal because it would require a fantastic amount of money to acquire, build, and develop the resources that would be needed. Releasing energy was one thing, controlling that energy was another thing, and being able to develop the engineering know-how to direct that energy for use was another staggering problem. But physicists rejoiced that for the first time the energy of the nucleus of a particular atom had been released by splitting it. Drs. Hahn and Meitner were awarded the Nobel Prize in physics. Then came the start of World War II in Europe and the real possibility that Nazi Germany was unstoppable, together with Italy and Japan as allies. People today forget that up until 1942 the United States and its allies were faced at worst with defeat and at best with an ignominious peace treaty which, given Hitler's record, was tantamount to total surrender. A refugee Hungarian physicist understood that if the United States, on the basis of Hahn and Meitner's work, initiated a crash program to develop and produce an atom bomb, it would prevent a Nazi victory. But that bomb had to be developed before the Nazis did it; they had superb physicists who undoubtedly had the knowledge to build the bomb. And if they beat the United States to the punch, the war was over. To make a long and fascinating story short, President Roosevelt gave the go-ahead and with seemingly unlimited resources produced the bomb in a few years. Absent the war, it would have taken scores of decades for the diverse potentials of atomic energy to be realized. And if in the light of subsequent decades atomic energy is not an unalloyed blessing, it confirms me in my belief that the most basic of all laws in human affairs is that there is no free lunch.

Unlike in physics and science generally, in education we today do not have a history of theory and research which make for crucial studies pointing us in new directions. Science has a very old tradition of speculation, formal theory, and research, a tradition whose "life" is understandable not in terms of years or even centuries but millennia.

Education in the form of schooling and an arena of issues is less than two centuries old. These issues were, as they still are, accompanied by controversies in which passion, opinion, and power were the dominant characteristics. That, of course, should not be surprising because the issues were about the nature and potentials of people, what they are and what they can become, what they *should* become. There was and still is more controversy about those issues than about how people learn, even though both are interrelated. For the sake of brevity and at the risk of oversimplification, let me say that two traditions were started which continue today. In one tradition, of which John Dewey was the foremost figure, the purposes and contexts of school learning were indivisible—they determined how students experienced the classroom learning context. The other tradition, exemplified by Robert Thorndike, emphasized that the nature of human learning had to determine pedagogical practice and how that practice can be quantitatively measured; his theory of learning consisted of what he considered several basic laws, e.g., the law of effect, association. Dewey did not seek laws of learning but took as a given that humans were quintessentially curious organisms, curious about themselves and their world, seekers of knowledge and experience that had personal meaning for them; it followed, therefore, that a context of classroom learning that ignored or was insensitive to this given was a dysfunctional one, an unproductive one. Whereas Thorndike saw himself as a psychologist and scientist rigorously studying the *outcomes* of school learning, Dewey's focus was on the experience of learning in contexts which were productive or unproductive for the life of the mind and the satisfaction of curiosity and personal meaning.

What Dewey's approach called for was a program of research to clarify and substantiate what he meant by learning and how and why those meanings were so different in outcomes in contexts of productive and unproductive learning. Dewey, unlike Thorndike, was not a researcher, although he knew the history of science extraordinarily well (Dewey 1960). Dewey had many interrelated interests for undertaking such a research program. That is no criticism of Dewey, but it did not lead his many followers to pursue, clarify, and put to the test what they meant by learning, at least productive learning. Even today, after a decades-old reform movement which has gone nowhere, what is meant by learning is not discussed. We are told about greater expectations for students, an emphasis on basics and literacy, teacher and school accountability, and other factors external to the child, but practically nothing about learning. In her much acclaimed book on a hundred years of reform effort failures Ravitch (2000) says next to nothing about learning.

This history explains why the studies I discuss are so relevant to what I have written about contexts of productive and unproductive learning. In this book I have endeavored to bring my thoughts together in a way I have not done before. This is why in doing so I devote Chapters 3 and 4 to a comparison of current classroom contexts to the implicit assumptions of parents, who are the teachers of their children in their earliest years, as they are talking, crawling, walking, manipulating, exploring. Those assumptions are rarely articulated because parents consider them glimpses of the obvious, "natural," but these home contexts are almost the polar opposite of the features of classroom contexts of learning. It also explains why I regard these studies as analogous in their implication to Hahn and Meitner's demonstration of the release of energy when an atom is split. They proved it could be. The studies I refer to do not have that level of proof, but they certainly justify the expectation that future replications will indicate by what criteria we can distinguish between contexts of productive and unproductive learning. If and when we reach that point, the context of learning in the modal classroom will be exposed for what it is: unproductive.

Children are not atoms. Nor are they puppets whose movements are totally determined by someone manipulating the strings. But children and atoms have one thing in common: just as the atom has a nucleus containing, relatively speaking, a fantastic, "bottled-up" reservoir of energy, so does the young child. That is not flowery, utopian sentimentality. Human history is both sad and glorious. Sad because of the obstacles to the quest for individual freedom and respect, glorious because of those times, places, and people who refused to accept defeat by those elites who considered the mass of people to have been born without a nucleus of mental energy, and, therefore, needing to be directed and protected by their betters ever on the alert to distinguish the deserving from the undeserving poor. That stance of self-serving, autocratic paternalism, over the millennia, influenced child rearing and what may loosely be called education of the young. For all practical purposes, even today the relationship between individuality and learning is honored in rhetoric and ignored in the classroom.

The concept of individual freedom and choice is basic to the rationale of the proponents of school choice and vouchers. No one has articulated that more clearly than Milton Friedman (1962), and with each passing year as reform efforts continue to flounder, a policy of school vouchers has gained more adherents. Several states have put such a policy into practice on a very modest scale. I have no quarrel with the principle of school vouchers but for reasons I discuss later, the Achilles heel of Professor Friedman's advocacy is that it totally bypasses any discussion of learning. The word or concept of *learning* is not like the word *chair* which refers to a thing to which you can point. Learning is a process that occurs in an interpersonal context and is dynamically comprised of factors whose strength is never zero. Those factors have such labels as *motivation, attitude, cognition, affect, self-regard.* The reader who will examine what he or she experiences in the learning process will agree that what he or she experiences is, to say the least, an ever changing complexity in which different factors came into play at different times. I regard that as phenomenologically obvious. So, for example, knowing a child's test score tells us absolutely nothing about the context of learning and the role of the different factors which are endogenous to the learning process and experience, and without which a test score is unrevealing unless it leads us to determine which factors in the learning context played how much of a role. A voucher policy that ignores these considerations will be unable to explain why some students have presumably benefited while others did not; a basis for improving the outcomes of a voucher program will be missing.

Most readers of this book may be unaware of the history of the largest educational voucher program in American history, a program that transformed America *although its justification had nothing explicitly to do with a concept of productive or unproductive learning.* I refer to the G.I. Bill for returning World War II veterans. I discuss that legislation in some detail in the last two chapters of this book, which are about vouchers. Bennett's (1996) recent book *When Dreams Come True* is a long overdue, comprehensive description of how World War II, following as it did the catastrophic Great Depression, set the stage, and explains why the veterans looked at the bill as manna from heaven. Never before had so many young people *wanted* so desperately to learn, because the fruits of learning had such relevance to their present and their future. Of all the factors comprising and influencing the process of learning, the strength of *wanting to learn* may well be the most fateful. School vouchers are given to parents who for good reasons very much want their child to be in what they hope is a more stimulating and intellectually challenging environment than the school the child is now in. We cannot assume that what parents strongly want is matched by the strength of what their children want. And we certainly cannot blithely assume that the school to which the voucher child will go is one whose personnel have a clear conception of what constitutes a context of productive learning.

I raise these and other issues in the chapters about vouchers because it would be sad if voucher programs were not aware of and able to deal with the predictable problems which all previous reform efforts have encountered: What do we mean by learning? How do we evaluate what we do in ways of improving what we do? They are two interrelated problems about which the proponents for vouchers have said absolutely nothing. And one of the consequences will be to short-change the need for and promise of a voucher policy. Because I am in favor of vouchers and I have lived through the post–World War II reform movement, I am allergic to any reform which fails to distinguish between contexts of productive and unproductive learning.

I do not pretend that I have done justice to the description and analysis of the features of productive learning. Whatever the short-comings, I trust they will not obscure the implications of what will be required if and when the features distinguishing between the two learning contexts are clarified and put to the test, and the outcomes confirm with credible evidence what the existing studies to which I refer have done. The selection and training of teachers and adminis-trators, the organization of schools, the leadership of schools, the size of classrooms, the role of parents, the ways and criteria by which we judge student performance and progress—all of these will have to change. These changes will be neither easy nor quick. They will take decades to accomplish because of the weight of tradition, understand-ably reluctant vested interests, and cost. Some people, even those who have agreed with my basic argument, recoil from the time perspective one has to adopt. It is like telling a person he has a terminal illness that cannot be cured now, but sometime in the future research efforts will come up with answers. But that is precisely what over the past hundred years we have not been told by educational reformers, up to today when politicians from the president on down proclaim their trust in what they think is a new reform effort that at its core contains opinion, hope, and prayer. It is as if they have come down from a Mount Sinai with what is akin to an educational ten commandments. They are well intentioned, puzzled, and desperate, especially when they see the status and outcomes of urban education and what it por-tends for the nation's future, cohesion, conflicts, and wasted human and material resources.

I can pinpoint the event decades ago which illuminated for me why my time perspective for any serious, noncosmetic educational re-form effort was mightily unrealistic. It was at a time when optimism about reform was high and I allowed myself to hope and believe that certain reforms might have their intended effects, even though at the same time I had my doubts. It was before the era of jets and I was fly-ing from Idlewild Airport (now JFK) to Dallas in a four-engine plane. It was a lovely day. I was looking out the window and suddenly black smoke came pouring out of one of the engines. I do not know why I did not pee in my pants as I remembered imagery from silent movie war films depicting single-engine planes enveloped in black smoke crashing on the ground. The plane was put down in Cincinnati to await another plane. While waiting, the pilot took a seat near me and I took the liberty to tell him what my fears had been. He replied, "There is only one thing you have to worry about in these situations. You cannot put these monsters down quickly." I realized then that what we call our educational system was a monster that could not be changed in days, months, and years. It was not a pleasant thought, but as my thinking evolved I had no alternative but to accept it. It took a long time for physicists to understand the composition and dynamics of the atom. They were dealing with inanimate matter, which is child's play compared to understanding and changing large, traditional, complicated human systems of which our educational system is a prime example. Is the time perspective I adopt unrealistic? Is it unrealistic to conclude that somehow we will muddle through without paying a price future historians will regard as disastrous? I will be indebted to those readers who will send their answers, pro or con or both, to my home: 775A Poodatook Lane, Stratford, CT 06614. At my age I cannot get around much to sample and exchange views.

Chapter Two

Words and Things

Trying to understand why educational reform in the post–World War II era has been a clear disappointment quickly forces on you the realization that the sources of the disappointment are many and that one has to assume that not all sources are of equal importance. After World War II there was a consensus that the inadequacies of schooling and its outcomes were explainable in large measure by society's failure to provide school personnel with the level of fiscal support that would enable them to apply their skills and knowledge to better effect. Today, more than a half-century later, there are many educators and citizens who feel that the relation between increased funding and improved educational outcomes is disillusioningly low. That, I should hasten to add, does not mean that money is not an important factor, but rather that its importance as a source of the inadequacies of school cannot be on the list of most-important sources. In identifying sources one must judge how the sources vary in their importance.

It was sometime in the early 1960s that a prominent cell biologist was asked how come his field had begun to make rapid strides that held such promise for understanding cells and genetics. His answer was "We began to study simple problems." He went on to say that by simple problems he meant those the field believed it understood, those "take it for granted" beliefs which under close scrutiny prove to be misleading or wrong or grossly oversimple. "What we thought we understood, but didn't, made us humble." In this book I take up one such simple belief, one we think we understand. More correctly, it is a belief we take for granted; we do not have to think about it, unless on those rare occasions when circumstances force us to grasp how taking things for granted can have untoward consequences. In ordinary living those occasions are rare and we see no reason to question our "obviously" valid beliefs.

The unquestioned belief has to do with the relationship between things and the words we use to designate them. Let me give some examples.

1. You read about a *culture* in which adulterous women are stoned to death.

2. A corporation is described as marked by a *culture* of competitiveness and greed.

3. An anthropologist spends a year living with and studying an isolated, exotic society in order to write about that *culture*.

4. We are told that a school has a *culture*, a university has a *culture*, and so do medical, law, and business schools.

We have no basis for assuming, let alone believing, that the word *culture* in the above examples has identical or similar meanings. It is obvious that *culture* is intended to convey meaning about some aspect or aspects of something "out there," but they are not aspects to which we are directed, the way we would be if someone pointed to the sky and said, "Look at that airplane." We look up and see the airplane and there is no doubt that both of you see the same object "up there." You can point to and say *airplane*, or *tree*, or *automobile*, or *house* and assume that another person knows what you mean; these words are not things, they are sounds we attach to things. The word *culture* is also a sound, but what is it attached to by *common* agreement? We use the word *culture* as if there is agreement that when one person uses the word, he can count on other people to know what that word concretely refers to. That is rarely the case and some would say it is never the case. The practical consequences of the belief that we are "communicating" (when we are not) may be nil or unimportant but they may also be enormously important and negative if the words we use are a basis for action. That, I argue in the pages that follow, has been a strangely unrecognized (certainly undiscussed) problem in education.

Let's examine another word.

1. You receive a bill which you have reason to believe is wrong. You call the company and you are told, "We will *research* the problem and get back to you."

2. You read in a newspaper that a particular *researcher's* claim to new and important findings is being criticized because it was published in a *research* journal which does not use a peer review process in which well credentialed, independent *researchers* read submitted papers and pass judgment about the quality of the reported *research*.

3. On the front page of the *New York Times* you read that a large, well-controlled *research* project has determined that a certain hormonal therapy for menopausal women has, contrary to all expectations and *previous research*, adverse effects. Clinicians and medical *researchers* are shocked.

4. You get a call from a survey *research* company which seeks to determine if and how your travel plans have changed because of the 9/11 catastrophe.

The word *research*, like the word *culture*, is not used to denote a thing "out there." If, as I have, you ask people what they mean by research, their answers are in one way or another that research is a way of finding out something, of getting an answer to a question. They were satisfied with their answer. They had, they thought, given a clear answer. I would then say, "You make research sound like a relatively simple affair." They would deny that was their intent. As one respondent put it, "I have read enough to know that research is a complicated affair." And what did he mean by "a complicated affair"? "All kinds of things can go wrong for different reasons. You have to be very careful, you have to be on top of things."

My respondents were well-educated people but with no research experience. What happened when I asked researchers what research is? Their initial answer was as short and unrevealing as those of my previous respondents. They knew as I knew that research was (again like culture) a very complicated affair which reflected personal, interpersonal, institutional, economic, and historical features, and more. But since these researchers were my friends, I could ask them, "Do you think it is an adequate answer to someone who has a question to which he or she seeks an answer?" I paraphrase their answer: "Of course it is not adequate. Research is not a thing you can touch and feel. Research is about ideas, theory, precision, mulling over, and interpretation. It is by no means a purely cold, rational, logical process which takes place in a social vacuum. You don't just decide to do research. You need time, space, funds, and materials or devices of various kinds. You need persistence and imagination, and the courage to be able to accept the possibility that your ideas were wrong, your methods inadequate, and you have to go back to the drawing board. There is research on piddling problems. There is research on important problems. Most research, and I do mean most, never gets published because it has nothing worth saying. The fact is that if you or I were to describe the research process, there would be researchers who would say our description is incomplete, we didn't give due weight to this or that aspect; and there would be those who would say that our description will mislead people, certainly overwhelm them. There is only one way to learn what is meant by research, and that is by doing it."

Someone once said that language is both our ally and foe. It would be more correct to say that the limitations of language inhere in how we use language. Blaming language is an instance of blaming the victim. When we use words as if they do not vary in what they signify or point to in the external world, as if two people using the same word intend the same meaning, we invite trouble which does not become apparent until the practical actions we take reveal that the relationship between words and things is far more complicated than we had unreflectively assumed. We learn, for example, that there are words which refer to concrete, palpable things and there are words which have no such relationship even though we use them as if they do have such concrete referents in the external world. There are words and there are words, and one way we distinguish between them is by saying that some words are concepts (like *culture* and *research*). You cannot see or touch a concept, which, as the word indicates, was invented or conceived to serve a special purpose: hopefully one that is productive and illuminating of the relationships between humans and the world. *Democracy, patriotism, bureaucracy, neurosis, science, philosophy* are (again like *culture* and *research*) words quite unlike words like *sun, moon, horse, milk, shoe,* etc. Two people may each say they are patriotic only to find that when they pursue what they mean—what the concept includes or excludes, what actions it supports or indicts—they come to a parting of the ways.

I am oversimplifying the problematics of the relationships between words and things. The purpose of this chapter is to alert the reader to the fact that literature on education is replete with examples of the use of concepts that are assumed to have shared meanings but do not. Worse yet, the failure to recognize this state of affairs virtually guarantees that educational reform is doomed. I am referring specifically to the concept of learning, undoubtedly the most frequent word to be found in the educational literature.

One more example. On June 21, 2002, the Supreme Court rendered a decision that on its June 22 front page the *New York Times* described this way: "Citing 'National Consensus' Justices Bar Death Penalty for Retarded Defendants." Let us begin with the concept of consensus. What is a consensus? Does it refer to most people? What do we mean by *most*? Does it mean a majority of people? How much of a majority? It was a 5-4 majority decision. Is that what is meant by consensus? Here is what Justice Scalia said about consensus.

> Moreover, a major factor that the court entirely disregards is that the legislation of all 18 states it relies on is still in its infancy. The oldest of the statutes is only 14 years old; five were enacted last year; over half were enacted within the past eight years. Few, if any, of the states have had sufficient experience with these laws to know whether they are sensible in the long term. But the prize for the court's most feeble effort to fabricate "national consensus" must go to its appeal (deservedly relegated to a footnote) to the views of assorted professional and religious organizations, members of the so-called "world community" and respondents to opinion polls. I agree with the chief justice (dissenting opinion), that the views of professional and religious organizations and the results of opinion polls are irrelevant. Equally irrelevant are the practices of the "world community," whose notions of justice are (thankfully) not always those of our people. We must never forget that it is a Constitution for the United States of America that we are expounding. . . . Where there is not first a settled consensus among our own people, the views of other nations, however enlightened the justices of this court may think them to be, cannot be imposed upon Americans through the Constitution.

You may not agree with Justice Scalia's vote but you have to credit him for indicating that the word *consensus* means different things to different people.

The court's decision brought back many memories to me. My first professional job after graduate school in 1942 was as a clinical psychologist in a spanking-new state institution for mentally retarded individuals. I have written about my experience in several books (Sarason 1985, 1988, 1994). For my present purposes the following is relevant.

1. Admission to the institution (through the probate court) required that the individual have an IQ of 70 or less. If he had an IQ less than 70 it meant that he had "it," the "thing": mental retardation. Even in the many cases where there was no biological-neurological evidence that there was anything wrong with the individual's brain, the low IQ meant that the

person had not been able or would not be able to cope with the tasks of living in the community. Mental retardation, therefore, implied assumptions, predictions, and explanations, the validity and logic of which frequently went unchallenged. The low IQ was used not only to explain everything but also to justify admitting the person and keeping him or her there for years. It was an instance of the self-fulfilling prophecy: you say someone is incapable, you treat him or her as incapable, and you end up "proving" you were right in the first place.

2. It was never the case that more than 2–4 percent of all children with IQs below 70 were institutionalized. What if you compared an institutional group of people with IQs between 60 and 70 with a comparable low-scoring group of people who were considered mentally retarded and were in special segregated classrooms in public schools? If mental retardation meant that these low-scoring people could not adapt to the tasks and pressures of community living, should not those in special classes have great difficulty in adapting, in demonstrating the cognitive and social competence necessary to become independent workers and citizens? Studies done at the time gave clear and unexpected results: after leaving school they were as a group surprisingly productive workers who married and successfully reared their children. At the very least, these studies indicated that the words *mental retardation,* if not meaningless, gave rise to actions and explanations of behavior that were illogical or unjustified or both.

3. Were psychologically troubled, mentally retarded, institutionalized individuals capable of benefitting from psychotherapy? The answer, I was told, was clearly no. To benefit from psychotherapy one must be able to introspect, to analyze, willingly to engage in an interpersonal relationship that has mutual obligations for the purpose of changing some aspect of behavior. My wife and I went ahead and demonstrated that there were *some* retarded individuals who could benefit from a sustained therapeutic relationship, a conclusion that years later came to be accepted. Although the arguments were many and different, it was long the conventional wisdom that for old people, say those above seventy, psychotherapy was not a treatment of choice. That conventional wisdom also has gone by the boards. The words *old* or *mentally retarded* do not refer to one thing or an observable action or imagery which lead to actions accompanied by the belief that what you and many other people mean by the words are obviously the same.

4. If your neighbor's child strangles a cat to death and people are told that that child has an IQ of 65, the odds are monumentally high that his IQ will be used to "explain" what he did. He did X because he "has" Y: cause and effect. But what if your neighbor's child had an IQ of 170? People would not say he strangled the cat *because* he has such a high IQ; they look beyond an IQ for an explanation. They are very unlikely to do that in the case of a child who is labeled mentally retarded.

The Supreme Court had to decide whether execution of a mentally retarded person was an instance of the constitutional prohibition against "cruel and unusual punishment." If the Supreme Court is noted for anything, it is their concern for what words mean. And yet, in neither the majority nor minority decisions is there even a hint of doubt about what the words *mental retardation* mean or signify. The lawyers for the plaintiff argued that a mentally retarded person does not have the ability to distinguish at all clearly what is right and wrong and what the consequences of a major criminal act could be. To execute such a person is unfair and, therefore, unconstitutional. Are we to conclude that *all* individuals labeled as mentally retarded are so incapable? As someone who has worked over the decades with several thousand such individuals, I can attest that such a conclusion is totally unwarranted. If when I entered the field in 1942 someone gave a paper at a convention predicting that within forty years many institutions for the mentally retarded would be closed, that their former residents would be living in the community with their families or in small group homes, and that many would be exercising a degree of independence and be gainfully employed, he would have been regarded as someone who had lost touch with reality and was in need of shock treatment. But he would have been right.

What is a woman capable of in life? Or, what are the defining characteristics of a woman? Or, what does the word or concept of *woman* "mean" to you? If you asked people those kinds of questions a hundred years ago, answers would have been something like this: a woman is best suited to have and rear a family, perform whatever chores are necessary to keep a clean and happy home, to support her mate in his endeavors, to do what is best for him and the family. If you then asked if women should participate in the political process by voting, a huge majority—including men and women—would have said no. Why no? Because women are not worldly creatures, nor have they that cast of mind necessary to participate in decisions about local, state, and national affairs; the mind and temperament of a woman, which are very different from those of men, are specially suited for the responsibilities of family and home. Note that the word *woman* has an unverbalized starting point: biologically a woman is not a man. Once that "observable" is taken for granted (a glimpse of the obvious) it becomes the basis for "explaining" women's capacities and role. Women are what they are because they are women! Men do not cause what women are, they only provide support for what they inherently are and protect them from activities ill suited to their "nature."

Now, what if a hundred years ago we had asked people if the time would come when women could create and sustain a large business, be active participants in military affairs and activities (other than nursing), seek and win public office, go to college and earn advanced degrees, become lawyers, doctors, engineers, and professors? The answer would have been that the question was stupid, an emanation of unbridled fantasy, it was not worthy of discussion, we should get our head examined. A hundred years ago there was a small number of people (men and women) who were challenging the "meaning" of women. Once the biological starting point was established its meanings for the future were also established.

Elsewhere (Sarason 1985) I have discussed in detail three children whom I labeled as mentally retarded, instances in which I was grossly wrong due to thinking in ways I am criticizing in these pages. Fortunately, my sloppy, conventional thinking was proved very wrong in each case by someone for whom a very low IQ was just that: a low number. Because the point I am making is so central to this book, I describe two of these children.

Case 1

There were certain times during the week when "children" could be admitted to the Southbury Training School. Our offices were in the administration building, situated so that we could see the cars pull up to the entrance to deposit the child and the adult (or adults). Occasionally, case material was sent to us before admission, allowing us to make some preliminary judgments about a suitable cottage placement. More often than not, the case material accompanied the child on admission, and we had to make some quick decisions about cottage placement. We took cottage placement seriously because being in a "high grade" or "middle grade" or "low grade" cottage was a difference that made a difference. We could, of course, later change a placement, but that could bring in its wake complications for child and staff.

It was an admission day. A car pulled up and from the back seat emerged a rather large man carrying cradle-like in his arms what from our windows looked like an unusually large child of three or four years of age. But we knew that it could not be a child that young because at that time children had to be at least six years of age to be admitted. We went to the front door of the building to greet the party and only then could we see that what we had thought was a young child was in fact a much older male. The accompanying material (quite sparse) indicated that he was thirty years of age and had been taken care of from birth by his mother, who had recently died. The father had died years before. Why was he being carried like a baby? He was as gnarled and contorted, as muscularly and neurologically involved, as any such case I had seen. His body was constantly moving: he was almost constantly drooling: whenever he attempted what seemed to be a purposeful movement, the diffuseness of his body movement became more intense and widespread; and his disfigured face had a wild, "monster-like" quality to it. I looked at this man with puzzlement because I could not understand why he had not been institutionalized earlier. What little material was in the folder that accompanied him indicated that the mother had been opposed to insitutionalization. If I was puzzled by that, I was not puzzled about the cottage in which he should be placed: a large, middle-grade cottage that, in truth, had as many low- as middle-grade individuals. Basically, it was a custodial cottage, unrelated to the institution's educational program. Mr. Humphrey (that was his name) was no candidate for an educational program. Of that I was sure!

It was our practice to do a formal psychological assessment within a few days after admission in order to make a final judgment about cottage placement, suitability for programs in the academic school, work assignment, special needs and cautions, etc. In the case of Mr. Humphrey, there was no need, I decided, to do an early assessment. Indeed, I was relieved that there was no particular point to a psychologic assessment in this instance. Those days were quite busy—the opening of Southbury's doors stimulated a stream of admissions, including children from schools that closed their special classes so that their occupants could be sent to Southbury where they became legal and financial wards of the state. Three weeks later, I was walking past the cottage in which Mr. Humphrey had been placed, and Mr. Rooney, the cottage "father" (there was no "mother" in *that* cottage) came out. Mr. Rooney was one of my favorite people and we began to talk about this and that and the state of the world. I remembered that we had not done an assessment of Mr. Humphrey, and I asked Mr. Rooney how he was doing. Mr. Rooney replied: "Now *there* is a smart person. He can read and he understands everything." I was surprised and my face must have shown it because Mr. Rooney, no shrinking violet and a rather good "natural" clinician, invited me to a demonstration of Mr. Humphrey's abilities. Mr. Humphrey was lying on the seat of a wheelchair, i.e., he was lying on the seat as if it were a bed. Mr. Rooney left us for a moment and soon returned with a checkerboard in each square of which was a letter of the alphabet, i.e., the top first square had a large A, the second a B, and so forth. The checkerboard had been one of the things accompanying Mr. Humphrey to Southbury. "Now," Mr. Rooney said, "you ask him a question that requires a one-word answer, then move your finger slowly from one letter to the next and when you have reached the first letter in the answer he will let you know, and you do that for each letter in the answer." How could he let me know if he was in constant motion and if his attempts at vocalization were unintelligible and only increased the level of diffuse bodily activity? I cannot remember what question I put to him, but I do remember that when my finger reached the square containing the first letter of the answer, immediately it was obvious that that was part of the answer—his facial and bodily responses were like a pinball machine gone berserk. He did know the answer to that first question and to almost all of the subsequent ones. I was dumbfounded and I felt stupid, guilty, and quite humble.

I shall not dwell on my diagnostic mistake, which was as unforgivable as it was understandable. I should have known not to go by appearances, or by what a person cannot do, but rather by what a person can learn to do, i.e., by signs of potential assets rather than by exclusive focus on deficits. I had reacted to Mr. Humphrey as if he were a thing, not a person. Instead of arousing my curiosity, challenging me to figure out how I might relate to this individual, forcing me to keep separate what I was assuming from what was factual, Mr. Humphrey's appearance short-circuited the relationship between what I ordinarily believed and practiced. To someone like me, for whom Itard was a major figure in the pantheon of gods, my response to Mr. Humphrey was, to indulge understatement, quite humbling.

Once I was able to overcome (in part at least) my feelings of stupidity, guilt, and inconsistency, I realized that there were questions far more important than my diagnostic acumen. *How did the mother manage to accomplish what she did? What kept her going? What did she recognize in the infant as sparks that could ignite the fires that power learning? What was her theory and in what relation did this stand to her practices? What could we have learned if we had the opportunity to follow and study Mrs. Humphrey in the rearing of her son?*

Case 2

A colleague called to ask if I would, for purposes of assessment, visit a retarded five-year-old boy in a residential nursery in another state. A friend of my colleague, the boy's grandfather, requested an evaluation because the nursery felt that the boy, Andrew, should be moved to another setting. I was reluctant to make the trip and told my colleague that I would prefer seeing the boy in New Haven. This, it turned out, was not possible for several reasons. The boy's parents had been divorced two or three years earlier, and the father had never visited the nursery; the mother, who lived hundreds of miles away, visited once or twice a year during her shopping expeditions to New York; and the grandfather, who footed all of the boy's bills including my fee, had never visited the boy in the nursery. The grandfather had arranged for a pediatrician in the local community to be available to Andrew. Again reluctantly, I agreed to visit.

I arranged to meet with the pediatrician before going to the nursery. He told me that Andrew had had a mild polio attack from which he had recovered; there was some nonspecific brain damage associated with a "sugar-loaf" shaped skull and with an awkward gait and other motor movements. Andrew was a nice, likable, obviously retarded child.

The nursery was a large ranch house in a residential neighborhood. I rang the bell, and the door was soon opened by a young boy who, from the pediatrician's description, had to be Andrew. He did have a markedly pointy skull and seemed both distracted and anxious. He said something that was hard for me to comprehend because his articulation was not clear; and he ran back into the house and quickly returned with the chief nurse. The nurse and I talked for a while in one corner of a large living room. Andrew was almost always in sight, not because he was asked to be but, it seemed, because he did not want to be far from the nurse. She told me that Andrew was the only ambulatory child in the nursery, all the others being bed patients. She, it turned out, was the one prodding the grandfather to move the boy to a more socially appropriate and intellectually stimulating environment. She obviously liked Andrew and would miss him terribly, but she could not justify his continued residence there. In fact, she asserted, it had become harmful to his development because there literally was no one there, aside from her, with whom he could have a relationship. After indicating that from time to time she had taken Andrew for a visit to her apartment (she was unmarried), she related an incident from several months earlier. She had to go to the local drugstore for supplies and, for the first time, took Andrew with her. She had started to go into the drugstore when she became aware that Andrew was not at her side. She looked back and there was Andrew, paralyzed by fright and unable to take a step forward or backward. Instantly she realized that Andrew had never been in a store and was fearful of what awaited him there. Aside from the handful of times he had been in her apartment, Andrew had not been out of the nursery and its immediate environs. She took him by the hand, went back to the car, and returned to the nursery. That incident was crucial in leading her to contact the grandfather to convince him to consider placing Andrew elsewhere.

Prior to testing, I tried to interact with Andrew. For one thing, I had trouble making out what he said. No less interfering was his clear reluctance about interacting with me. It seemed to be a reluctance powered by anxiety, which at the time mystified me, although the thought did occur to me that Andrew did not view my visit as being in his best interests. There was something very likable and pathetic about him. As soon as I tried to administer some intelligence test items, his anxiety noticeably increased and, in the most indirect ways, he let me know that he wanted no part of what was going on. It was as if he sensed that I was somebody who could be harmful to him. He whimpered, became tearful, and once or twice got up from his chair to depart. I stopped my efforts at formal testing. I had already concluded that Andrew was markedly retarded, although I did not know how seriously. I had also concluded that, regardless of the degree of retardation, this nursery placement had become dramatically counterproductive and that he had to be placed elsewhere. Finally, and crucially, what concerned me most was the implications of the fact that Andrew had one and only one significant relationship with another human being: the nurse. Psychologically, she was his mother. That is the way he related to her and she felt about him. Theirs was *not* a nurse-child relationship. I related all of this in a report to the grandfather and urged that it was essential that the nurse accompany Andrew to the new setting and stay with him until he had made some kind of positive adjustment. The thought that Andrew would be picked up at the nursery and taken (psychologically alone) to a new setting interfered with my sleep! I received no reply from the grandfather.

A year or so later, my colleague called me up to say that the grandfather was requesting another evaluation. The nurse, my colleague related, had been persuaded by the grandfather to give up her job and to devote her time and energies to caring for Andrew. He had been placed in a kindergarten in a public school and the immediate question was: *Should he be promoted to the first grade, which the school recommended?*

I did not need to be urged to visit the nurse and Andrew. Obviously, somebody was selling somebody else a bill of goods! What fool or knave was recommending that the Andrew I had seen a year or so earlier was ready for first grade? The nurse had moved into a garden apartment development. When I steered my car into the development, I had to go at about one mile an hour because the area seemed to consist of more children than blades of grass. I parked the car very near their apartment and, as soon as I got out of the car, a young boy approached. It was Andrew, but what a different Andrew! There was that pointy skull, his motor movements were not graceful but they were far more smooth than when I had first seen him, he spoke with a clarity that amazed me, and he seemed to know and to be on very good terms with the other children. He guided me to the apartment, chit-chatting with me. However, even in those early moments, I sensed that he was very ambivalent about my visit, as if he wanted to be his usual giving self but was suspicious about what my agenda was. This became more noticeable later when I tried to test him and, again, I stopped because it seemed upsetting to him. We did enough, though, with my observations, for me to conclude that Andrew tested in the normal range. Whereas on my first visit there was a question about how seriously retarded he was, the question now in my mind was how bright he might be. If on my first visit I intuited a mother-child relationship, I did not have to resort to intuition on my second visit a year or so later. She was a mother constantly seeking ways to stimulate the boy and to help him overcome a pervasive anxiety and self-deprecatory tendency. She told me that within a year or so, she would like to move south and take Andrew with her. What did I think? I, of course, said that Andrew should go where she goes. As for promotion to the first grade: of course. Two years later I received a call from the nurse. She and Andrew had moved south and they were both happy and doing well. The reason for the call was that Andrew's mother had visited a number of times in the past year, developed a real interest in the "new" Andrew, and now wanted him to come live with her. How should the nurse respond? I was explicit in recommending that she try to avoid such a change. I also wrote this to the grandfather.

I shall assume that no reader will accuse me of stating or implying that parental love, devotion, and energy are unmixed blessings and that, if these characteristics could be appropriately channeled, scads of retarded persons would become "unretarded." Nor do I wish anyone to conclude that as a group parents possess knowledge and wisdom that professionals do not, as if parents possess a productive interpersonal sensitivity and "natural" acumen that is in short supply among professionals. These are arguable issues, but they are irrelevant to the reasons why I have presented these cases.

The relationship between language and things is far more complicated than I have indicated, and it is the recognition of that complexity that accounts in part for the explosion of scientific advances in the twentieth century when the language of science, especially in physics, came to be seen as a major source of confusion. Words or concepts such as *time, space, energy, measurement* could no longer be used as if the meanings conventionally attached to them could be logically and unreflectively used in science. That is why so many people did not understand, and still do not understand, the meaning and significance of Einstein's contributions. He used familiar words like *time, space, motion, energy,* and *mass* but they didn't mean what people generally meant by those words. To my knowledge the first person who systematically analyzed and described how we use everyday language in ways that unjustifiably confuse the relationship between words and things was, of all people, a Utica, New York, banker Alexander Bryan Johnson, who in 1836 gave a series of lectures to a town forum. He put the lectures together in a book he titled *A Treatise on Language.* For all practical purposes it was read by no one. It took more than a century for it to be rediscovered in a San Francisco bookstore by David Rynin, a professor of linguistics, who realized that Johnson had anticipated the complexities of the relationship between words and things. Professor Rynin wrote a long introduction to the book (1947) in which he says that Einstein regarded it as a major achievement. Johnson is a mystery. You could say he was a genius but if he heard you say that, he would say that by using that word you were defining one word by another word and the mystery remains a mystery. Todd and Sonkin (1977) have written a biography of Johnson, and I have written a chapter about the mystery (1994).

In this chapter I have tried to give the reader some idea of why this book has the title it has. The word and concept of learning have gone as unexamined as they are important. More correctly, the word has been used with so many different meanings that it has earned the status of an inkblot in a Tower of Babel. When we use the word or concept our intentions are honorable, but as is frequently the case in human affairs, a hellish road is paved with good intentions. When these good intentions turn out to result in total or partial failures, we are disappointed and puzzled, and we direct blame to various factors but rarely (if ever) do we ask: is it possible that our conception of learning was faulty, grossly simplistic, and in need of an overhaul or even discarded?

The title of this book is not a rhetorical device intended to capture the attention of readers. It is explicitly intended to suggest that like most everyone else (including me) you use or have used the word or concept of learning in grossly simplistic ways, unaware and unable even to entertain the *possibility* that what you say you mean is part, a large part, of the problem and in no way a solution to the improvement of school learning. I italicize the word *possibility* to make the point that when one of our treasured beliefs is so taken for granted that we cannot and do not subject it to scrutiny, the consequences can be disastrous in varying ways and degrees for the individual and/or the larger society.

My most recent book was titled *Educational Reform. A Self-Scrutinizing Memoir* (2002). In it I go back over my decades in the educational arena to try to identify my errors of omission and commission, issues I wrongly deemphasized or avoided or skirted, and why it took me years to say out loud that the one thing the history of educational reform indisputably proves is that the more things change the more they do not remain the same but rather do or will get worse. But the one thing in that book that caused me to cringe was the realization that I never came to grips with what I thought I meant by learning, even though I was never in doubt that in the countless times I observed classrooms I came away with the feeling, "That is not learning, that is anti-learning." Having said that, let me assure the reader of two things. First, I never blamed teachers, because that would be an instance of blaming the victims; they, like most everyone else, had been "taught" what learning is and schools were organized to make that kind of teaching possible. The second is that there were, as there always are, those rare exceptions in stark contrast to the "rule"; the word *exception* is a word, not an explanation, and the mystery of exceptions remains a mystery, to me at least, much as Alexander Bryan Johnson remains a mystery after you label him a genius for writing his *Treatise on Language*.

Where should I start in my attempt to shed some light on what I mean when I use the word *learning*? That was not an easy question to answer. I started with an indisputable learning context unconnected with schools, familiar to and fateful for every human being, and yet one allowing me later to direct attention to the relevance of these meanings to the school classroom. My starting point is on the surface dramatically different from the school classroom but it contains all of the ingredients of the classroom context. So, in the next chapter I turn to the relationships between parents and their newborn child.

Chapter Three

Infant and Parental Learning

The relationship between parents and children can be said to begin when it is established that the mother is pregnant. And by *relationship* I mean that from that point on the embryo is not for the parents an "it" or *just* an embryo but a fantasized, concretized little person, a stimulus to their imagination, hopes, fears, and obligations. That is true not only for each parent as individuals but for their relationship with each other. Yes, they were married to each other but now the word *married* takes on concrete meanings and imagery that inevitably alter what they mean by *married*. These alterations may or may not be subtle, or even verbalized, or with or without positive or negative consequences. At the same time that each parent's fantasized relationship with the child-to-be begins to develop and elaborate, the "real" relationship between the parents inevitably changes: what they say to each other, how they should plan for the future, what health precautions should be taken, how space in the apartment or house should be organized, whether they should seek to determine the sex of the child or test for indications of developmental defect or malformation, whether the financial resources are adequate, how life- and work styles will change, etc.

In my professional, personal, and social experience no one has denied that knowledge of parenthood brings in its wake surprises about oneself or one's mate. Most relevant here is the fact that in the early 1940s I was a member of a team in the pediatric department of the Yale Medical School where Drs. Edith Jackson and Grover Powers were creating the first rooming-in facility for mothers who did not want their infant to be in the nursery for newborns but instead wanted their newborns in the same room with them. These mothers were interviewed a number of times at intervals before and after delivery. It was the rare mother who did not say that before delivery she "learned" things about her husband that surprised her, frequently but certainly not always pleasant and comforting. Now, what did these women mean when they would say, for example, "I learned how deeply he cared for me" or "I learned he was a Grade A worrier" or "I learned he wanted me to make all the decisions even though I knew he wouldn't or didn't agree with me." What each woman meant was that her husband had an attribute, a habit, a proclivity that surprised them. They were labeling him, pigeonholing him as if the newly discovered attribute was characteristically him in other contexts. No woman ever indicated that she in any way played a role in the attribute she was describing; he had "it" and she played no role in how, when, and to what degree the attribute was displayed. They did not mean that they were part of an interpersonal, transactional *process* occurring in a particular, ongoing *context* in which each was affecting the other. And, it should be noted, what they said they learned—what caused surprise—was a perceived change in *overt* behavior: a description.

Let me be more concrete by relating personal experience.[1] After eleven years of marriage it was clear that my wife, Esther, and I could not have children. We decided to go the adoption route even though we were advised that the newborn we desired might take years to get. We were in our mid-thirties and had begun to adjust to life without children. It would take me many pages to recount the many avenues we took, all of which were dead-end streets. In 1954 a friend had mentioned our plight to a physician friend who told him that there was a Dr. Krall in Hartford who had helped many couples like us by finding newborns for them to adopt. I should call him up. I called and told him I was an associate professor at Yale and my wife, also a credentialed psychologist, was a clinical psychologist in Yale's student

---

1. Precisely because the word and concept *learning* does *not* refer to a "thing" (like *stick, stone, house*), or one point in time, or a single person existing in isolation, or only what is observable and audible, I know that my use of words and concepts such as *process, context, covert, transactional* is an instance of defining one concept by resort to other concepts, which is not illuminating and may even be misleading to the extent that it leads the reader to conclude that these concepts are other than opening gambits in the pursuit and integration of concrete phenomena. The concept of learning is cold and impersonal and only comes alive when we are forced (for whatever reason) to ask and begin to examine two questions: What do I *mean* when I use the concept of learning? What am I *referring* to and is that what others *refer* to?

counseling service. Dr. Krall told me he was a Yale alumnus, and then *immediately* said, "I am sorry you did not call last week because I had a newborn but I promised it to someone else. Why don't you write me a couple of paragraphs about you and your wife and I will see what I can do." The entire phone conversation took no more than three minutes. Dr. Krall came across as cheerful, ebullient, hail-fellow-well-met. I thought he was either a nut or a peddler of babies, an out-and-out sleazy character. What did we have to lose? So I wrote the letter and my wife and I never spoke about him. That phone conversation was in March of 1954. In August of that year we went on vacation and returned on the Friday of the Labor Day weekend. We were not in the house more than a half-hour when the phone rang. Esther picked up the upstairs phone and I the downstairs one. It was Dr. Krall, who cheerfully said, "Your daughter was born yesterday. Come pick her up on Tuesday." Just like that. Esther began to run downstairs, I started to run upstairs. She looked at me with amazement and said, "How does he know that we are not schizophrenics?"

I chose to relate this experience for two reasons. The first is that it is an instance of two people literally catapulted into a situation they no longer thought would ever occur; their lives would never be the same again; and by "same again" I mean they would be *changed* as single individuals and as married partners, and those *changes* would impact on a newborn. That brings us to the second reason: the word *learning* is very frequently used to mean that an observable change has been noted in a person's overt behavior and performance. The change may be judged as desirable or undesirable, as of major or minor import, or explainable or mystifying. But that narrow conception of learning—restricting it to changes between two measurable points in time—is in no way an explanation of the change, especially in instances where the two points in time are explicitly chosen to determine if a change has occurred (which is why and how tests are used in schools). That narrow conception of learning is not embedded in or integrated with the major factors that impact on learning, factors of content, context, or unverbalized covert attitudes, feelings, and motivation. If the stock market goes steadily up or down over a period of weeks, you are not content if your stockbroker tells you that it is "one of those things that happen." What you want to know and what the Dow Jones average cannot tell you is, What are the major factors that can explain those dramatic upswings and downswings? If you went to an economist for an explanation, he would tell you more than you want to know, or even understand: the complexity of our economic system, and why knowing that one aspect of it has changed over a period of time, is understandable only by relating it to how other economic measures have changed. Economics has been called the "dismal science" but that derogation should not obscure the fact that it has illuminated how complex our economic system is. They respect that complexity. They take it seriously. That is not the case in psychology and education in regard to identifying and integrating the ingredients of the complexity to which the concept of learning refers. It is not a dreamed-up, manufactured complexity, as I shall endeavor to show in the pages of this book.

Let us return to my wife and me in the situation I described. I ask the reader to indulge the fantasy that you are the mythical man or woman from Mars in a spaceship over our house, possessed of technologies and visual powers which allow you, the celestial observer, to see and record everything I and my wife do, singly or in interaction with each other. And to indulge farfetchedness you have been "studying" us for the previous eleven years of our marriage. But you do have two handicaps: you can see and hear everything but you have no comprehension of the meanings of the sounds we make (our language), and you do not have a clue that inside our skulls is a brain. In brief, your data are observables, and only observables. And because your technology is so advanced it automatically records when an observable recurs, when it becomes part of a pattern of observables, and if and when they change. Your fantastic technology has the virtue of providing you the existence of *overt, behavioral regularities* and if and when they change.

I trust it is clear that what I am asking the reader to do is a way of asking whether a discernible change in an overt behavior or performance can be a basis for saying anything meaningful about learning. The change may be a desirable one to us, but does our concept of learning caution us that it may not be so viewed by the learner? The change may be undesirable and disappointing but does our concept of learning direct us to what aspects of the learning process and context we should give attention? There may be no change at all, but does the concept of learning allow us to pat ourselves on the back because the individual is learning precisely what we wanted him to learn?

I consider it a glimpse of the obvious to say that what and how we learn is a very complicated process that occurs in a complicated context of interpersonal, transactional relationships in which overt and covert factors are always in relationship to each other but not readily discernible by the participants. I also consider it a glimpse of the obvious that people resist or are unable to take the obvious seriously. Someone once criticized me for introducing too many variables into the learning process and thereby making a difficult problem an impossible one. My answer was that I was not introducing new variables but rather trying to identify and take seriously how I could account for how and why *I* experienced learning, a process I had to conclude had been and was grossly, scandalously oversimplified. Introspection has its drawbacks but that is no warrant for throwing the baby out with the bathwater. If your concept of learning makes little sense for understanding you as a learner, why not, at the least, say it out loud?

I start with an overt behavior regularity you, as Martian, would have noted in the first eleven years of our marriage, which later would change in the daily lives of me and my wife. Would anyone deny that we were in a context in which we would adapt to each other, inevitably experience each other in new and old ways, undergo changes in how, when, and why we relate to parents, new and old friends, in how we think differently about our careers? Is it wrong or inappropriate to say that we were two people learning a lot about ourselves? If we had gotten divorced after one or two years, would you not conclude that we had learned a lot about ourselves and each other that we wished we had not learned? But what would justify you to draw such a conclusion? The answer is that either by personal experience or those of friends or what you have read in the professional literature on marriage and divorce or what you have read in novels; you know that marriage plunges you into a context of mutual learning that is extraordinarily (in this day and age) complicated and that to say "they learned they were not for each other" is a description and not an explanation of the content and process of what was concretely learned.

I shall restrict myself to revealing overt behavioral changes the Martian would have recorded.

1. During the preadoption phase of our marriage we rarely did anything apart from each other (work settings aside). We ate breakfast and dinner together, listened to music together, we went to the movies and theater together, we went food shopping together, we went clothes shopping together (for her and for me), we prepared meals for social occasions in our house together, we cleaned up afterwards together, we watched TV together. In fact, we rarely were not in the same room together. As a friend once remarked, "Where you will find Esther you will find Seymour." The Martian would have noted one other thing: shortly before any of these observables we uttered sounds to each other, which the Martian had no way of decoding. All he could conclude was that these sounds were followed by overt actions. If he became creative enough to understand the sounds coming from our lips, he would learn that the overt behavioral regularity far more often than not involved decision making. We would say he

learned something about the regularity that had puzzled him but we would also say that he had no way of comprehending why it existed and persisted. The existence of a correlation does not constitute an explanation. What you see is what you get, but what you require for explanation causes you to take other factors or regularities into account for purposes of explanation. Over the past century, decade by decade, the average height of men and women has increased. We know that but what puzzles us is that what we want to learn is why it has occurred and the explanation is by no means clear.

2. The above overt regularity changed almost instantly and dramatically with the telephone call that a newborn would be entering our lives. We literally had none of the things you need when you bring a newborn home from the hospital. No crib, diapers, powder, pins, infant formula, bottles, nipples, blankets, wash basin, container for used diapers, carriage, etc. Could we find a practical nurse to help out for a few weeks and where do we start looking for such a person? On what basis do you select such a person? Where should we put the crib? In our bedroom or in an adjoining room? With the passage of the decades my memories about these early weeks are all about my incompetence and anxieties. I was in a situation where I had to acquire new knowledge and, as or more important, use that knowledge in practice. The first time I held Julie in my arms I thought she would waft off into space. Phenomenologically, to me she seemed to weigh several ounces (she weighed seven and a half pounds), and I feared that my slightest movement would crush her. None of this would be recorded by the Martian. I have not been describing observables. And to understand why, I turn to Esther's behavior, her observable behavior.

Esther took over, by which I mean that minutes after the phone call she began to pose and answer questions about what we needed, who could help us (e.g., lend us a crib), and called several stores to find out if they would be open on Sunday and Labor Day, since this was at a time when many stores were closed on those days. She manifested no anxiety; she reacted as if she was faced with a familiar situation for which she was competent. To me she was more than competent, she was no less than my Rock of Gibraltar. I could conceal my anxiety and incompetence; you would not be able to record my internal states, although that concealment and her competence mightily increased the pace of my learning in the month after Julie arrived. It was not that

Esther "taught" me; there was none of that. It was that I watched her with awe and relief. If I asked questions about why she was doing what she was doing with Julie, she would explain, but if I internally had any doubt about what she was doing, I said nothing. On the surface the overt behavioral regularity of talk—decision—action, which characterized our relationship had not changed for the Martian. In fact, it had changed dramatically where Julie was concerned. Esther made decisions, I gladly went along with them. I learned a great deal about Esther, Julie, child development, and parenthood that the Martian had no way of noting or explaining. Learning involves more than observables, when and how they change. The *more* that is involved is significant (if not crucial) depending on the purposes leading you to record observables and the uses you will make of them. *If your purposes are to be a basis for action, you have to go beyond observables.*

3. The pace of human learning is fastest in the first three or four years of life. I knew that as "knowledge," a fact, not something based on personal observation and experience. I was primed to try to be a careful observer of Julie's overt behavior but I was not a Martian with the luxury of his omnipresent, out-of-this-world technology and unlimited time. But I was kin to the Martian in that in the first year of Julie's life my data were only observables. If I noted anything that aroused my attention or curiosity I could not ask her to help me understand what was puzzling to me: crying, refusing the bottle, making the babbling sounds she did, smiling, or why her entire body would go into action when the mobile hanging above her crib started to move. If you had asked me why I found her behavior interesting and puzzling, I would have gone beyond observables and said, "The movements of the mobile obviously delights. It is as if those movements stimulate her to move." I was going beyond observable and *deducing* something about her internal state. That is what all parents of infants do—they are seeking correlations between overt behavior and internal states in order to have a basis for determining whether they can or should take action that will reinforce what you consider to be productive learning. Whether right or wrong, superficial or not, parents employ a conception of what and how infants can and should learn, and that conception is based on or seeks to establish correlations between overt behavior and internal states, as well as to note changes in those correlations. By inevitably starting with the observables, parents are Martians. But from day one the new parent is always going from observables to the infant's internal states.

The above is obvious but it obscures, if not ignores, some facts about what learning involves (although I regard these facts as also obvious, they are given short shrift in practice, especially when children enter school). The first of these is that parents are *motivated* learners using cognitive processes in their attempt to (a) make practical sense of their infant and (b) to become skillful in employing those conclusions in ways important for how they desire that infant to develop. Just as you do not need or have one theory for the oxygen atom and another for the hydrogen atom, you do not need one learning theory for children and one for adults. Of course the developing child and the adult differ in many ways, but that in no way means that the learning process of one is not the learning process of the other. I said that parents are motivated learners. We do not say that infants are motivated learners because that would imply that the infant has internal processes and contents he or she does not have. But what if, say, when an infant cries and wails and you try x, y, and z with no success? The parent may say, "He's trying to tell me something by crying. Maybe he is in pain because he has gas or God knows what. Something is causing, driving him to cry." She may pick up the infant, place it by her shoulder and then pat it repeatedly on the back even though the crying continues, and then the child gives out with a very audible burp and the crying ceases. What about the adult who does not feel well? He has a headache and stomach pains, he takes an antacid pill but it has no positive effect. Suddenly he runs to the toilet and vomits the meal he had at lunch. He begins to feel better. We are likely to say that unlike the infant, he was *aware* he was sick and in pain, which motivated him to take a medication, and soon he was *driven* to run to the toilet to vomit. Granted, what I described is more complex than what I described for the infant where I did not use words that suggested awareness and conscious purpose, but in both cases there was an internal state driving the organism to overt behavioral acts. The words *driven* and *motivated* have conventionally different meanings but that should not obscure the fact that what are called drives in infants are soil for or precursors of what we mean when we say an adult is motivated. So, if we use the word *drive* in the case of infants, let us bear in mind an aspect of the learning process which becomes transformed and increasingly differentiated.

You cannot comprehend infant learning without comprehending parental learning. That brings me to a second fact that narrow conceptions of learning have tended to ignore or not take seriously. I refer to the fact that learning is a process, social-personal-transactional in nature, that takes place in an observable context which has purposes which may give it an observable formal or informal structure or a nonobservable, covert structure. Crucial to describing and explaining the context is the role of the participants in defining the purposes of the context.

For example, in regard to Julie and the mobile over a crib, someone could ask me, "Why did you put a mobile over the crib of a newborn?" The question correctly assumes that Esther and I created a circumscribed context with a purpose or purposes in mind. My answer would have been, "When Julie was awake in her crib and we were not in the room, we did not think that her staring up at the ceiling would be perceptually stimulating, a source of interest, a spur to a discriminating perceptual apparatus. We thought the mobile might have value for learning, for development." We did not know what to expect. (Julie was about two months old at the time.) The first time she saw the mobile she just looked at it fleetingly. I flicked one of the seemingly weightless birds with my fingers, causing all the birds to move. We did this several times, by which time her eyes were wide open and her body the opposite of inactive; this, of course, accompanied by loud expressions of parental delight. Because the mobile was so light and attached to the crib, her bodily activity kept the birds in motion. Several times in the next several weeks, when one of us entered the room, we found Julie and the mobile in action. Julie had learned something and so did we. I do not think it is unwarranted speculation to suggest that Julie learned that there was a relationship between her bodily activity and the mobile's movements. I am not saying she was "aware" of the relationship. All I mean is that she could do something which could alter something else in ways pleasurable to her. No one would say that Julie learned nothing. I trust no one would deny that these types of learning contexts in very young children play a role in the development of a sense of competence, depending, of course, in the individual case on their frequency as well as on experiences in other contexts. Was Julie *driven* or *motivated* to do what she did? It never occurred to me to use the word *driven* as if there was some very strong internal or external force propelling her. *Motivated* was far more appropriate a word to describe her behavior.

The point of this anecdote is that the context I described had purposes and a rationale, all relevant to what we should mean by learning. The first purpose was based on the belief that infants can and should be exposed to patterns of stimuli which generate interest and attention, and contribute to the development of perceptual discrimination. The second purpose was that Esther and I wanted to test that belief, to learn what we could learn. That is but another way of saying that those who create contexts of learning for others should be obliged to see that context as a learning one for them. If that obligation is neither assumed nor taken seriously, the context is still one of learning for others but can mightily decrease what these others learn or do not learn. *As soon as you or someone who wants or needs to learn about how another person learns, the chances mightily increase that you will be sensitive to what the other person may be experiencing.* There is a world of difference between teaching as a unidirectional process and learning with and from each other. That difference is very infrequently recognized or respected in too many school learning contexts.

In this chapter I have indicated that learning is not a thing you can point to but a process that takes place in a describable context in which participants are in a transactional relationship with each other and, therefore, mutually affect each other's learning experience, and brings into play in seamless ways cognitive content and processes: motivation, attitudes, and emotions. Some of these aspects of the complexity of this concept of learning are not observables, but that does not mean that these aspects cannot be elicited, reflected in language, cannot become shared knowledge, appropriately judged and dealt with for the purposes of the context of learning. That cannot happen, of course, if your conception of learning is narrow and renders you insensitive to these aspects. As I shall indicate in later chapters, the few aspects of learning to which that conception of learning refers go a long way to explaining the failures of educational reform. *Conceptions of learning are not developed for the hell of it but as a basis for informing action. As William James would have put it, the "cash value" of your conception is determined by the degree to which your actions have the consequences you desire.*

For centuries doctors resorted in many cases to "bleeding the patient" as a way of purging the body of the causes of their serious illness. They did that despite evidence that the cash value of their well-intentioned actions was less than poor. And up until several decades ago doctors prescribed bed rest of several weeks for patients who had heart attacks, and that prescription was based on a conception of how injured or weak heart muscles could begin to be repaired. Initially, doctors resisted basing their actions on an altered conception that led to action which required getting patients out of bed within a couple of days and encouraging them *to begin* to use their body in normal ways. That resistance vanished when it became apparent that the altered conception and new actions had very substantial cash value. Still another example is that up until three decades ago American surgeons were never in doubt that there was one and only one action dictated by their conception of the bodily dynamics of breast cancer:

mastectomy. There was published evidence that British surgeons frequently, by no means always, performed lumpectomies, which are not as invasive or disfiguring as mastectomies. Two different conceptions, two different actions. When it was clear that outcomes in the two countries were either similar or somewhat better in Britain, the use of lumpectomies in America steadily started to rise. It is worthy of repetition to say that the cash value of conceptions depends on the consequences of the actions those conceptions dictate.

Before taking up the conception of school learning, which has led to actions and consequences whose cash value is, so to speak, nothing to write home about, I devote the next chapter to several examples of learning in early childhood (long before the beginning of schooling) that illustrate why I regard learning as a very complicated process. *Learning is a process that occurs in an interpersonal context and is comprised of factors to which we give such labels as* motivation, cognition, affect, attitudes *(about self and other). These factors are always part of its process to some degree; their strength is never zero.* Test scores have their uses but knowing scores tells you absolutely nothing directly illuminating of the content and contexts of learning. I should emphasize that the psychological aspects I listed as comprising the learning process do not, so to speak, enter and leave the process; they are always in the picture, although their interrelatedness can vary considerably in strength. To understand, grasp, or intuit what is "going on" in the mind of a learner is no easy task, especially if the individual feels you will not understand, or you will criticize or downplay what he is internally experiencing. For example, there is very credible research that students ask very few questions. At home they spontaneously ask many more questions; indeed, parents learn a great deal about what goes on in their child's head from the questions their children ask. Why the difference between home and classroom? The answer I have gotten from students in school or my clinic office is that they fear their teacher will consider their question in some negative way, e.g., the question is silly, irrelevant, or stupid. Students who have a "don't ask, don't tell" stance play it safe. Interpersonal safety is one of the major concerns of the young learner. Unfortunately, the preparation of teachers inculcates in them a conception of learning that renders them insensitive to what the learning process engenders. Ironically, when teachers are required to learn and demonstrate proficiency in a new curriculum, they experience what they are insensitive to in their own students. How you conceive the learning process is a difference that makes a world of difference on the level of action, and that goes a long way to explaining why past and present reform efforts have failed.

Chapter Four

Parents as Teachers

Before their newborn arrives parents have questions, wants, needs, and fantasies about what it "will be and look like." For example, many parents are more than curious about the gender of the newborn. Their curiosity may be so sufficiently strong that the pregnant mother undergoes the procedure by which gender can be determined. Why is that important to such parents? Briefly, there are two integrally related reasons. The first is that they, like all parents, are future oriented; they know that whether it is a boy or a girl is a difference that will make a big difference in their lives. The second reason is that they know—they do not have to be told—that *they* are obligated to adapt to what they find out, that although rearing boys and girls has many of the same features, there are differences which parents recognize or are told to recognize. I entreat the reader to see the movie *Carousel* so as to see and hear the male lead sing "My Boy Bill." The first two-thirds of this very long soliloquy are a fantasy about what his son will grow up to be; he revels at how masculine and macho the boy will be, just like he is. The music and language are stirringly macho in quality. Suddenly he stops singing—a questioning, somewhat fearful expression appears on his face. What if he fathers a girl? His voice becomes strikingly tender as he fantasizes how distinctively smart and pretty she will be. Then the words and music pick up speed and force as he realizes that his lifestyle and low work status have not prepared him for the obligations he will have. The sequence ends with the resolve that he will have to change. *Carousel* is a musical (what an unrevealing word!), a creative work of art illuminating the role of fantasy in those facing parenthood and its impact on expectations and obligations. *Although parents-to-be would not put it this way, their fantasies have at their core the parent's role as teachers.*

In this day and age technology has complicated matters for parents-to-be. What if the "it" is more than one "it?" What if the "it" is in one or another way malformed or a carrier of a genetic defect? Decades ago, before the technology was available to determine the number of babies in the womb, a colleague of mine who became a renowned child developmentalist, Dr. William Kessen, became the father of triplets. He was in shock and so were his friends. How, on his assistant professor's salary, could he afford the requisite housing and help? Would it not negatively affect his research career? And, I should add, he already had two children! Over the years we talked about the experience. Bill, for obvious reasons, had become very interested and knowledgeable about schooling, especially the preparation of teachers, which may account for what he said to me about his experience decades before: "You act and learn, you act and learn, you pray you are doing justice to the kids. The textbooks were worthless. There are no lesson plans. We changed our lesson plans at a dizzying pace. The name of the game was adaptation without getting discouraged. We knew we were learning: we were fearful of what the kids were or were not learning." If before the arrival of the triplets his conception of learning did not give appropriate emphasis to context, it certainly did thereafter.

Before the newborn appears, parents hear much from and discuss with friends, parents, classes for parents-to-be about what to expect from their transactions with the newborn. Many do a lot of reading. Each era has its own pediatrician whose book attains a best-seller, bible-like status. Parents have, so to speak, something akin to a curriculum which tells them what to do, why, and when. But as soon as mother or child come home from the hospital that curriculum loses in varying degrees its comfort-blanket quality. No curriculum prepares you for the unpredictabilities and complexities of "real life"; it is a guide placing on you the awesome responsibility for deciding whether you are implementing it appropriately, and it is the rare parent who is so self-confident of her diagnostic powers as to be nonchalant. Parents differ widely and wildly in personality characteristics. Some follow the curriculum rigidly, some are constantly plagued by anxiety, questions, doubts. Some are nonvigilant observers because they implement the curriculum rigidly, others are disposed to observe and interpret everything the newborn does or does not do. Fortunately, newborns are a resilient lot and in those early weeks their fast growth is accompanied by the fast growth in parental learning. However, there is a not infrequent feature of the relationship that can make positive mutual learning very problematic. I refer to those instances where there is a mismatch between parental and newborn temperaments. Just as two people who decide to marry or live together may find they are temperamentally unsuited for each other—one is passive, quiet, unspontaneous, the other active, explosive, impulsive—parental and newborn temperaments also clash; the parent experiences it as a clash, a mystifying and frustrating one, the infant is only able to display the overt signs of bodily discomfort or displeasure. You could say that it is a clash which neither one understands or wills but it is a mismatch that feeds on itself.

I bring up these instances for two reasons. The first is that these mismatches—which can vary in strength from slight to gory—affect the parent in the role of "teacher." At this stage of the game of infant rearing, parents do not see themselves as "teachers" but as nurturing caretakers of a dependent, helpless organism. But they are teachers in the sense that they have assumed the responsibility to aid the infant to adapt to and learn a curriculum that fosters growth. They are an indispensable part of the infant's context of learning at the same time the infant is part of the parental context of learning. Phenomenologically speaking, the parent is constantly concerned with two questions: Do I understand the needs and overt behavior of my infant child? Am I satisfying those needs in ways productive of growth? Every parent, mismatched or not, asks those questions. In the case of mismatches, what sends the parents up a wall is that whatever they do to help the infant learn and adapt to the prescribed curriculum does not seem to work.

The second reason I brought up mismatches is that among the hundreds of classrooms I have observed there were numerous instances where there was an obvious mismatch between the temperament of the teacher and those of at least two students, and in some cases more than two. Elsewhere (Sarason 2002) I have described one classroom in which the mismatch was between the teacher and the entire class. I should also add that only a few teachers with whom I have had private discussions denied that these "types" of students could be annoying, or irritating, or so phlegmatic as to cause the teacher to wish the student were elsewhere. As one teacher put it, "I try to reach out but I am rebuffed and I give up trying. Sometimes I feel guilty because I know I don't like or take to all my students in the same way. Yes, I have my likes and dislikes." These discussions made me realize that in the school culture teachers are expected to be equally effective with all their students, regardless of differences among them in personality. You do not have to observe classrooms to know that such an expectation guarantees mismatches. To expect that there should be no mismatches between parent and infant is ludicrous.

My purpose here has been to emphasize that in the context of parent-infant transactions, both "actors" are learning with and from each other, for good or for bad. The parent is a learner and a teacher, the infant is a learner, capable only of sending "signals" for the teacher to decode and respond. How the parent interprets and reacts to these signals is the crucial factor in the infant's learning in that context. Learning is a transactional process, whether in infancy or the school classroom. That fact has been obscured by our conventional imagery of what a classroom teacher does, a conventional imagery which emphasizes what and how a teacher does and ignores what a teacher is learning; not only the neophyte teacher but any teacher, whether a kindergarten teacher or a college professor. The teacher who is not learning something new about himself or his students is shortchanging himself and his students. That is an infrequent disconnect between parents and their infants.

Perhaps the most obvious feature of the mother of a newborn is what I would term vigilance. It is as if everything, and what everyone in the home does or does not do is judged by the potential effects on the infant: loud noises or loud talk while the infant is sleeping or feeding, who picks up the infant and how, who prepares the formula and warms it, the sterilization of bottles and nipples, whether a visitor has a cold or puts his or her face too close to that of the infant, whether the father can be trusted to diaper or give the bottle to the infant when the mother is not there to observe, etc. Vigilance is a form of scanning, looking, examining a context (small or large) to determine whether something is amiss or "normal" or puzzling; you scan overt behaviors and regularities from which you deduce covert needs or intentions which require you to act or not. The parent never only scans but rather seeks to understand the overt-covert relationship for a reason the parent takes for granted: what she does can make an important or unimportant difference in the short or long term, but it will make a difference. I emphasize this because in a context of productive learning you expect the parent-as-teacher to be sensitive to the overt-covert relationship. As any parent will attest, that does not mean that what the parent then does will have its intended effects; if the effects are not what she expected she has to reexamine her understanding and decide on another course of action. That is an obligation she has assumed to enable her and the infant to learn. No parent (no classroom teacher) discharges that obligation in an ideal manner, nor should they be expected to; but we expect that they never forget or minimize that obligation because it is a crucial element of a context of productive learning, an assertion I have yet to hear a parent deny. In fact, in my professional experience I have never known a parent to deny that there were times she experienced guilt because she minimized or short-circuited the implications of the obligation. Parents quickly, very quickly, learn that there are no cookbooks containing recipes for how they should deal with their concrete newborns in concrete contexts for which the cookbook in some small or large way is unhelpful. And let us not gloss over the obvious fact that parents-as-teachers are concrete, complicated organisms who vary considerably in their predispositions, thinking, attitudes, sensitivities, and personal and learning styles.

Nothing I have said above was intended to suggest that lapses or mistakes in discharging the obligations of vigilance are serious, let alone unforgivable. That they are frequent I have no doubt. There are two kinds of lapses or mistakes. Those that are occasional or time limited and have little or no adverse consequences, and those mistakes which are repeated over time in relation to a particular behavior and which have adverse consequences (which is not to say they are life long). My limited purpose here has been to emphasize that parents of newborns are quintessentially vigilant observers and actors.

The significance I attach to vigilance both for parent and newborn or infant can be illustrated by a personal experience. A professional friend of mine had returned to work two months after she had given birth to her first child. It was not a decision she and her husband made lightly but her developing professional career would have suffered if she had not returned to work. (She was in a residency program in a medical specialty.) Before giving birth she and her husband, also a young physician, had visited several daycare programs for infants and had selected the one they judged the best; it was in a church which rented out two large rooms to a social agency which created and supervised the program. One room was for infants less than a year old, the other room was for children between one and two years of age. The children were brought to the site at 8 A.M. and could be picked up no later than 6 P.M. On my own initiative I spent one hour observing the room with the youngest children. There were seven infants in the room together with three young women who at most were twenty years old. There was a supervisor for the two rooms but I never saw her in the hour I was observing.

Each infant was lying on its back on a small mattress, all but two of them awake. On one of the walls was a sheet of paper for each child containing the telephone numbers of parents and pediatricians, instructions about time and amount of feeding, and whatever special instructions had been provided by parents or pediatricians. The young women were well spoken, seemed bright and interested, and were likable (to me at least); they were usually talking to each other at the same time at least one or two of them were watching the infants. It was a clean, relaxed, pleasant atmosphere. It was also expensive.

It was not until I left the site and was ordering my reactions and observations that I realized several things. First, there was surprisingly little crying. When a child did cry more than a few seconds, one of the young women would go to the child, make eye contact, stroke it fondly, utter a few words in a soothing voice, but never picked up the child. Second, when a diaper change was necessary, it was done gently but almost always unaccompanied by talk or sustained eye contact or followed by picking up the child. I definitely got the impression that the young women were somewhat fearful of physically handling the infant (the way I was for several weeks picking up Julie). Third, there was no visual or auditory stimulation of the infants (e.g., music, singing).

Let me say that if circumstances *compelled* me to place my infant daughter in a daycare nursery, I would thank God if she were in the one I have described. Having said that, I have to go on and say that I would be guilt ridden because she was not being stimulated in ways an infant should be if its potentials for *sensory discriminations* are to be exploited. Generally speaking, there are two types of learning contexts: where we are learning with peers and where the substance and direction of the learning is the responsibility of someone with delegated power. In the former, power is more or less equal among participants; in the latter, it is a relationship of unequal power. With power comes responsibility. For what purposes? The answer is (or should be) that the person with power is expected to elicit, stimulate, and sustain the development of the learner's capacities, knowing all the while that discharging that responsibility is not a simple rote process and that the context of productive learning is one in which the child and teacher learn from, with, and about each other. Such a context of learning is not unidirectional but bidirectional. What I observed in the day nursery was far more unidirectional than bidirectional. Even when they think they are messing things up, parents of very young children know that the context is inevitably bidirectional. Indeed, it is when they think that they are messing things up that they are most aware of the bidirectional relationship and therefore alter their actions, and altering is an indication that the parents are trying to learn something. Parents do not have to be taught the concept of bidirectionality; they confront and experience it, although they do not articulate it as I have if only because it would not clarify anything they do not already know! I cannot say that for the young women caring for the infants in the nursery.

I observed the nursery for one hour and it may be that if I spent one or two days there, I would have observed more of a bidirectional context of learning. I have used that one-hour observation only as a way of emphasizing that a context of productive learning is a bidirectional one. There was another reason: if I were asked to conduct research evaluating such nurseries, I would, initially at least, study the frequency, quality, and observable consequences of bidirectional transactions. Who is learning what and from whom, and what is the conception of learning undergirding what one has observed?

Let us turn to some examples of what more is involved in the context and process of learning between parent and the young child. What I shall say and describe will be to parents glimpses of the obvious, but as I shall indicate in later chapters about contexts of school learning, the obvious is not only not obvious but frequently absent or simply not taken seriously. What if we asked parents why their six-month-old infant does not walk? Let us leave aside the parent's reaction that she is surprised that we ask such a stupid question. We entreat her to answer. In light of our stupidity she asks that we come back the next day by which time she will have organized an answer. Here is what she might say:

> For one thing, the musculature of the six-month-old infant is not developed to the point where he or she can stand alone. Even if we hold him upright so that his feet touch the ground, his knees would buckle and he might even start to cry because we are holding him in a way strange to him. He cannot see me holding him and he evinces no pleasure at all. If I gently propel him forward his legs are dead weights. Let me put it this way: if the pilot of an airplane high above the ground said I should get in his seat and fly the plane, I would react the way the infant would when being made to make the motions of walking. If I put the infant face down on the floor, he cannot use his hands to lift his body from the floor and he is not able to keep his head up. You don't ask a child to do something he cannot do; even if he were aided to do it, he couldn't, and you would have an unhappy child. They say you have to crawl before you can walk, but it is also true that you have to learn to crawl, the child has to be *motivated* to crawl, to get satisfaction from crawling, and you have to seize the moment when the child indicates in some way that he no longer wants to crawl but to walk.
>
> The child does not wake up one day, stop crawling, and start walking. When you think he is able to stand alone, albeit very unsteadily, you take the child by the hand and walk ever so slowly with him, expressing your delight that he is walking. Eureka. I want

him to know how pleased I am. I want him to develop self-confidence and confidence in me. When I first saw him get up by himself and try to walk, I knew he would fall, and when he did I would sing, "All fall down. Up and down, up and down," from a song we played and he loved. Why exclaim or sing? Because it is the only way I could think of to indicate to him that he should continue to try to walk. I try to motivate him to do what he clearly would be able to do. I'm motivating a motivated child. On one occasion when we were both in the kitchen, I saw him fall, hit his head on the leg of a chair, and begin to scream. I ran and picked him up, saw no blood on his head, and held him closely. I kept kissing and soothing him until he quieted down, at which point I directed his attention to the chair. I wagged my finger at the chair and said, "Bad chair. Bad chair." If you ask me why I did and said what I did, I'm not sure I know. It may well be that I didn't want that experience in any way to interfere with his desire to walk alone. One thing I do know. I was not about to deliver an admonishment which would cause him not to trust that I would *understand* and comfort him. He could *trust* me not to make a bad situation worse.

One more thing and I'll end my mini lecture. It's so obvious that we come to take it for granted. Once a child begins to crawl or walk he becomes an explorer, more of an explorer than he ever was. His curiosity explodes, he is into everything to an extent that can drive you crazy. As any parent will tell you, once a child can crawl or walk your responsibility as a parent increases. You don't want to stifle his curiosity, but you also don't want him to get hurt. How can you handle this so that he remains curious about things, places, and people but is not endangering himself? His curiosity and need to be competent contribute to learning. And, believe me, he is learning a lot even though you as a parent are riveted on the crawling or walking. He is learning more than crawling and walking. It's like when you learn to drive, you are learning far more than you would see from a video of learning to drive. The video gives you the observables, the overt, not the amalgam of covert attitudes and feelings. If you kept a diary of your learning-to-drive experience it would confirm what I have just said. After one lesson from my dad, he insisted I go to a driving school. He simply did not understand what was going on inside of me. It was different with the driving school teacher. She understood. I didn't feel like a klutz and a failure.

A child talks before he or she can talk. That assertion is strange only if by "talk" you mean "being able to say words or sentences." What we conventionally call *talk* are sounds, and long before a child can make the sounds we conventionally call *talk* he has made many thousands of sounds, beginning with his first cry after coming into this world. As parents we may be amused by the child's babbling, gratified that he appears to be developing normally, and then eagerly looking forward to when he can "really" talk. The babbling may have no meaning for us except as a developmental marker, but that overlooks the fact the child hears the babbling. He does not know, of course, that he is causing what he hears but hear it he does. If you closely watch and listen to a child's babbling over time, you will frequently observe that he seems to be getting pleasure from the babbling and that his arms and legs are in action, indeed the entire body. (I know that was the case for our Julie, and when I have queried friends they too said that they had made similar observations.) I offer the hypothesis that when the babbling child hears the sounds he makes, continues to react to what he produces and hears, and takes pleasure from it, it is one of the earliest origins of the sense of competence. After all, he can turn the sounds on or off, quite an accomplishment, although he is, of course, incapable of understanding what is going on. That's what I mean when I say that a child talks before he can talk.

What I have just said is blatantly inadequate in regard to the major factors that clarify how, when, and why children learn to talk. Let us seek to identify those factors, keeping in mind the role of those factors I briefly discussed in the case of walking.

From its earliest days the young infant is exposed to sounds made by parents. The sounds may take the form of words, cooing, singing. Some parents may have music playing on the stereo not only because they enjoy music but also because they want the child to be stimulated by and responsive to the melodies and rhythms of music. Where the mother is the primary caretaker and the father works outside the home, it is the voice (or voices) of the mother that the child hears much more often. We do not know when the child is able to make a discriminating response *to and between* parental voices. One would expect that it would be the primary caretaker who is most with the child and whose modes of auditory stimulation reflect a conception of what every young child needs for normal or optimal development; the mother's modes are not randomly chosen. The caretaker is in the role of parent-as-teacher, although she will not describe herself as such. Over the decades when we would visit homes in which there was an infant and could observe young mothers talk, coo, or sing to their child, I took the opportunity in a handful of instances to say (in what I hoped was a naïve manner), "It's a delight to see how much pleasure you get from talking the way you do to your child. But why do you do it? What do you want to accomplish?" There was an initial unanimous response. It was a facial expression that, so to speak, said, "He is, God help us, a psychologist who knows absolutely nothing about kids and mothers." The other response was also unanimous, although there were differences in what was emphasized. Here is a paraphrase: "I can't help doing what I do. I can't contain my love for her, I can look at her all day long and sing and hug her. Sometimes when she is asleep and I look at her, I want to wake her up and kiss, hug, and talk to her. It's obvious why I do it. It's the only way I have to give her the feeling that she is loved and she can count on my always being there for her. I want her to take pleasure from the pleasure she gives to me." What these young parents wanted their child to learn describes the parent as teacher; they fertilize the present to reap fruits in the future.

I chose learning to talk and walk because they so clearly involve a context in which the processes and contents of learning not only involve attitudes, cognitions, and feelings but other sensory modalities as well. Learning is a *multisensory process* for child and parent-as-teacher. To say that when a child learns to talk he has learned to decode the meaning of language he has heard and can articulate words appropriately is a gross oversimplification which too frequently causes us to take actions characterized by tunnel vision. Learning is a very complicated *indivisible* process. We are a complicated organism when we are born and because of indivisibility of the learning process we become dramatically more complicated over time. We enter the world as a psychologically solo creature. That changes when we are born and the interpersonal living and the socialization process begins.

What happens thereafter very much depends on a combination of parental temperament, expectations, a largely implicit conception of learning, and the young child's temperament and activity level. There are parents who believe a child should be fed on a schedule, and there are parents who believe you feed the child when you think, for whatever reason, that feeding the child will be satisfying. There are parents who believe that when you put the child to sleep and he cries, it is all right to let the child cry himself to sleep and not to "learn" that crying leads to being picked up; other parents feel that to let the child cry itself to sleep will have untoward effects. There are parents who believe that you should not start toilet training until the child gives signals that he or she is ready; other parents believe that such a view leads to a permissiveness not in the best interests of the child.

None of these parents is a "good" or "bad" parent. It is the rare parent who will knowingly do something which by her lights is not in the best interest of her child. There was a time when it was believed that a particular rearing practice in the early years would be correlated with the child's functioning and personality when he or she reaches adulthood. Research has effectively disconfirmed such predictions. Just as a too-simple conception of learning blinds us to the complexity of the context and processes of learning, it also leads us to ignore the even greater complexity of the developmental process. It's like forecasting the weather for next week on the basis of today's weather. You can make such forecasts as long as you take seriously what meteorologists have learned: the prediction increasingly loses validity after the first two days.

The practical significance of any conception inheres in the actions we believe it justifies us to take. Each of us is a partisan for our particular conception, especially if we are in the role of parent as teacher or of a classroom teacher. That is both understandable and predictable because we have been given and assumed the responsibility to facilitate learning in others who have less power. In fact, the more equal the power or authority between teacher and learner—both of whom are adults—the more obvious it is that too-simple conceptions of learning are unproductive, that there is more in the picture than our conception contains.

What I have attempted to indicate in these pages is what our conception should contain and why, not because I dreamed it up in an armchair but because I have been a learner; I have been a student, parent, and teacher; I have observed and talked with learners (students) and teachers (parents and classroom teachers); I have been a clinician and researcher trying to understand and help individuals failing or unhappy in a context in which they are learners or teachers, and in the course of these experiences I found I had to *unlearn* a lot of my conventional preconceptions. That unlearning was neither quick nor without humbling struggle.

I am not by temperament or interest a theoretician. I have respect for, and in no way do I devalue, those who attempt in a systematic way to give us a picture of the nature of human learning. The problem for me in regard to those attempts was that they left out a good deal, and what they left out were factors *always* part of the learning experience, not occasional, unpredictable intrusions; their strength and consequences may vary widely but are never zero. Here are the factors of which the learning process is composed in, for example, the classroom.

1. Learning is a process that takes place in a circumscribed context with the publicly stated purpose of aiding students to acquire new knowledge and skills deemed by educators and other adults to be important for desirable change and growth of students.

2. Students come to this context with curiosity, attitudes, expectations, emotions, and feelings the strength of which depends in large part on previous learned life experiences. These features of the learning process will undergo transformations in strength and

consequences depending on what students begin to experience in the new context of learning. Learning is not a point in time but a process over time. Not all the features I have mentioned are always observable. Nevertheless, it is not an unwarranted act of faith to say that their presence can be taken for granted. It is totally unwarranted to assume that what is not observable or articulated is not playing a role.

3. What I have said about students is no less the case for teachers who approach a new school year with curiosity, attitudes, expectations, emotions and feelings, again depending on previous learning experiences in the school context. It is also the case both for students and teachers: how they experience the classroom context of learning is related to what they experience outside of the classroom and school. That relationship may vary considerably but it too is never zero; it may vary from being dramatically disruptive to being dramatically supportive.

4. In the learning context the teacher is front and center, a figure the student seeks to understand, characterize, and overtly to conform to the teacher's instruction style and rules. At the same time the student hopes and expects that he will not only like the teacher but also that she will like him, that he can trust her to understand him and to treat him with fairness and respect, to be someone who will not disparage him or make him feel inadequate or like a failure or embarrass him before other students whose friendship and respect he very much wants. The student is a neophyte psychologist very much aware of himself and a scanner of his social surround, all in the service of being seen as worthy in the learning context.

5. The *beginning* teacher approaches her role agonizingly aware that the moment of truth has arrived. She will be on her own teaching a group of students. She is anxious and curious. Will she be adequate? Will the students "take" to her? Will she take to them? Will the children know or sense that this is her first real experience as a teacher? Will there be a couple of students who will be hard to handle? Will there be incidents she will handle poorly that other teachers and the principal will learn or hear about and that will cause them to see her as inadequate? What if more than a few students are not learning what she expects of them? The questions are many. In brief, the teacher knows she is a learner beset with questions only time will answer and that the answer will depend on what she has done. She may feel secure in her knowledge but she

also knows that the bottom line by which she will be judged will be how well her students do on achievement tests. By the end of the first year the beginning teacher may have concluded that her preparation for the role left much to be desired and/or that she is temperamentally unsuited for the role of teacher.

There is more to the learning process than I have given above and I shall discuss these elements in later chapters. But I hope that what I have said indicates to the reader that the concept of learning should refer to and in action make us sensitive to personal and interpersonal, cognitive and affective, overt and covert features that are always in the picture, their strength never zero.

I did not dream up this encompassing, complex conception. In fact, I have never met a person who denied that the components I listed were operative in their learning experiences, however weak or occasional. For fifteen years I was engaged in a research program on test anxiety in college students and elementary schoolchildren (Sarason, et al. 1960). We would administer a simple oral set of questions to all children in a particular grade, to which the children would encircle a *yes* or *no* on a sheet of paper. We would make a distribution of scores and, as previously agreed, we showed the distribution (no names) to the classroom teachers. In each instance the teacher was more than surprised that a dozen or more students admitted to experiencing very high or somewhat high anxiety when they were given tests, and some teachers said that you could not trust how children respond to a questionnaire. Support for our conclusions was provided by subsequent longitudinal studies. I mention our project here to emphasize the point that if your conception of learning is one that leads you to rivet on overt behavior, you are rendered insensitive to important features in the experience of the process of learning. The artistry of teaching inheres in the ability to elicit and make those features overt. But you cannot do that if your conception of learning does not direct you to these features and issues.

Take the case of a high school student who on the final achievement test gets a high score. What significances are we justified in attaching to that score? The teacher, of course, is gratified and we assume the student is as well. Why ask about other significances? He learned what he had to learn, period. But what about formal research which confirms what many middle and high school teachers have told me and others: as students go from elementary to middle to high school their interest in school learning steadily goes downhill, and that is true in suburban and urban schools. What if we found that our high-scoring student experienced the course as uninteresting and a bore and he thanks God that he will never have to take any more courses in that subject; he can enjoy the forgetting process. Does your conception of learning permit you to be content that aside from subject matter he learned other things not so gratifying as getting a high score? *Is that question irrelevant to your conception of learning?* If your answer is yes, then you would have to say that how a person learned to make a lot of money is testimony to his abilities regardless of what he learned in amassing his fortune and how that learning influences what he does with it. Similarly, you may take your body temperature and be gratified that it is normal, but that does not mean that you are healthy or have learned how to sustain a state of health.

What makes it so important to have or flesh out your conception of learning? The answer is that as parents of very young children we have a picture of what we want them to learn to be and become. As parents we judge what we observe and do by what it portends for the future. We may not realize that that concern implies, among other things, the assumption that learning is a *continuous* process by means of which the parts of the picture become more complexly integrated and enable the child to adapt to and master new tasks and responsibilities consistent with the picture. For parents the goals or purposes of learning are in the present and future. And that picture and its goals are never about one aspect but about many which we label as *cognitive, affective, emotional, motivational, attitudinal.* It is not a surrealistic or cubistic picture whose parts appear to be unrelated but a picture of an individual living and learning in accord with it.

An analogy may be appropriate here. Parents of a very young child will tell you, if asked, whether a time will come when that child will be of age to learn to drive a car and they, the parents, will give assent. "Of course," the parents will reply. But when that time comes parents find themselves wrestling with several questions. Why is he seemingly obsessed with learning to drive? Why is it such an all-consuming need, as if his life will be transformed? From time to time he has done some silly things that were dangerous, can I trust him to be careful and show judgment when he is behind the wheel? Should we say that for a while at least he cannot drive the car with his friends in it, leery as a parent may be that a couple of his friends are on the wild, impulsive side? Should we for a while say that he cannot drive the car without a parent present? Will he rebel if we tell him that he cannot use the car on school days and only occasionally on weekends? Do we tell him that when he uses the car to go someplace, he should call us up to say he arrived safely? Will he regard that as a sign that we do not trust him and we are treating him as a little child?

The questions are many but they do not include any doubt that the child will learn what we conventionally mean by driving; that it will be no problem for him. It is a mélange of noncognitive factors that concerns the parents. Learning to drive is a quintessential example of an activity that contains a number of factors bearing the imprint, style, and quality of those factors from past contexts of learning. Most parents know that from personal experience, just as they know that the test scores their child gets—be they high, middling, or low—reflect more than cognitive factors.

I have said and tried to illustrate that parents are teachers who implicitly or explicitly have a conception of learning undergirding their actions—a conception they believe will be productive in the sense that the child will be enabled to be and become the kind of person they deem desirable. I can assure the reader that parents differ widely in their consistency, sensitivity, flexibility, or even competence. What I have tried to do in these introductory chapters is to give a few examples of learning contexts which most parents create and by which the very young child learns to perform certain functions which she is capable of and which are essential to performing other functions. And I did this in order to contrast the learning process in early life with school learning contexts. That these contexts of learning are radically different needs no emphasis. That the conception of learning of the two contexts is radically different does require emphasis, because those differences go a long way to understanding why educational reform has been and will continue to be disillusioning and in some ultimate sense catastrophic for the society.

Chapter Five

Home and School Contexts
of Learning

What are some of the most obvious differences between a child's home and his or her school as a context of learning? Let us try to answer the question in the case of young children starting school. Certainly the most obvious answer is that a school is a much larger place than the home. It not only is larger and contains many more rooms but the chairs, desks, windows, eating site, toilets are also very different; the halls are much wider, the floor coverings are bare and the walls more often than not are bare. The child is taken to his room where he will "reside" five days a week over a period of ten months. It is an encapsulated room in the sense that the child has little or no opportunity to visit other rooms and get to know other teachers and students. He may hear or know that there is someone called a principal who is king or queen of this realm, not someone to trifle with. It may take more than a few weeks to see the principal, maybe even hear her talk; she is an important but remote figure, the kind young children associate with danger. Not so incidentally, I have met more than a few children who near the end of the first grade could not tell me the name of the principal; some of those who knew it were told her name by their parents or older siblings. If you doubt or are surprised by what I have said, I must report that on a visit several decades ago to a large midwestern high school with two thousand students and 154 teachers, I, in my innocence, asked a teacher what a faculty meeting with so many teachers was like. Her answer was, "We have departmental faculty meetings. Once or twice a year the whole faculty meets in the auditorium but it is really not what you would call a faculty meeting where issues are raised and discussed. All meetings last for less than an hour." She then said something I never forgot, which was confirmed by what other teachers in comparable high schools told me: "There are teachers in this school I would not recognize if I saw them on the street. I would say that I have never had a face-to-face interaction with more than half of the teachers." We like to think that schools are places where educators have similar outlooks and work together to implement an educational vision and publicly proclaimed goals consistent with that vision. That is frequently not the case in middle and high schools. On the surface it is more frequently the case in elementary schools, which are much smaller, but anyone who, like me, has discussed faculty meetings with teachers (especially in urban schools) will conclude that these relatively brief meetings are conduits for directives from central office and antithetical to a sense of community, of a context of shared learning. There are exceptions, of course, but they are just that: exceptions.

Let us return to the child starting school from the standpoint of this question: What are some of the differences between learning contexts in school and those at home? The first and most obvious difference is that in school the child is placed in an encapsulated space in what we call a classroom, whereas in the years before elementary school much of what he was experiencing and learning occurred not in one place but in a variety of sites in and out of the home. He may experience the shopping mall, the supermarket, homes of friends and relatives, the park, the outdoors after a snowstorm, traveling in a car (locally and elsewhere), a trip to a zoo, celebrating Thanksgiving and religious holidays and birthdays, going to parades, being read to at bedtime. These and many more events and sites make up childhood experience. But those experiences are in varying degrees contexts of learning. They can, again in varying degrees, satisfy curiosity and be exciting. The child is not a physically and mentally passive character; he or she, so to speak, eats up new experience. Indeed, most parents seek to enlarge the child's experience. They may be rich or poor, educated or not, but they make some effort to expose the child to new contexts of learning. If the child has older siblings, the variety of new contexts increases. What, if anything, a child learns in and from any of these experiences depends on the extent to which parents are sensitive to and exploit them for the purposes of learning. And, one must add, parents are well intentioned but that does not mean that how and when they handle these experiences may not be antithetical to productive learning. It is certainly not my intention to portray the years before school as nonproblematic for children and their parents. It is my intention to indicate that those are years in which the child's curiosity, motivation, attitudes toward self and others, and feelings become interrelated and a basis for and part of the process of learning: they are the child's phenomenology in learning contexts.

All of the above changes when the child starts school. The child may approach school with unalloyed curiosity and enthusiasm, with no doubts about her competence to do well, to be seen as worthy, to be understood; at the other extreme are children who have all kinds of doubts about their competence, their worthiness, their likability. Aside from curiosity, the other thing all children have in common is hope; hope that they will now begin to experience that transformation from being a dependent child to one on the way to adulthood.

The child finds herself in a strange-looking room. She may have come there in a school bus with other children, most of whom are strangers to her. In the strange-looking room there is another stranger: the teacher. The child takes or is given a seat, her seat for one year. The teacher calls the class to attention, gives her name, and offers words of welcome. I am not aware of any study focusing on the teacher's welcoming words. Do they in any way speak to questions in the minds of the children? Do they, for example, say anything about the rest of the school? Does she say they will have an opportunity to see the rest of the school, e.g., the gym, the cafeteria? Will they meet the principal? Why does a school need a principal? Do her words contain any humor? How do the children feel on their first day of school? She will ask each child to stand and give his or her name. She will not write their names on the blackboard nor will she ask if the child has a friend or friends in the class.

The reader may feel I am attaching great importance to words of welcome. I do not attach great importance to them, but neither do I want to gloss over the obvious fact that the children inevitably do not regard them as perfunctory; children form first impressions the way we do. First impressions are first impressions, which may or may not undergo change. I rivet on those words because it is the first opportunity the teacher has to begin to speak to the child's unverbalized expectations, questions, and hopes. I like to put it in this way: in a context of learning for new students it is the teacher's obligation to know and adapt to where the child is psychologically coming from, which is akin to saying children in the class are not coming from the same psychological place. That variation—which every teacher is aware of before she sets foot in the classroom—is a bedeviling problem for teachers and I am only saying here that however inconsequential welcoming may be, it should not be regarded as devoid of any significance, however transient, to students.

By the end of the first day the students have begun to learn what I have termed the constitution of the classroom (Sarason 1996a): what students should or should not do, what is expected of them, and what is off limits. That sounds right, natural, and proper. However, at home, preschoolers between, say, ages two and five are told what they can and cannot do, but frequently (certainly not always) they are given explanation; e.g., "You have to drink the milk because it will make you strong, and then you will be able to do or pick up things you are not able to now." "You must not light a match because it may give off sparks that burn you," "You may get very angry at Mommy and Daddy but you must not hit us, because it's wrong to hit people," "You cannot play with your friends outside in front of the house because it is too near the street and you or one of your friends could get hurt by a car if you don't see it coming. You can only play there if Mommy or Daddy are out there watching," "You can ask Mommy and Daddy any question you want about something you do not understand. We will try our best to give you an answer that will help you understand. You learn by asking questions."

Parents differ considerably in the frequency, clarity, and persuasiveness of their explanations. Parents are not born with the ability to explain everything to young children, who at these ages are normally egocentric and governed by the pressures of instant gratification; they can make childrearing test the limits of parental tolerance and dull sensitivity. If you put a hungry rat into a complex maze, it does not take long before it learns that when it makes contact with a bar at a certain point it will receive a pellet of food. That is no model for the context of mutual learning, which parent and child are inevitably in over many years. It is not easy for parent or child. The explanation of one can be the frustration for the other; it can also be one with which the child agrees, however reluctantly. Someone should do a systematic study of the whens, hows, and substance of parental explanations and compare those frequencies and their observable consequences with instances where explanations were not given but should have been given. I consider explanations a form of respect we owe children even though this or that explanation may have to be given or altered many times. And by respect I in no way imply anything resembling permissiveness. In a context of productive learning, respect is a way of openly acknowledging that the learner needs and wants explanation of your behavior, words, and directives. For example, before the child starts school he or she has become interested in sexual matters: Why do boys (or Daddy) have a penis and girls (or Mommy) do not? How are babies "made"? How do babies come out of women's bodies? Young children can manifest their curiosity in diverse ways but certainly one of them is to ask questions of parents. Most parents expect those questions, they do not view them as indications in any way abnormal, and they know they should offer explanations even though all of these parents are never totally secure about the adequacy of their explanations and are very insecure about how the child is interpreting the answer. But these parents try in their own ways to accord respect to the child's needing and wanting an explanation for something that is the opposite of trivial to him or her. Then there are those parents who for one or another reason do not or cannot respond to the questions and may seek to divert the child's questions elsewhere, or say the time will come when he will be able to understand an answer, or by words and body language indicate that the subject is off limits and that is that.[1]

I said that by the end of the first day—and certainly in my experience by the end of the second day—the children starting school are told what the constitution of the classroom is, the rules of the game of classroom life. *It is a constitution constructed by the teacher that appoints her or him to perform the executive, legislative, and judicial functions.* One thing is clear to students: they are expected to obey and support that constitution and if they do they will learn what they are supposed to learn. And with rare exceptions they do obey. Besides, most (really all) parents have told their child to obey the teacher because that is precisely what they, the parents, were told and did. Parents are aware that classroom and home are two very different contexts of learning and that their constitutions are far from identical. More than a few parents will be concerned with how their child will "take" to the new learning context, e.g., Will my Jimmy be able to sit still for most of the several hours of the school day? Will he be able to refrain from talking to other kids when he is not supposed to? Will my sweet, demure, noncompetitive Mary volunteer an answer to a question the teacher has asked the class or will she be content to go unnoticed? Will my Cathleen be able to tell the teacher that she already knows how to read? Will my Jeremy, who has learned to do what other children do except that it takes him longer, feel dumb in the eyes of the teacher? If starting school is a momentous occasion for the young child, it also

---

1. I trust the reader will understand that I am not writing a textbook where I would be obliged to (a) describe the complexity of dealing with children's sexual questions, (b) when and why parental explanation can be a productive or unproductive learning experience both for child and parent, (c) cite line and verse from a huge theoretical, research, and clinical literature on curiosity, question asking, and their consequences. My purpose in these pages is the limited one of indicating that your conception of learning is fateful for how you stimulate, respond, and sustain the need to get answers to questions.

is momentous for the parent who has brought up the child and knows him in ways the teacher cannot. For the parent, his child starting school raises what I call the "marital question": Are the teacher and my child a match that will withstand interpersonal potholes?

One of the unverbalized assumptions undergirding the school and teacher's approach to young students is that the teacher is knowledgeable and sensitive to a degree that will allow her relatively quickly to determine the nature of the individuality of each child and to adapt to it. That assumption is patent nonsense. Discerning a child's individuality in the context of the classroom takes the most unusually sensitive teacher weeks. As I have discussed elsewhere (Sarason 1993a), teacher preparatory programs are scandalously inadequate as preparation for understanding individuality. (Gifted teachers were gifted before they entered a preparatory program.)

There is an irony here. It is only in the last few decades that educators have emphasized that parents and educators have to be partners in the educational process, a belated reaction to a past when parents were restricted to raising money for special needs of a school. It was a past that was more like a cold war which occasionally heated up; parents were tolerated and were not greeted warmly and neither were their ideas about school policies. The reaction was belated and a recognition that the public generally was more than concerned with disappointing educational outcomes. The irony is that, history aside, no sane teacher has ever denied that parents know their children in ways teachers cannot. The knowledge a parent has may vary from being largely correct and helpful to being grossly subjective, skewed, and misleading, but in either case the parent is conveying a picture of the child in a context of learning which is not irrelevant to how the teacher approaches the child in the classroom context of learning. Let me be more concrete. Decades ago (Sarason 1976) I suggested that in the month before school opens a teacher should meet with the parents of each child he will have in his class when school opens. This is what the teacher would say:

> I am going to be your child's teacher and I want to be of as much help to your child as possible so that he (she) finds school and learning rewarding. You know your child in ways and to a degree I obviously do not. You are his parents, which means that you have also been his teacher. You can be enormously helpful to him and me by describing him to me. For example, what interests him the most? What turns him on or off from this or that kind of task, situation, or person? Every person, young or old, has assets and vulnerabilities. How would you describe him in these respects? What do you think I ought to know that would make me effective in teaching him? Also,

> I have to feel that anytime I have a question I can call and discuss it
> with you. Similarly, I want you to feel that you can call and talk
> with me about any question you have. Like you, I do not wait until I
> am sure there is a problem. I find it comforting and helpful to use
> parents as a sounding board because far more often than not what
> they tell me erases the question in my mind. I want you to feel you
> can use me in the same way.

You cannot or should not say the above (or a more felicitous version) unless you truly believe that parents have something important
to tell you about how you will go about understanding and teaching
their child. Most parents can sense the difference between sincerity
and empty rhetoric. All parents pray and hope their child will have a
teacher who will try to ferret out their child's individuality, and parents want to feel that they can *safely* voice their opinions and observations. *And by* safely *I mean that the parent-teacher relationship has changed
from a formal, distant, and unproductive context of learning to a productive
one which, of course, should be a feature of the teacher-student context of learning.* When you say (and mean) that parents should have a role in their
child's schooling, the parent-teacher relationship becomes one of mutual learning, otherwise the concept of relationship—like that of
learning—is narrow, empty rhetoric which has the effect of missing
the forest for the trees. When a child enters the school context of
learning, he or she continues to experience a home context of learning. The pressing, practical problem both for parent and teacher must
be to be vigilant to the degree to which the two contexts are influencing each other, always keeping in mind that in the mind of the child
they are always related to each other, a fact of which parents are more
aware than are teachers. Why is it as predictable as night following
day that after the first day of starting school, parents ply the child with
questions? "Tell me what happened in school. What did you learn? Do
you like your teacher? Did you get a chance to talk with any of the
other students? Did the teacher call on you for any reason? Did you
like school as much as you expected? What did you like best about
school today? What did you like least?" Parents vary in the number
and content of their questions on that and succeeding days depending
in part (sometimes a large part) on the questions they had about how
their child will take to the school, especially to the teacher. When in
the preschool years parents for the first time have need of a baby-
sitter, they will not choose anyone. They seek someone they feel they
can trust to deal appropriately with their child when he or she mani-
fests x, y, and z types of behavior, someone about whom they have
judgments by others about competence, maturity, and trustwor-
thiness, someone who will respect the individuality of their child.

Parents have a degree and quality of investment in their child—a long-term investment—that teachers cannot have, if only because the classroom obviously has far more than one child with whom the teacher's relationship ceases after nine or so months. That is reason enough to suggest that a teacher should forge a relationship with parents who may provide information very relevant to a child's context of classroom learning; it may be the difference between a context of productive and unproductive learning. *How you react to my suggestion depends on your conception of the ingredients of a context of productive learning*, i.e., the degree to which you take seriously that the process of learning involves more than the acquisition of subject matter. That in no way lessens the crucial importance of subject matter, it simply underlines the obvious: how the child comes to regard subject matter and school learning—what the child is learning about school learning—is not intrusive, background noise in the learning process, it contributes to who the child is becoming as a thinker. Again I remind the reader of studies clearly indicating that as children go from elementary to middle to high school the value they attach to school learning goes steadily downhill and that is true in suburban and urban schools; it was what hit me with full force when my test anxiety research brought me into schools. High school teachers knew this long before I did or the studies appeared. Within a handful of years after World War II a movement began around the question, How do we make learning more interesting to students? You would think that that question would have stimulated discussion and study of the defining differences between contexts of productive and unproductive learning but it did not, the usual exceptions aside. Then came the sizzling sixties, when the word *interesting* was replaced by the word *relevant*: how do we make school learning relevant to students' life experience outside of school? But no one asked, What context of learning will make the "from what to what" productive and not an exercise in mindless thinking, let alone a devaluation of subject matter? All this happened as indices of school achievement declined year by year. Then, predictably, came the "back to basic" reaction which, generally speaking, was based on the most narrow conception of learning, as if the history of education did not contain scads of red flags saying that the more things change the more they remain the same. It is as if the motto of this movement was, If the test scores are declining then, by God, we will make sure that scores on tests of subject matter will go up. Improvement by fiat. It is like telling a child he is going to be toilet trained and the feat has to be accomplished in three weeks. Or else.

I have said that the parent-teacher relationship, like that between teacher and student, like that of parent and child, is a context in which mutual learning and adaptation occurs, for good or for bad and why. In regard to my suggestion that teachers and parents begin to forge their relationship before the school year begins, I make two assumptions. The first is that the reader does not regard my suggestion as off the wall, as possessing no persuasive rationale bearing on the goal of increasing the likelihood that the context of school learning for the child will be a productive one: motivation will be engendered and sustained, attitudes about the significance and rewards of learning will be reinforced, feelings about self and subject matter will contribute to a sense of growth, and future school learning will be willingly embraced.

Before going on to the second assumption I feel compelled to assure the reader that I do not regard my suggestion as an initial magical potion that will put the child, parent, and teacher on the royal road leading to the exploitation and fulfillment of their capacities, hopes, and dreams. I know we live on Earth and not in a heaven. I know that in the realm of human, social affairs we are never dealing with problems that have solutions in the sense that four divided by two equals two is a solution. And I like to quote H. L. Mencken's caveat that for every societal problem there is a simple answer that is wrong. As we shall see below as well as in a later chapter my suggestion is by no means simple. I offer it here as a way of discussing what the concept of learning refers to.

The second assumption is that some readers, especially those who are teachers, administrators or city or state officials, will say that my suggestion vastly underestimates predictable practical problems affecting its implementation. For example, educators will not take kindly (if at all) to a suggestion that they work the month before school opens or even two or three weeks before the new school year. But, they would say, even in the unlikely event that they went along with the suggestion, would public officials agree to pay educators for the time required? City officials (even boards of education) are not noted for their willingness or enthusiasm or ability to support a "good idea." There are a lot of good ideas. Why is your idea better than a lot of other good ideas?

I brought up my apparently not-so-simple idea for several reasons. First, I needed to make the obvious point that the parent-school relationship is at best distant or superficially ritualistic or downright insincere and at worst marked by resentment, divisiveness, adversarialism. (The parent-teacher relationship is remarkably similar to and as unproductive as that between teachers and those in the hierarchy above them. In terms of role, recognition, and power, teachers see themselves as at the bottom of a pyramid-shaped educational mountain, at the top of which are a few people who proclaim policies informing teachers what they should think and do. Teachers do not see their kinship to parents.)

The second reason was to indicate that when and how the parent-teacher relationship begins should not be a matter of empty ritual and certainly not when a parent has a complaint, or when the teacher thinks there is a problem she will have to discuss with a parent with whom she has hardly spoken, both occasions of a type which is truly emotionally loaded and frequently has adverse consequences. My suggestion derives from a conception of mutual learning which says, so to speak, "You start when there is no painful problem on the agenda, when the parent can experience acknowledgment for what she knows, when the seeds of trust can be sown, when both teacher and parent begin to feel safe with each other, and when the responsibilities of each in the future are recognized." My suggestion does not derive solely from the obligations of courtesy or noblesse oblige but from the recognition that the two people need each other, need to learn from each other in order to do what they can to make school learning productive for the child.

The third reason was to make a point that is central to this book: When you examine the organization, culture, and interpersonal relations in and around schools, and when you begin to understand the many problems schools have, it is clear that the conventionally narrow conception of learning on which schools are based (the usual exceptions aside) is not only the major culprit but also the major obstacle to any self-searching scrutiny of an alternative, more encompassing, more realistic conception of learning. And by realistic I mean that the process and contents of learning are a configuration, a gestalt, of features for which we have labels like *attitudes, motivation, emotions, thinking, problem solving, curiosity, judgment,* etc. *We use those labels as if they are isolated parts that "happen" to come into play in the learning process, thus glossing over that they are always present and their strength is never zero.* When in earlier decades psychologists spent their days putting hungry rats in a maze to see how quickly they could learn to get a pellet of food, they were not interested in what was "going on inside" the rat or even why rats varied (as they did) in their overt behavior while running the maze. They were interested in time, degree of hunger, and difficulty of the maze and what they could deduce about motivation. Human learning is a different ball game in a different park with a different audience interested in multiple goals. In one respect, unfortunately, the two games are very similar: The narrow interest of the rat psychologist, mirroring their narrow conception of learning, is highly similar to what we are seeing in the educational scene today, where test scores are center stage and mirror a ludicrously narrow conception of learning. And that brings me to the fourth reason which in an ultimate sense is the most important of all: *The compulsive, pressured concern with test scores as an explanation of learning totally ignores the distinctions between contexts of productive and unproductive learning, distinctions without which test scores are just that: numbers which tell us next to nothing and lead to reforms (when they do) which essentially are based on the same narrow conception of learning that sets the stage for future disappointments.*

When over the decades I would meet with groups of teachers, I would ask this question: Take the twelve-year period of life beginning with age six, and pick out one or two instances in which you experienced learning something you did not know before and which impacted on you, the significance of which has stayed with you so that you can recall it today. Ponder that for a few minutes because I want you to tell me the features of that experience, and we can determine what if anything is common to what all of you relate."

I deliberately did not use the words *classroom* or *school*, although the time period I indicated probably was interpreted as referring to school. The teachers had great difficulty coming up with instances. But I persisted and encouraged them to persist. But in each group the ice would be broken by someone who related, for example, a particular camp experience, a long family vacation trip, staying with grandparents and listening to the stories of their lives, being told their parents were going to be divorced. I could but will not elaborate on the fact that what teachers very briefly described contained or implied many of the features of a context of productive learning. *I bring up what teachers described to make the point that not one instance took place in a classroom or school.* That did not surprise me because during the years I met with groups of teachers, my eyes had been opened to the obvious: Generally speaking, again the usual exceptions aside, classrooms are dull, boring, unstimulating places both for students and teachers. And it was also at that time that John Goodlad (1988) was saying the same things in his heroic study described in his book *A Place Called School*. As I said earlier, that assertion is most applicable to middle and high school classrooms.

Parents of preschoolers do not have to be told that their children are question-asking characters, albeit they vary in how they react to and answer those questions. But they have no doubt their children are curious about this or that aspect of the human and physical world around them, reflected in facial expression and questions. Parents will attest that questions beget questions. For example, when my daughter Julie was about four she held up her hand, fingers spread apart, and pointing to the spaces between her fingers asked me, "Why don't we have fingers here?" I was flustered. Of all the questions I had heard or read about, questions young kids asked, Julie's was not one of them. I played for time to come up with an answer which at the least I thought might be satisfying to her, although I intuited that there was more to her question than she conveyed. So I said to her in what I thought was a nonchalant manner, "That's the way people are made." To which, looking me straight in the eye, she responded, "Daddy, how are people made?" That cat was out of the bag! One question begets an answer which begets more questions and on and on and on. I never felt I handled it well but I was always at pains to show her my respect by answering them, however much I would mumble and jumble. A context of productive learning is one in which you expect, encourage, and stimulate questions. A context of unproductive learning is one in which you do not expect or want questions, or give answers that are essentially brush-offs, or you tell the child to stop asking "silly" questions. There are parents, of course, who would act on the knowledge of the children's curiosity but have never been given or acquired that knowledge.

So let us take up question asking in the classroom. I still find it mind-boggling that in the past one hundred years the number of studies of question asking in the classroom is no more than fifteen. You would expect that in light of the truly voluminous literature—one that would fill a modest-sized library—on the significance of children's question asking for learning, that the research literature on *question asking in the classroom* would be high. Educational researchers apparently do not consider intellectual curiosity and question asking important and worthy of study.

I ask the reader to take a few moments to ponder and answer this question: In fourth-, fifth-, and sixth-grade social studies periods of fifty minutes, in a suburban school, how many questions relevant to the subject matter will students *spontaneously* ask? How many questions will teachers ask? The last study on those questions, and the most rigorous of all previously done, was in 1969 by Dr. Edward Susskind. Before relating his findings I should report that since his study (done at Yale in the psychology department) I have asked scads of groups and individuals those questions. In regard to questions by students the answers ranged from zero to five; for teachers the answers ranged from twenty to sixty. What was striking to me was the facial expression of respondents. A knowing smile would appear, as if they knew from their experience as students that the discrepancy was very large. Susskind's finding was two questions by students—it could be two questions by one student—and from forty to well over a hundred questions by teachers. *Those results are a defining feature of a context of unproductive learning reflective of the most narrow conception of learning; students are passive recipients of knowledge from teachers.* I trust the reader will understand that when I say that the modal American classroom is, generally speaking, a boring, unstimulating context of learning, I did not dream up this idea out of whole cloth, just as I did not use whole cloth to dream up the assertion that as students go through the grades their interest in and value attached to school learning goes down steadily. Dr. Susskind was one of my graduate students, and when I learned that he and my colleague, Dr. Murray Levine, were going to study question asking in the classroom I was much more than interested, because they would provide me with a check on my own observations of classrooms which lead me to conclude that efforts of educational reform were doomed because of the lack of recognition of the differences between contexts of productive and unproductive thinking. I was and am aware of the risks you take and the mistakes you can make when you rely only on personal observations, which is why Susskind's proposed study was so important to me.

Both today and in the past, critics of our schools have said that schools are not educating students who can think, who can become critical thinkers. Those critics are well intentioned, their assessment is valid, but what they say is empty rhetoric because of what they do not know and, therefore, cannot say. I take this up in the next chapter where we return to differences in the context of learning between school and home.

Chapter Six

What Do We Mean by Critical Thinking?

What do we mean by thinking, critical thinking? What do we mean when we say you learn to think, to be a critical thinker? The second question implies that we are not thinkers at birth, that whatever we mean by thinking has a long, developmental history. No one would deny that by the time a child starts school he or she is already a thinker. Indeed, an obvious feature of parental phenomenology is that from their child's earliest days they try to understand what is going on "inside the child's head"; even when the child is not yet able to use language and the parent can only vigilantly observe what the child overtly does, the parent interprets (gives meaning) to what may be "inside" the child. They know the child has a developing mind and that it is their responsibility to influence that development in ways they deem appropriate. And no parent will deny that they look forward to the time when the child can talk and give the parent a better basis for understanding how the child is thinking about this and that. Thinking is not synonymous with talking. If you ask parents if their child could think before he or she could talk, they will say as one parent did to me, "Of course, that is obvious, but as often as not I wasn't sure, sometimes I did not have a clue what was going on inside that little head." When the child is able to talk, the quality and content of the parent-child dialogue changes except in one very important respect: the parents' need to know what their child is thinking continues and gains strength and scope, and the same is true for the child. In the inevitable role of teacher the parent feels the necessity to know what the child is thinking as a basis for determining how to react and what to say so that it will be understood and assimilated in the child's thinking in ways the parent judges appropriate or "right." As the parent's "student" the child wants to know a lot, which may or may not be a sign to the parent that the child's thinking is or is not on the right track. For my present purposes I am emphasizing two things: a parents' need to know what she is dealing with, and the exposure of parent and child of the contents and values of each. And, to labor the obvious, those dialogues can be peaceful or stormy or in between, productive or antithetical to further exposure of each other's thinking. By the time the child starts school, parents are not in doubt that their child has a distinctive style of thinking, doing, and of self-expressing which the parent prays and hopes the child's teacher, his substitute parent during weekdays, will comprehend. The child comes to school eager and curious about beginning to learn how to acquire and think about the competencies of "big people," adults.

When critics inveigh against schools because their students do not know how to think, to be critical thinkers, they unwittingly imply that it is only in school that children will learn to think. That is patent nonsense. They were thinkers before they set foot in school. They had learned a lot, ranging, for example, from eating with a spoon, urinating and defecating in the toilet, talking and walking, putting on clothes, enjoying being read to, enjoying perusing books appropriate for their age, scribbling and finger painting and, of course, playing with and solving puzzles and games graduated in difficulty, discriminating between dreams and external reality, and in increasing numbers learning the rudiments of the computer. The question that the critics do not ask is how come preschoolers are the thinkers they are? Nor do they ask the question, What is it that parents think, arrange, and do that accounts for what children learn and do before they start school? Does the classroom context of learning differ markedly from the parental one in recognizing and exploiting the variables in the learning process, intrinsically related variables whose strength is never zero?

The most glaring feature of the preschooler's daily existence is that he or she is active: exploring and doing, more often than not with intensity, causing parents to say, "He would be into anything and everything if I wasn't watching." However you define *thinking*, it is going on in that activity, and with each passing month the role of thinking in that activity becomes more noticeable and remarkable; the activity comes from "within," it is usually self-initiated. We may have difficulty understanding why this or that object or activity is so interesting, even fascinating, to the child but we are never in doubt that he is thinking, that he shapes and is being shaped by the activity. All this is the case whether the child is in or outside the home. For example, if you observe mothers coming into a supermarket with, say, their three-year-old child and placing him in the seat of the shopping cart, you may see the child actually resist this restraint on his movement. Most children do not initially resent restriction but after ten minutes or so some of them become insistent and give vocal expression to it by angry crying or words. Battles can ensue and some parents will pick up the child and place him in the larger part of the cart. What I have described also takes place between parent and child on long auto trips. Placing constraints on movements of young children engenders resistance because for the child it is also a constraint on his curiosity to experience the world around him by touching, manipulating, studying, exploring, changing, and understanding it. And, I must add, all of this can be so taxing on the patience of too many parents that they are content to let their child sit for hours before the TV set passively watching cartoons; the child is a passive viewer interpreting and thinking a virtual world, and God knows how what is being viewed is shaping his thinking. What a child acquires by passively watching TV is not the same as what he learns by self-initiated activity. I know of no credible evidence whatsoever that both are equally productive of critical thinking.

When the child starts school his psychological situation changes dramatically. First, he is restricted to being in one room for almost the whole day. Second, he is usually restricted to a particular seat from which he is expected not to roam, even to go to the toilet without the teacher's permission. Third, he cannot talk when he wants to, except to the teacher, but only after raising his hand and receiving the teacher's permission. Fourth, it is made crystal clear to him that his thinking and attention must be directed to what the teacher is saying and teaching, all else is off limits. Fifth, he must not talk to, help, or seek help from another child; he becomes the encapsulated child in an encapsulated classroom in an encapsulated school. He becomes spatially-geographically a very "bounded" individual. In brief, in these and other ways the child is not in doubt that school and home are two very different places for living and learning.

Decades ago when I became actively involved in educational reform I asked teachers this question: What are the goals of the period during which children go to the gymnasium? (Not all schools had a gymnasium, an absence their teachers deplored.) There were two answers. The first was almost always given in a perfunctory, single phrase: To learn the skills of organized sports. The second was never as perfunctory or as brief; it centered around the unreasonableness of expecting that young, healthy, active children "can sit still all day"; several teachers spontaneously volunteered that it was standard practice among teachers to have reading, arithmetic, and writing in the morning and less demanding subject matter the rest of the day, when children were more restless and inattentive. It was true that in the morning the children were eager, interested, highly motivated learners, engrossed in what they were expected to learn. My classroom observations confirmed what these elementary school teachers said because by the end of the day the clang of the closing bell was greeted by most children the way a prisoner must feel when he is freed from jail, at which time the students instantly came alive.

I did not ask my question of middle and high school teachers because I did not feel I had to. Having observed in such classrooms I was appalled by students' silence. Only a rare student would ask a question, and students' facial expressions did not bring to mind adjectives such as *eager, motivated, interested, lively*. Students in these schools have several different teachers during the day (the schools are departmentalized and are much larger than elementary schools). After each period they move from one room to another one. The difference between what most students look like in the classroom and in the halls is the difference between night and day. In fact, "hall behavior" is often a problem in these schools; behavior problems vary from the minuscule to the severe.

In light of what I said about elementary schools, some readers may have concluded that I painted a picture of young children entering a place where teachers are martinets lacking warmth or the desire to develop and exploit the potentials of children. Such readers would be grievously wrong. Teachers did not create the modal classroom I described. Teachers teach the way they were taught to teach, and the nature and power of the school culture reinforce what they were taught in preparatory programs. To place sole blame on teachers is a blatant instance of blaming the victim, a mistake I have zealously tried to avoid in my writings. In my experience there are teachers, albeit a minority, who come to the conclusion that schools are not organized in ways conducive to critical thinking and/or productive learning. For example, I observed several high school classrooms for students who wanted to learn to speak Spanish; the number of students varied from twelve to twenty. Both the students and teachers were having a hard time for several reasons, but the one each teacher deemed most important was these classes were held on alternate days of the week in fifty-minute periods. In conversation with one of the teachers I gingerly said that it appeared that students were not what you would call enthusiastic or highly motivated, even though they had elected to take the course. My remark opened up a minor floodgate, from which came the conclusion that three weekly fifty-minute periods over the course of the year were inefficient and self-defeating for teacher and students and violated what has been learned about how to acquire practical use of a foreign language by total immersion in several weeks in a context where only that language is spoken. "If I had these students for the entire school day for one month, they would learn more, much more, and experience a real sense of competence and self-satisfaction." I asked the teacher how she had become fluent in Spanish. "I went to Mexico and lived for most of a summer with a family who for all practical purposes couldn't speak English. It was hard, challenging, funny, but at the end boundlessly rewarding. But the way high schools are organized makes learning a foreign language an unrewarding battle."

I gave a lot of thought to the conversation with that teacher (who also indicated that given her fluency in Spanish she might decide to use that fluency in the business world or, best of all, in government foreign service). I had already learned that devising a high school's class schedule to accommodate the many pressures to teach this or that deemed educationally important by some person or group or tradition or the state department of education can be little short of traumatic for those who are given the responsibility to figure out how to apportion limited time and space. But the question is not whether you can do it but rather whether by doing it as is currently done you are almost guaranteeing that certain types of classes, such as the teaching of foreign languages, will be contexts of unproductive learning.

Are there alternatives to how high schools apportion time and space? Of course there are. We are not dealing with problems that have one and only one "solution." There is always a universe of alternatives varying from the doable to the flagrantly utopian. But can you explore that universe of alternatives without keeping in mind that you should (I would say must) judge each alternative by the degree to which it contributes to sustaining contexts of unproductive learning or creating improved contexts of productive learning? After all, a high school's schedule can be justified only by an educational rationale about what is conducive to learning, not simply by whether a menu of needs has an assigned box in the schedule. It is beyond the purposes of this book to discuss the alternatives I came up with. I brought up the concept of the universe of alternatives as a way of discussing critical thinking. You think about and devise a high school schedule in a way similar to, if not identical with, doing a jig-saw puzzle where you have to put the pieces together. That pretty much describes the current practice I have gotten from talks with personnel who devise these schedules. My distinct impression is that they do regard it as a game which has to be solved in a short period of time with as little hassle as possible from those whose ox has been gored by the schedule. Few negative reactions, or (improbably) none, means a job well done; what it means for learning is not in the picture.

What is meant by those who criticize schools because their students are not taught to be critical thinkers? As best I can determine they mean that the student does *not* unreflectively accept what he is told, hears, reads, as locked in concrete gospel truths. The student may very much want to believe that something he has been told or read or heard is true but in his or her self interest, that student should be prepared to ask if the received knowledge is incomplete or wrong in some ways. The critic does not mean the students become ritualistic contrarians or naysayers but rather that they should feel comfortable examining the adequacy of received knowledge. Although critics do not put it this way, they clearly imply that critical thinking should become a *self-initiated stance* in the student grappling now and in the future with an increasingly complicated world. Helping students acquire that stance is something schooling should not continue to short change. The way some people talk about critical thinking can be summed up by the expression "to be able to think 'outside the box,'" to unimprison yourself from the force of convention, to resist the force of conventional thinking and practice.

Critics are by no means clear or helpful about how teachers can plant the seeds of growth for critical thinking. I use the word *help* instead of *teach* precisely because the conventional imagery engendered by the word *teacher* is one in which the minds of students are being filled and enriched by what the teacher tells them. That is especially true today when "standards and accountability" have become center stage in our schools and the pressure is on teachers to pour knowledge and a very narrow range of cognitive skills into the heads of students who on tests should be able to demonstrate that they have acquired that knowledge and those skills. Critical thinking? *Ever since the standards and accountability movement began to pick up steam, the words* critical thinking *are absent from public discussion.* You could say that the logo of the movement is "Get students to meet standards and then we will worry about critical thinking." Famous last words, testimony to an utter inability to distinguish between contexts of unproductive and productive learning and also testimony to employing a scandalously narrow conception of learning.

Decades ago the truly great gestalt psychologist, Max Wertheimer, wrote a book called *Productive Thinking* (1945). It is not a book about schooling. To my knowledge he had never written anything about classroom learning; his interests were sensory perception, critical and creative thinking. (He and Albert Einstein were long, close friends.) At the end of the book Wertheimer discusses in detail Einstein's *style* of thinking in the course of his major discoveries. Well, for some reason Wertheimer decided to observe a class being taught geometry, specifically the theorems necessary to solve the parallelogram problem. After the class was over he met with a group of the students and started by asking them if they could come up with a way of demonstrating a solution that was an alternative to what the teacher said and what the textbook contained. The students were puzzled and quickly said no. Wertheimer then demonstrated an alternative way of using the theorems and he asked for their reactions. Each of the students firmly said that Wertheimer's way was wrong and the teacher's way the "correct" way. Need I say more about the absence of critical thinking, of the acquired stance which makes it virtually impossible to recognize and accept the fact that there is a universe of alternatives?

Let us now return to the child's preschool years with this question: Is the preschooler a critical thinker? Let us initially employ the word *critical* as referring to instances where the child disagrees with, refuses to accept what a parent tells him or her to think and do. Consider the following example.

> It is well past midnight and you are asleep in your room and your child is in his or her room. Suddenly you are awakened by the crying and shrieking of your child. You bolt into his room, embrace and pick him up, and he then tells you there is a bear in his room.

How do you think about it? What should you do? If you are like most parents, you are hardly thinking, you want to calm your child down. And again if you are like most parents, you are likely to attempt to reassure him that there is not or was not a bear in his room, at which point he is likely to start crying again and angrily say you are wrong. If the parent was ever in doubt that very young children confuse dreaming with reality, that doubt is gone forever.

The parent has an immediate problem: how to reassure and calm the child so that he will go back to sleep. My personal as well as clinical experience is that solely depending on language may, depending on the quality of what the parent-child relationship has been, achieve your purposes, but do not bet on it. One parent quickly realized that conversation with her distraught child was going nowhere. She said to her child, "You and Daddy and I are going to go into every room, look in every closet, under every bed, and when we make sure there is no bear in the house, we will go back to your room, and Daddy will stay with you until you fall asleep." I asked her how she hit upon such action. She laughed. "I really don't know. All that I was aware of was that we had to reassure him that we understood and would protect him. I thank God it worked. At breakfast the next morning we began to discuss that everyone dreams, that some dreams are really real to us. And he agreed with my suggestion that at breakfast each of us would relate the dream we had, if we could remember it, which we often cannot. If I could not remember what I dreamed I either said so or made one up that made the point I wanted to impress on him."

I relate this anecdote to illustrate several points.

1. The mother almost immediately recognized that the situation was one in which you do not try to reason or think with the child; it was a situation in which her first obligation was not to do anything that would make a bad situation worse or give the child cause to mistrust what she says or does. Reasoning and thinking would come later when they stood a chance of having productive consequences.

2. The mother knew she would have to begin figuring just how to begin helping the child to understand that things are not always what they appear to be. The mother would not have put it that way—she said nothing to indicate that she would generalize from what happened—but she was intent *in this situation* on helping her child to *begin* to be able to take distance from what he experiences or thinks is true or real. I emphasize *begin* because it is a long process determined largely on whether other spheres of parent-child interactions reinforce or weaken that emerging stance. If there are people who tend to believe anything they are told via the Internet, there are others who heavily discount almost everything they are told on the Internet.

3. Together with the child, the parents engaged in an *activity* to reassure the child there was no bear in the house. And the next morning the mother engaged the child in another activity to begin to help the child recognize and accept the difference between appearance and reality.

It would be appropriate to say that both in their role as parents and teachers the parents' goal was to influence the child's reality testing. It would be appropriate, however, if the emphasis was on testing. In the above anecdote the child had absolutely no doubt what his reality had been; he had no way of psychologically taking distance from it, to examine or reflect about it or to question it. The parental-pedagogical task is how to plant the seeds for critical thinking or, to put it in another way, how you avoid rearing a child who passively accepts what he sees or hears or is told. The critical stance is an acquired one and the origins of it are in the preschool years. It is by no means a congealed one or a cognitive habit, it is a stance in progress. (Preschoolers are also singers, musicians, and artists. Whether any of these activities are developed after the preschool years, is also a work in progress, depending in significant measure on whether schools seek to exploit such activities, which, unfortunately, they minimally do.)

I did not know at all well the mother who related the above anecdote and I cannot say how typical her actions were in other more mundane situations where it was possible to sensitize her child to be a critical thinker.

I present one more example of a problem which, sad to say, some (not a few) feel obliged to deal with, especially with their preschool child. I say especially because they rightly know that such a child is not capable of recognizing dangers of diverse kinds. So, for example, some parents will say and often repeat this message: "If you are down the block playing with friends and a person you do not know is driving a car and stops, calls you over, and says he is a friend of mine or Daddy and that we asked him to get you and bring you home, you are not to listen to him and get into that car. We will never, but never, ask a person *you* do not know to do that. You come home, run home immediately. Do you understand?" The child may say yes, a rule is a rule. The child may assent and ask no questions. He may be puzzled, he does not understand why his parent is telling this to him with such seriousness; he does not ask why. Other children will ask why. The answer likely will make two points: "Most people who act nicely and friendly are nice and friendly people. But you have no way of knowing if they are really nice or just acting that way. So if a stranger stops his car and asks you to get in, he may be a person who wants to hurt you or do bad things to you. There are such people and you must never do as he asks."

The parent is dealing with and trying to explain and illustrate the appearance versus reality problem: You should not necessarily believe what people tell you, there are times when you must disregard what they say, you have to learn to think and not get hurt or disappointed. The parent is going from the particular to the general but to the young child who cannot arrive at generalizations, what the parent says is applicable or makes sense only in the case of strangers in their cars. We hardly know how, when, and why in young children one instance interacting with similar instances *begins* to become a generalization, another complicated work of cognition in progress.

In the preschool years parents have innumerable opportunities which obligate them to try to help the child to unlearn impulsive and unreflective ways of thinking and acting and to learn to think and act in ways that are more adaptive and productive for growth. No parent wants his or her child to be dumb, they want him to be smart. If asked what they mean by smart, their answer in one way or another is that at the least they want their child to be adequate to the predictable tasks and problems their child will confront. If you, as I have, ask parents whether by smart they mean normal or average, some parents will say yes but they hope, they would be delighted, if the child came to be judged as "really" smart. Other parents say that by smart they mean their child would do "better" than most other students, that he would be a better thinker and learner. Regardless of type of answer, parents will not deny that especially in the preschool years their obligation is to help the child learn how to think.

If parents differ in what they mean by smart, those differences are minuscule compared to differences in when and how they recognize and exploit opportunities to help their child to think, to begin the arduous and complicated process of becoming a critical thinker, if only a beginning one. In this process the parents are more than just parents, they are also in principle teachers.

The students in the classroom are in a new kind of space, they have become part of a larger group, the rules of social living are by no means identical, the formal subject matter to which they are exposed is different; nevertheless, their teacher's major goal is identical to that of parents: students who will be better knowers and thinkers. That is no more than to say that in the preschool and school years whatever you mean by critical thinking and learning takes place in a social-interpersonal context.[1] Although I regard that as a glimpse of the truly obvious, as I am sure readers and everyone else will agree, the fact is that for all practical purposes its implications and obligations are virtually ignored.

---

1. In regard to the preschool years there have been few studies bearing on the frequency of contexts in which parents seek to influence the way in which the child thinks or parental justification of what was said or done. My prediction is that once the child can talk and walk the most frequent situation is one in which the parent is responding to a child's physical activity. That is in marked contrast to the classroom, where the child is not in action but is a relatively passive recipient of what the teacher is saying/teaching about how to think. Especially in the elementary school years that type of context is far less conducive to thinking, let alone critical thinking, in comparison to what occurs in the preschool years.

If you take the obvious seriously, you then have to confront the question: What are the distinguishing features of contexts of productive and unproductive learning? That is a question those who bemoan the fact that students are not, generally speaking, becoming critical thinkers seem unable to ask and confront. Critical thinking takes place in the same classroom context as all other school learning does. Just as you do not need a special theory for the oxygen atom and a special one for the hydrogen atom, you do not need a special classroom learning context for critical thinking and a special one for this or that subject matter. For students to begin to be critical thinkers and learners requires that (a) they feel *safe* to make their questions and puzzlements *public*, (b) the teacher seeks to understand and respond to the student in a way that does not discourage or implicitly criticize him or her for thinking as he or she does, (c) that the teacher is a consistent and sincere advocate of the stance that learning to think, to learn anything important, is serious hard work which takes time and has its frustrating ups and downs; (d) that learning to be an independent thinker, and not to believe everything you hear or read is right, even if it comes from the teacher, is what growing up is all about.

You cannot say a student is thinking *critically or uncritically* unless he makes his thinking public in some form in a social context. That is why I have placed such emphasis on question asking by students in the classroom; more correctly, why I am appalled at the few questions they ask. It is not because their minds are blank but rather because teachers do not encourage students to ask questions or encourage it in a way that does not engender in students the feeling they may be regarded by the teacher and other students as dumb or odd. And if teachers do that, it is in part because *their* conception of learning is narrow to the point where the role of question asking in the learning process is not in the picture. If, in addition, the public's conception of learning is equally narrow and leads them to accept as fact that test scores are valid and meaningful indices of learning and thinking, even critical thinking, the situation remains as it long has been: grim.

Test scores are or can be meaningful. (I am no mindless critic of them.) *Keep in mind that the act of taking a test is not an act of learning, it is a response to items which others deemed important for the students to be able to answer correctly.* By themselves test scores tell you absolutely nothing about the classroom context of learning for students. The potential significance of a test score is in the degree to which it directs you to examine students' classroom context of learning. So, for example, when scores of children in classrooms of a particular school are considered unacceptably low, it leads to wailing, moaning, and action. But far more often than not the remedial action has been to do more of the same but to do it "better" by putting more pressure on teachers and students, by expecting more from teachers who in turn expect more from students. The context of learning remains virtually the same, with the result that test scores remain what they were or go up a notch, and it is claimed "we are going in the right direction." It is like saying that if a child got a score well below the norm last year and this year he or she gets a score three or four points higher, that child has become a better learner. If his score goes down three or four points, does that mean the student is more dumb, a worse learner than he was before? H. L. Mencken said that for every major problem there is a simple answer that is wrong. Today the answer to our educational ills is elevated standards, higher expectations, and accountability. Mencken is turning over in his grave. Given my advanced age (CA 84) it will not be long before I join him. What I have been saying in these pages I began to say, orally and in print, in 1965. The Horse Story is relevant here; it was placed several years ago in the mailbox of my late friend and colleague, Dr. Emory Cowen, at Rochester University.

Horse Story

Common advice from knowledgeable horse trainers includes the adage, "If the horse you're riding dies, get off." Seems simple enough, yet, in the education business we don't always follow that advice. Instead, we often choose from an array of alternatives which include:

1. Buying a stronger whip.
2. Trying a new bit or bridle.
3. Switching riders.
4. Moving the horse to a new location.
5. Riding the horse for longer periods of time.
6. Saying things like, "This is the way we've always ridden this horse."
7. Appointing a committee to study the horse.
8. Arranging to visit other sites where they ride dead horses efficiently.
9. Increasing the standards for riding dead horses.
10. Creating a test for measuring our riding ability.
11. Comparing how we're riding now with how we did ten or twenty years ago.
12. Complaining about the state of horses these days.
13. Coming up with new styles of riding.
14. Blaming the horse's parents. The problem is often in the breeding.
15. Tightening the cinch.

No one is opposed to schools inculcating a stance of critical thinking in students. We are not born with that stance just as we are not born with a knowledge of history or chemistry or literature. The initial context of that learning is in the preschool years when parents are the teachers. During those years parents will not say that one of their major goals is to help their child become a critical thinker. Nevertheless, it is during these years that in diverse ways in concrete situations the child is helped to give up impulsive, unreflective ways of thinking and acting, to begin to think and make judgments about the consequences of actions, to begin to resist the force and appeal of what is palpable and its possible dangers. The seeds of what becomes critical thinking are implanted in the preschool years and their sprouts begin to become discernible.

Whereas parents have innumerable opportunities to observe the child in a wide variety of situations—most frequently involving the child in physical activity—the child's classroom teacher has far fewer opportunities because he and the students spend almost all of the school day in an encapsulated space where, unlike at home, the child is much less free to walk, talk, play, roam. The teacher's main window through which to observe the child's style of thinking is in relation to subject matter: reading, writing, arithmetic. The child is hardly in motion or a spontaneous talker. She is expected to be task oriented and there may be penalties if she is not. Phenomenologically speaking, the teacher is not concerned with critical thinking of any kind but rather the teaching of subject matter. If asked, the teacher will say that he certainly does not devalue the importance of critical thinking but with young children, helping them learn subject matter has to take precedence. That this may be an unduly or unjustified narrow conception of learning is simply not in the picture. That there may be much more going on in the child's mind than being able to demonstrate that she knows the correct answer or that she does not know the answer is hardly in the picture.[2]

I return now to the classroom constitution issue I raised in earlier pages. I said there that teachers *solely* determine the classroom constitution which will shape life in the classroom. Do first-grade students have a conception of what is fair and unfair? Do they have

---

2. I am being descriptive here, not judgmental. In a later chapter I discuss why blaming teachers for the inadequacies of our schools is a scandalous instance of blaming the victim. Will the day ever come when the critics of schools will be able to take distance from their overlearned peeves and become critical thinkers who explore the universe of explanations? Unfortunately (for me), I'll not be around if and when the critics and the public policy gurus experience that epiphany.

the potential to begin to examine why issues of fairness in the class-room are no simple affair? Are they capable of participating in a dis-cussion of why and how they must take responsibility for their own learning? Are they capable of being introduced to and becoming in-terested in what makes schooling interesting and worthwhile? Why must a student feel safe to tell a teacher he thinks the teacher has done or said something that is wrong and unfair? After all, if the teacher can safely tell a student he is wrong and unfair, why can't the student tell a teacher he is wrong and unfair?

The preschooler's ability to generalize, to formulate a principle is, of course, limited, but before starting school the parent and child have, so to speak, locked horns in countless concrete instances implied in the above questions. It is a struggle between an adult who is clear about a principle and a child who is not, between a parent who knows what the constitution delineating her relationship to the child is and should be and a child who has difficulty understanding or abiding by that consti-tution. But by the time schooling begins the child has more than a glim-mer of the fact that he lives in a world of adult-determined rules. He knows one other thing—if only because parents (or siblings) have told him—and that is that the rules and expectations by which he will be governed in school will be different from those at home. I trust, there-fore, that the reader understands where I am coming from when I say that raising and discussing—not just telling—the constitution is impor-tant and of great interest to the child. He or she is primed for it.

Most important to me for returning to the constitution issue is that the questions I posed above refer to the major features of a con-text of productive learning. For one thing, those questions do not de-rive from a narrow conception of learning which primarily focuses on *cognitive* processes, as if they are not concurrently intertwined with, shaping and being shaped by, other factors constituting the learning experience. For another thing, it recognizes that now and in the past students have *attitudes* and *feelings* toward self and adults, especially adults who are authorities with power; the child's strong (and it is strong) need to feel and be judged by others as *competent* is dominant in the preschool years and takes on added saliency when he or she starts school, for good or for bad depending on what the child has ex-perienced and concluded in the preschool years. He or she wants to be *accepted, respected, understood,* and *trusted* (just as he hopes he can trust the teacher). The child *wants* to learn, to meet *expectations,* and when he falls short of expectations (occasionally or frequently) he hopes the teacher will help him and do and say nothing that will humiliate him in the eyes of other students.

Please note that I have labeled the ingredients of which the learning process is composed. Labeling too frequently has the consequence of creating boundaries, as if they exist apart from other things that are labeled and are either absent or present in the process of learning. What I have described and labeled is always present, albeit in varying strengths, in his or her classroom learning. They make up an operative system which is dynamic in the sense that at different times the relationship of parts to each other can change, depending on perceived changes in the context.

It may sound outlandish (or crazy) for me to suggest that the first few days of school be devoted to the ins and outs, the dilemmas, of constitutional issues and the nature of learning as children say they see it and then how the teacher sees it, with emphasis on the obligations of both. My hold on reality is not so fragile as to lead me to expect that children will come away from those discussions with other than a vague understanding (if that) of the significance of those discussions. But once those discussions are over and "real" formal learning begins, the teacher will have numerous opportunities, concrete instances, to illustrate how those instances require her and the students to go back to the substance of the discussion in the beginning days of school. Just as parents use instances in the present to remind the child of what was discussed an hour or a day or a week before, the classroom teacher can and should do the same. Parents do it because they believe the stakes are too high if they do not do it, and as any parent will attest, it is personally demanding and taxing of patience, and seems to be a neverending process. No parent will prevent a child from crawling because they want him or her to walk instead. But there comes a time when a parent believes the child should experience with the parent's active help what it feels like to be standing erect and he is encouraged to try with the parent's help to move his legs. The parent is crystal clear what her goal is and that it will take time to reach that goal. It is that understanding and time perspective by which I ask the reader to judge my suggestion: The child starting school is still an intellectual crawler on the long road to being an independent, critical thinker and learner. I am reminded here of the admonition that Rome was not built in a day.

Some readers may have concluded that I have said nothing new, that I have dressed up old ideas in somewhat new garb. They are correct. I confess to intellectual plagiarism from the writings of people who long antedated my involvement in educational reform. And there is nothing new in my observation that, the very few exceptions aside, the great bulk of American classrooms violate the conception of learning I have presented in these pages. If the reader desires to read about some exceptions, they should read an account of a Providence (Rhode Island) high school by Levine (2001) who describes what Dennis Littky and Eliot Worshor demonstrated (with data) and accomplished. Also, they should read Bensman's account (with data) of what Debbie Meier spearheaded at Central Park East in New York's Spanish Harlem (2000). And if you are interested in the poetry that students in a Spanish Harlem elementary school came to write and why, you should read a book written by the late poet Kenneth Koch (1970), after which you may want to read his book containing the poems of aged, poor, physically and neurologically handicapped residents of a depressing, unstimulating nursing home in New York's Lower East Side where its residents dozed and dozed, rarely said anything to anyone, and waited to die (1977). Kenneth Koch was a poet, not a psychologist or educator, but he certainly knew what a context of productive learning is.

The educational reform movement gets much of its justification (and funds) because of the wide gulf between the educational outcomes of suburban and urban schools (like those in Spanish Harlem) as those outcomes are measured by tests. If only urban schools can become more like suburban ones in regard to these outcomes! I have long regarded that goal as misguided in the extreme, an opinion based on my classroom observations in suburban middle and high schools. And some of those observations were in classes for gifted children, meaning in those instances that students had IQs of 130 or above. They were small classrooms of no more than fifteen students. I observed each for one day, after which I met with the teacher primarily to thank her for agreeing to allow me to observe and to tell her the truth: she had a very interesting bunch of students. I was not there to pass judgment of any kind. I said one other thing: The students seemed to be surprisingly and dramatically heterogeneous in personality. (I could make that remark about any classroom. It is a glimpse of the obvious. The statement was innocuous and nonjudgmental.) In three of the four instances what the teachers said is captured in the following paraphrase. "Heterogeneous? That they certainly are. Obviously they are bright. Look at their IQs. Of the fifteen kids there are three who really sparkle. I never know what they are going to say and come up with. They are challenging, creative, but almost always they make me think and I have learned that I sometimes have to tell them that I don't know the answer to their question. They are a delight, but are they ever creative and probing. I sometimes think they can teach themselves. Then there are seven or eight kids who are smart, they master what they are supposed to master, but there are few signs that they want to go further. I can't call them creative or even gifted like my top three. I don't know if it is motivation or lack of ambition but they are not impressive thinkers. They are nice kids, I'm glad they are in my class but despite their IQ I cannot call them gifted. Then there are three or four students I consider dumb. They don't know how to think, sometimes I wonder if they are thinking, and I am always looking for signs or sparks of creativity. They are not dumb, I know, but they are not in the same thinking league as my top three. It's puzzling."

I did not relate this anecdote to point out the obvious: conventional test scores tell you little about thinking style or, in the case of achievement tests whether subject matter they measure has been absorbed in ways that reinforce or increase motivation. As I said earlier, the majority of middle and high school students who get passing grades and get passing achievement test scores do not indicate much interest in school learning, and that holds true for urban as well as suburban schools. The problem that bedevils suburban high school educators is drinking, and drugs of one sort or another are second. The hope that urban middle and high schools can become more like those in suburbia has its problems which will continue to go unchallenged as long as the word and concept of learning is as narrow, ambiguous, and unexamined as it is.

As a result of my experiences giving talks to educators as well as groups of noneducators with more than a passing interest in and knowledge of the problems of schools, I have to assume that some readers will have concluded something like the following: "I agree with most of what you say but you do not seem to realize that the implications of what you have said for changing schools are enormous and unsettling. You are not being realistic and practical." Anyone familiar with my writings will agree that the implications of what I have written, especially in regard to the selection and preparation of educators, are unsettling (Sarason 1993a, 1998). I have not and do not kid myself that personnel of colleges of education will take kindly to the prospects of institutional upheaval over time, *even though not one of them has said or written that what I was proposing was wrong.* In fact, the reviews of my books have been what is called a critical success. (That they have not been financial successes is not relevant!) I am, I know, not regarded as a practical critic. It is fair to say that many educators regard me as overly critical, unable or unwilling to recognize progress.

For example, in the past few years we have witnessed the promotion and in some states the implementation of a policy of smaller class size. Why? The first part of the answer is the admission that reforms tried in the past had been failures. The second part is also an

admission: the many students who need understanding and attention can only get them if class size is small. That is to say, the context
of learning depends on the frequency and quality of interpersonal
dimensions. Reducing class size is a necessity, not a luxury. Despera-
tion was a spur to change.

It is obvious from what I have said in these pages that a context of
productive learning requires teacher time that is next to impossible
with a large class of students. I have, therefore, been very much in favor of the policy of reduced class size. But—there is almost always a
but—it should remind us of the numbers game in which all that matters are the test scores. Now, in previous books (Sarason 1999, 2002a)
I have discussed why I conclude that at the present time the cohort of
teachers contains a large fraction who either should not be teachers or
are subpar teachers. If you were to assess teachers by whatever set of
criteria, the results when graphed will resemble a normal, bell-shaped
curve. If so, that means that many teachers will be subpar; that is a lot
of teachers. If I were to go by the criteria derived from features and
obligations of a context of productive learning, the results would be
depressing. *A below-average teacher with a class of twenty-five students is as
likely to be a below-average teacher with fifteen to twenty students.* Therefore,
I have predicted reducing class size will not have as robust consequences as expected. Unfortunately, we will never know why, say, in
small class X scores went up and in small class Y of the same grade
they did not go up. Why? Because the advocates are not able to ask
and support efforts to determine where and why small class size has or
has not resulted in expected outcomes. But that is an old story in matters educational. I would like to point out to the reader that it was in
1910 that Abraham Flexner published his report on the quality and
competence of physicians in the United States and Canada. Flexner
was no muckraker or dyspeptic critic when he describes medical education and practice as more than deplorable; it was scandalous, far
worse than the preparation of educators today. His report had revolutionary consequences. What I have said about class size I have said
about charter schools.

In regard to medical education Flexner knew the difference between contexts of productive and unproductive learning. Flexner was
not a physician. He was one of the two preeminent educators of his
day. John Dewey was the other one and he too knew the difference.

Chapter Seven

Practical versus Impractical

When we say an individual is a practical person, we usually mean that faced with problems—his own or those brought to him by others—he has the knack of coming up with a course of action that works, in the sense that the problem is no longer a problem or its negative impact is significantly reduced. The individual may regard himself as practical but those with whom he lives and works may or may not agree he merits such a badge of virtue. If a person describes himself as a practical person, we have no basis for agreeing or disagreeing because we know how easy it is to deceive ourselves. It is when other people independent of each other come to the same conclusion that he is a practical person, that he has a track record in this regard; we accept the designation because our personal observation has been confirmed by others who also know him. We do not think of the practical person as a theorist, a conceptualizer, or scholar. Indeed, such people are often the butt of humor and satire when we learn how impractical they can be with such specialized, circumscribed knowledge and talents in "real" life, in dealing with problems in the quotidian world, especially those involving social and/or family relationships. If we unjustifiably overgeneralize from such satire, it nevertheless underlines how when we say an individual is a practical person we frequently mean he or she "knows" people and adapts that knowledge to "people problems" about which she is asked to be helpful. I am certainly not implying here that the practical person is a psychologist or sees himself as a psychologist. The practical person can be found in all walks of life. I have been a member of the psychological community for six decades, long enough to conclude that it does not contain a much higher percentage of practical people than would be found in all other professions, keeping in mind the way I have characterized the practical person. Clinical psychologists, clinical social workers, and psychiatrists can be helpful to patients with their individual problems of living but that in no way means that outside of their offices they are more practical people than surgeons, engineers, etc. The literature on social networks contains a great deal of description and discussion of individuals who have a role in sustaining the network and who are recognized as practical people even though they operate informally and have no assigned title. Elizabeth Lorentz and I have described such individuals in a resource exchange network of which we were members (Sarason and Lorentz 1989, 1998).

The practical person is one who deals with problems of a circumscribed nature in a relatively circumscribed social-geographic arena in which the consequences of the course of action he or she advises or takes can usually be judged in a matter of days. The practical person infrequently thinks "big" in the sense that he or she has or develops a vision of what can or ought to be beyond his or her dealing with this or that discrete or local issue. When that happens the practical person may become an activist, no longer a responder to people who come to him for advice and advice only. He is now in unfamiliar territory, he has to persuade others that his vision should be realized, others should join even though they will have to, in a discernible degree at least, change the way they have been thinking and acting. The practical person quickly learns that he is in a new ball game in which by no means everybody he had reason to believe thought the way he did cottons to be part of the new game; the reasons are many but none more intimidating than the fact that the desired consequences are in a distant future and there is little or no basis for asserting that those consequences will indubitably be evident. Besides, it will predictably arouse the resistance of many people who consider the venture both radical and impractical.

Let me concretize what I have been saying by referring to a historical event, the repercussions of which are daily fare in our mass media. I use that event and what it led to because it has been described and discussed in great detail from different vantage points in scores of books, articles, and symposia, allowing me to identify what is considered practical and impractical and why. Although the example had nothing to do with education and its reform, it came to have, as I shall indicate later, a very direct bearing on educational reform in terms of policy, the practical and the impractical. So bear with me.

It had long been the dream of physicists to demonstrate that two atoms colliding with each other at tremendous speeds would release energy. If the dream was realized in the laboratory, even if the amount released was tiny, it meant that it should be possible sometime in the long, long future to create the conditions whereby the amount of energy released would be huge and the dream of an endless supply of energy would become a reality. It was a dream because no country would be willing to allocate a galactic amount of resources over a very long period of time to such an endeavor. Atomic physicists had to be content with their dreams.

Around the time of the start of World War II (in Europe) the tiny release of energy was demonstrated, an accomplishment of which the world took little or no notice. That changed when America entered the war on December 7, 1941. There were a few European refugee physicists alarmed at the possibility that German physicists of renown would alert Hitler that it was possible to develop an atomic bomb capable of such devastation as to ensure Nazi victory; this was war, and it was in the self-interest of the Nazi regime to allocate the resources necessary for such a weapon. The refugee physicists' alarm was fueled by the fact that the war was not going at all well. Indeed, a Nazi victory was a realistic possibility. High-level scientific advisors to President Roosevelt needed no convincing. But how could they convince the president to approve a project of unprecedented scale that might not work as hoped or could not be successfully completed before the Nazis' project? The president respected his American advisors, but he might not respond approvingly to such an unprecedented venture with so many ifs, maybes, and buts. They had a practical problem that was by no means new in human history: Can you come up with something that increases the chances that a leader, ruler, executive will look favorably on a course of action you propose? They decided to have Einstein write a letter to President Roosevelt in which he said the requisite scientific knowledge on which the proposal was based had been established.

There is no reason to believe that Einstein's letter was decisive, but there is reason to believe that it was helpful. The point is that whoever came up with the idea to get the letter was thinking practically about decision making in the context of knowledge of the pressures on a president in a situation of war. It was a practical ploy intended to achieve a short-term goal but one with enormous, long-term consequences. The phrase "street smart" is frequently used to describe a person who in a particular arena of life knows how to adapt his actions to achieve his purposes (which may be good or bad). We say he knows the territory, by which is meant he knows the people in it: their needs, characteristics, likes, dislikes, pressures, and more. The practical, street-smart person does not label him or herself as such, it is a label pinned on him by others who know his track record. In other venues of his life he may be a theorist and conceptualizer but when it comes to dealing with and persuading people, his focus is on what will be considered doable, believable, and important by this or that individual and group. I need not elaborate on the fact that not all practical, street-smart people are moral and virtuous; and when they are not, they are regarded by others in that arena as untrustworthy. "Honor among thieves" is a myth. In the arenas I talk about in this book those who say somebody is practical or has street smarts intend the designation as an honorific.

As soon as the atom bomb project (later called the Manhattan Project) got the green light a major practical problem immediately arose: Who would lead a top-secret project involving literally scores of existing industrial companies (small and large) scattered all over the country; new sites that would have to be created; university research laboratories; and a major new site which had to be created in a rural nowhere and which would house scores of scientists developing theories and methods for the construction and testing of an atom bomb; all of this to be accomplished by what prewar physicists would have regarded as a bit less than the speed of light.

In light of the decision to place the project under the aegis of the military, the decision was made to appoint Leslie Groves, whose status was not yet that of a beginning general. Groves had overseen the building of the Pentagon and he had accomplished it on time and under budget. He was a no-nonsense type of person, and no one who worked under him had any doubt what he expected of them, or else. This is not to say that he was unfriendly or insensitive or a tyrant. He had a job to do, the most important aspect of which was to make sure that people did what they were supposed to do. He did not suffer fools gladly. When he was asked to oversee the Manhattan Project, he agreed, but with one condition: that he be promoted to the status of a general. Why? Because, he explained, he would be dealing with generals and he knew that if he had an inferior status, it would be a source of many problems. He was promoted.

Groves' request is a clear example of a practical response. He did not ask for the promotion to feed his self-esteem; he was a very self-confident, task-oriented person. But Groves knew the military culture: the interpersonal competitive dynamics within and between the military's rigid, bureaucratic hierarchy were governed by a long tradition. He knew the territory like the palm of his hand and that governed the one condition he set, and it was a condition which those who selected him readily understood. In his military career Groves had dealt with and come to know many executives in a variety of private sector companies. He knew how they saw the world and the federal government and he was as comfortable with them as they were with him, a fact that was of immeasurable importance in getting companies to make things they had never made before.

Having accepted the job, Groves was faced with a practical problem truly new to him in two respects. First, he lacked experience about the science and engineering aspects of developing an atomic bomb. At best he was an educated layman. He knew a lot about engineering but that knowledge was hardly applicable to the arcane knowledge required to think about the strange world of the atom. The second aspect of the problem for Groves was that he would be ultimately responsible for hundreds of scientists at Los Alamos and a number of universities, and that number included Nobel Laureates in physics and a fair number doing work of a caliber that would earn them a Nobel Prize. Groves knew he would need a director with interpersonal skills who was regarded by the field as an important figure in physics. He would lead and administer the largest collection of "stars" ever to work together in one place.

The president's science advisors as well as others Groves consulted suggested Robert Oppenheimer of Berkeley. The two met several times. Groves said that Oppenheimer seemed to know a lot about everything, except baseball. It would be fascinating if we had tapes of those meetings, because I am certain that directly or indirectly Oppenheimer conveyed to Groves the message that academics, in this case physicists, were a breed apart in when and how they worked. I mention that because of Groves' visits to Los Alamos, where he saw people presumably not "working" but talking and arguing, talking and arguing for a good deal of the day and late into the night. That bothered Groves, and Oppenheimer never really succeeded in getting Groves to understand that these scientists *produced*.

One final note. Oppenheimer's appointment had to await FBI clearance for security. They reported that Oppenheimer was a leftist, had friends who were probably communists, and cautioned against the appointment to be in charge of a project as top secret as the Manhattan Project. Groves used his status and connections to go ahead with the appointment. He never had reason to regret his choice. Even after the war, and after Oppenheimer had become a consultant, when the Atomic Energy Commission essentially took away Oppenheimer's security clearance, Groves testified in support of Oppenheimer. I doubt, and this is clearly my opinion, that very few generals would have appointed Oppenheimer and testified in his favor.

I did not present these isolated vignettes from a very complicated context and story only to illustrate what I mean by a practical reaction to a problem or decision that has to be relatively quickly dealt with, not a theoretical problem but one in the here and now, that will have short-term consequences even though one may hope that it will lead to desirable long-term consequences. I had other reasons for bringing up the Manhattan Project. The first can be put in the form of a question: Why is it that the physicists who pressured for an atom bomb project would never have done so before World War II, when the threat of Nazi Germany to the world was plain to see? Why would it have been viewed as impractical bordering on a loss of reality testing then, but practical a few years later? The answer, of course, is that our country and what it stands for were imperiled. We could not afford to dismiss a possibility that would ensure victory.

Let us now ask this question: How do we explain why in the post–World War II era educational reform as never before steadily, year by year, became a focus of national concern with political, racial, ethnic, religious, constitutional ramifications? Why is it that despite differences of opinion about practical actions to take to remedy our educational ills, there was unanimity that as a society we should and must do something about these ills or our society would change in untoward ways? The "enemy" was internal, not external. We had to look into the mirror and admit that we had gone wrong somewhere, we had been asleep at the switch. Like it or not, we had to act. So let me relate, as I have done in previous books, a story about a meeting of a president with his cabinet, when education reform was on the agenda. Dr. Sam Brownell, who was at the meeting and was in his later years a dear colleague of mine at Yale, is my source of what follows.

Sam was the director of the federal Office of Education in the early years of the Eisenhower administration. The Office of Education was a piddling, unrespected, uninfluential entity, a reflection of the fact that education does not appear in the constitution because the founding fathers believed that education was the responsibility of states and local government and not, God forbid, a federal government which inevitably will seek to increase its powers to influence the minds of people. (They did have history on their side!)

Sam was an educator. Early in his federal position and as a result of visiting cities around the country he became more than upset by what he saw: cities whose tax base was utterly inadequate to deal with overcrowded schools due to the immigration from farm to city, stimulated by the need for workers in war-related manufacturing or shipping sites; the postwar baby boom; and the state of disrepair of existing schools because of the priorities of war and the Great Depression which preceded the war. In addition, the juvenile crime rate was steadily escalating and already was a source of national concern. The cities, Sam concluded, not only did not have money to deal with what they faced but would also need help to determine what they might do.

Sam was a gracious, soft-spoken, cautious, conservative individual. He was the polar opposite of a banner-waving social crusader. He was quite upset by what he had learned. He arranged to have a meeting with the president. (Sam's brother was Attorney General.) At the meeting he explained what he had learned and the conclusion he had reached that the federal government should seriously consider aiding the cities to repair and reform their schools. Eisenhower listened attentively and said that he assumed Sam knew that he was suggesting a course of action that represented a *dramatic* break with all past federal policy, which had been to play no role in public education. Sam said he knew it was such a break but he feared what would happen to urban areas and their schools if nothing was done.

Eisenhower asked Sam to make a presentation at a cabinet meeting. After Sam's presentation the president asked each cabinet member to react. With no exception they advised against a new policy, even though some (but not all) agreed that what was called the "urban problem" was truly worrisome. The president then turned to Vice President Nixon and asked him to express his view. In the most clear language Nixon said the federal government should act in ways to aid public education, otherwise the problems of urban education would have percolating adverse consequences for the nation. At that point Eisenhower said he agreed with Nixon, and he asked Dr. Brownell to draft a legislative proposal. From that point on educational reform became big business. It must be emphasized that it was the president's expectation that once the cities were helped to deal with the urban educational crisis the federal policy would revert to one of noninvolvement in schooling. Famous last words, especially because two years later the Supreme Court's desegregation decision was rendered.

It is far beyond my purposes to compare the meeting Dr. Brownell described with the one in which the atom bomb project was approved. I shall restrict myself to those comparisons most relevant to the central focus of this book: What do we mean by learning and how do we distinguish between contexts of productive and unproductive learning? How you answer those questions will determine whether the actions you take are practical or impractical, successful or failures.

The physicists came with experimental *evidence* that the collision of atoms (of a certain kind) released tiny but measurable bursts of energy. The evidence came from only one experiment but it had long been predicted from accepted and fruitful atomic theory. They were not selling President Roosevelt a bill of goods. In fact, they well knew there would be thorny engineering as well as equally thorny product manufacturing problems. And they knew before they began that they would have to determine how to control the energy released by colliding atoms. They had little or no doubt that these and other problems could be overcome but they did doubt whether they could do so before Nazi Germany won the war and could dictate the terms of a peace.

The proponents of federal action about education certainly had evidence of the fiscal plight of the cities, which was bad and would get worse. From the federal standpoint the problem was how to provide funds that would allow cities to ameliorate the problems of failing schools. That was an understandable and practical response. However, it was based on the assumption that the administrators of schools would implement the legislation in educationally productive ways. That assumption, however understandable at the time, had no basis in credible evidence. In fact, there was credible evidence that for decades before World War II, those directly responsible for running school systems were part of the problem and not of the solution. That is to say, their schools were riddled with problems. There were school systems mindlessly mired in stultifying, problem-producing traditions, and there were systems which latched onto the latest nostrum coming down the pike. There had long been critics of American schools; the arguments of some are as unheeded today as they are relevant to the current scene. I said that the change in federal policy and action was understandable, by which I mean that there are times when you have to act, to do something, even though you know that at best it is a short-lived Band-Aid. It is a practical response in that it buys you time to think and reflect (maybe even read?). At the same time it was an impractical response because no one in officialdom saw it as more than a temporary measure, a way of "getting over the hump" and returning to a presumed normal past. They were utterly unprepared for the failure after failure that has characterized efforts of educational reform. Unprepared then as they are today. And they will continue to learn little or nothing until they have credible evidence that we can distinguish the features and consequences of contexts of productive and unproductive learning in the classroom. I have described sites of contexts of productive learning and I am sure there are more, but they are isolated instances of which federal and state policy makers are unaware. That is why in my 1993 book *Letters to a Serious Education President* I say that the president should support a major research effort to demonstrate the differences between the two contexts. It will not be easy or quick, just as demonstrating the release of energy by colliding atoms came after numerous failures.

But there is one huge difference between the atom project and a proposed, kindred educational one. The physicists were dealing with *things* that ultimately would produce one big thing: a bomb. If and when consensus has been reached about the differences between contexts of productive and unproductive learning, we then confront the problem of getting thousands of *people* in our schools to change in ways appropriate to those findings. In addition to death and taxes, we can be certain that resistance to change will be considerable.

There are those who have argued that the Manhattan Project was an *impractical* one because it ignored the possibility that a practical short-term success would lead to a time when nuclear energy would endanger man's existence on Earth; by solving the problem of defeating Japan and finally ending the war we, the argument goes, opened up a Pandora's box we would come to regret (assuming people were alive to experience regret). That dysphoric view of the future was expressed by some of the Los Alamos scientists when they observed the consequences of the first successful testing of the bomb. Those consequences were considered so awful that some of President Truman's advisors counseled against using the bomb, and others advised that a "demonstration" bomb be dropped in some remote, unpopulated area in Japan so that Japan would decide to sue for peace. The argument has continued to today. The point is that what is deemed to be a practical, short-term response to a problem may come to be seen as impractical. The law of unintended consequences has not and can never be repealed. Man may be the highest form of life but that should not be confused with perfection.

The story of educational reform is one in which the impractical has not led to the practical; nothing has been learned. If someone wrote a book describing in detail every reform effort funded by the federal governments and foundations, it would be more like a heavy weapon than a book. It would not be pleasant reading, although as I have emphasized, one can point to isolated instances in which the differences between the two contexts of learning have been taken seriously and with credible success. *But those isolated instances remain isolated.* In the development of the atomic bomb a crucial problem was how to get and control the energy released by two colliding atoms to facilitate the collision of surrounding atoms and thereby create a massive amount of atomic energy. The problem in education is how to get the findings of one isolated success to cause surrounding sites to follow suit. That is a daunting theoretical *and* a practical problem which has hardly been posed and discussed, and it is one that I firmly believe is beyond the competence of one person, at least one like me. I have lived through and am knowledgeable about almost all of the major efforts of reform in the post–World War II era and I have to say that each of them, however well intentioned, I regarded as impractical from the get-go. They were going to go nowhere, which is where they ended up. Am I unduly pessimistic or cynical? If people think that I am vastly underestimating what has been learned and done by reform policies, they are living on a different planet than I am.

For example, from the president on down we are told, especially during political campaigns, that charter schools rival the invention of sliced bread and their accomplishments will stir regular schools to compete with them. I am in principle in favor of charter schools. But in two books (Sarason 1998, 2002a) on charter schools, I explain why I have to make two predictions. First, the number of charter schools which cannot be considered successful will be far from small. Second, we will never be secure in understanding why this charter school failed and that one is an apparent success. Why? Because the enabling legislation for charter schools simply did not include funding for a searching, credible assessment of these schools. We are left with personal opinion, empty rhetoric. *How more impractical can a policy be?* (The number of charter schools that were approved and never got off the ground deserves special study.)

Another example from the current scene. The recent federal legislation requires states to set educational standards students have to meet and to determine by yearly testing how many of a state's schools are below those standards; those will be identified as failing schools, in which case certain types of aid would be available to them. If that does not work, those schools will be closed and the students distributed to other schools, or parents may request a voucher to be used to place their child in any school of their choice. Now, a number of states had already elevated standards and they already had learned that if they adhered to those standards it meant that many—in some cases most—of the schools in the states were failing. With the foreknowledge of what the federal legislation would probably contain, what would you predict the states would do? Yes, they will discernibly scale down their standards. On the first page of the *New York Times* for October 15, 2002, there is a long article with the major heading "Law

Overhauling School Standards May be Weakened." Underneath that in smaller type is the heading "State Actions Upset U.S." And below that is a third heading, "Federal Steps to List Trainees as 'Highly Qualified' Are Also Being Criticized." Here is a short excerpt.

> Federal education officials are concerned that states are seeking ways around the law, and they are hammering out a statement warning of "the need for a change of culture in an American education" says Eugene W. Hickok, the under secretary of education."

Anyone familiar with corporate America—and that includes the president and his cabinet, plus many members of Congress—should know, especially if they graduated from a business school, that the top-down, autocratic, take-it-or-leave-it style of governing has had a huge number of gory failures in its history. In fact, corporate America each year pays many millions of dollars to consulting firms to advise them about how better to secure the understanding and support of its employees to policies and practices of executives and managers. This is not done because the well of altruism is at a higher level than before but rather because of bottom-line considerations. If life in a large corporation has some of the features of a jungle, executives and managers have by the dynamics of self-interest become sensitive to the attitudes, feelings, and ideas of the much larger number of employees below them. What decades ago would have been regarded as coddling is today, at least on the level of rhetoric, considered practical thinking. The situation is in all respects similar to the relationship between the federal government and the states, a relationship of marked ambivalence and conflict. In regard to the recently passed reform bill of 2003, states did not look upon it with enthusiasm and approval, and the administration never hid its opinion that states had been neglectful and they would have to change or else. What is ironic here is that this (and past) administrations have learned nothing and proclaimed something they could not apply in their thinking and approach to the recent education legislation. What they have learned was limited to the large federal bureaucracy and its response to efforts to change it. They put it this way, "The bureaucratic culture is opposed to change. It goes through the motions. It knows how to roll with the punch. It knows it will outlive us."

I confess that when the present administration expresses surprise and displeasure about the efforts of the states to bypass and weaken the new legislation, I do not know whether to laugh or cry. On the one hand it is high farce, on the other hand it is symptomatic of truly egregious, self-defeating, impractical thinking. You may agree or disagree with the goals of the legislation, but whatever your position you do not have to be a high-level sage, psychologist, sociologist, constitutional historian, or political scientist to predict how the states would respond to the new legislation.

I said earlier that one of the features of a classroom context of productive learning is that the teacher seeks to understand where, so to speak, the learner is psychologically coming from, to exploit that knowledge to help him or her change and *want* to learn more about a particular subject matter; the teacher knows the starting and the end points, in between is the hard part. It is a feature or principle applicable to the context of past and present federal-state relationships. It is not unfair or unreasonable to say that the present administration could and should have known where the states would be coming from in reacting to the new legislation. If they had known, they stood a chance of preventing what is now a situation of repair. The practical approach is one that does not make a bad situation worse.

Let me now return to my suggestion that before school starts in September a teacher will meet with the parents of each child she will have in her class.[1] Assume this can be accomplished in two to three weeks. We know what the major obstacles will be: money, and the unwillingness of some parents to have their vacation time altered or interrupted. But let us assume that money is made available and a large majority of parents and teachers are willing to participate. Is there any basis to believe that the proposal is impractical in that we are ignoring something that may give us the kind of positive consequences envisioned? Keep in mind that a practical course of action is one based on a knowledge of the territory, which in this instance includes teacher skills, knowledge, and personal style. The more general way of putting it: What do we know about the school culture and how teachers are prepared to be a part of it? As I have pointed out umpteen times in my writings, we have a great deal relevant to the question. First, teachers are rarely admitted to a preparatory program on the basis (as one criterion among others) of some direct observation of their interpersonal style. In fact, in the post–World War II decades when there have been frequent severe teaching shortages, preparatory programs admitted students who were borderline or worse on several criteria, including interpersonal style. Second, al-

---

1. I say this in regard to the elementary schools where the potential fruitfulness of my suggestion is easier to grasp and discuss. Middle and high schools are far more complicated places: they are larger, departmentalized, and students have far more teachers.

though every teacher must and does have to interact with some parents, usually when there are problems, they receive no training in how one should think and act in a meeting with a parent. How you think and act in such a situation is not determined by the genes, it requires training and is not acquired by a lecture or reading, although that would be an improvement over totally not recognizing the nature of the issues. Third, although everyone in the school culture will nod assent to the assertion that parents should have an active role and interest in their child's schooling, the new teacher soon learns that other teachers and administrators are deeply ambivalent about a direct, active role because it touches on sensitive issues of professional prerogative, power, and decision making. Teachers are experiencing and reacting to what physicians have been confronting. From their standpoint, the good old days were when patients did not question what their doctor advised or did. That is no longer the case. The image of the physician as a god is not held by an increasing number of patients, and doctors bemoan the passing of the good old days. That is how most educators feel about parental involvement. I have discussed this in my book *Parental Involvement and the Political Principle* (1995) and shall not attempt to say more about it here, except that the problems are most acute and serious in urban schools when teachers bemoan the fact that parents are not as interested in their child's schooling as they should be. That myth, and it is a myth, has several sources, the most germane of which is that educators cannot entertain the possibility that they have played a role in creating that myth (Sarason 2002b, Chapter 8). And I say it is a myth based on my direct observations of inner-city schools around the country where parents were encouraged to and did actively participate in the educational affairs of their child's classroom and school (Heckman, et al. 1995; Shirley 1997; Levine 2001). In a context of productive learning a major responsibility of a teacher is to engender or reinforce a child's *wanting* to learn. Absent wanting, what the child learns is dry knowledge which contributes little nutrition to his psychological bloodstream; it ends up in a "file and forget" mental category. The significance of wanting is no less crucial in teacher-parent relationships.

I would have no objections whatsoever if I was told that several schools in different states were taking my proposal seriously. I would not call them up and give them my wet-blanket message. I would sincerely wish them well, if only because there are, as I have said, a few schools who in their own way recognized the problem and went about implementing a course of action in their distinctive ways, not like my proposal but accomplishing a similar goal. I have no basis for saying to the schools that were implementing my proposal that they will not accomplish their goals. They defined the problem, plunged ahead, and I was later told they achieved their purposes. They had thought and acted in what to them was a very practical way. I would send them letters of heartfelt thanks and congratulations. But at the same time I would be thinking, "All of the few schools I have observed and the few I have heard about that altered school-parent relationships were unrelated and unknown to each other. We then usually have a few more about whom that can be said. Furthermore, in no instance did it influence any program that prepares educators, even though a few of the few had come to the attention of those administering such programs. There are many scores of thousands of schools. The few (less than piddling) have not, cannot, and will not change anything beyond their particular schools. In education the noncosmetic reforms do not spread."

If in these schools the participants had said that their aim was not first to change their schools but to influence schools generally, I would have called them with as soaking a wet-blanket message as I could formulate. It is one thing when parents in a school are galvanized by the idea intended to alter their relationships in order to change the context of learning of students; at the least they have identified a problem they *willingly* seek to confront in a noncosmetic way, reflected in the title of Heckman's (1995) account of one such inner-city school: *The Courage to Change*. The word *courage* applied both to teachers and parents, each group aware it would not be easy because each had to unlearn stereotypical conceptions of and attitudes toward each other. What was accomplished is not comprehensible apart from the fact that Dr. Heckman and his colleagues had created a context of productive learning in that school. I directly observed that process over a period of years. In their initial book and one that is scheduled to be published in 2004, the phrase "context of productive learning" does not appear, but the more I have reflected over what I saw there, the more that phrase is a summing-up of what happened. If Dr. Heckman did not use that phrase, he did not need to because he had in his head the features of a context of productive learning before I began my visits to Tucson. Those visits crystallized my thinking.

It is quite another thing if federal or state government, or a superintendent of schools, were to enact legislation that would require schools to alter teacher-parent relationships reflecting the letter and spirit of what happened in Tucson's Ochoa school (or in a few schools scattered around the country). Why? For one thing, generally speaking, educators are and would be resistant to changing highly overlearned stances about how to think and act about parental involvement. Also, there are pitifully few schools who have or can call on a Dr. Heckman, who can over time help them begin the unlearning process; unlearning is no smooth, easy process because everything in us (I use that pronoun advisedly) seeks to avoid changing what we have overlearned as right, natural, and proper. Finally, such legislation would be formulated and enacted by people who are not only far removed from the sites they seek to change but are also ignorant of the complexity, organizationally speaking, of those sites.

It is obvious that I think that altering parent-teacher relationships in the way I described is a good idea. But it is utterly impractical for the reasons I have given. Good ideas are not in short supply. What are in short supply are ways of avoiding implementing them that guarantee their intended consequences will be minimal, or nonexistent, or worse. That is the major lesson that should have been but still has not been drawn from the history of the reform movement. The other and more basic lesson is one central to this book: When year after year, efforts to reform schools generally have failed, it is because of how the problem is wrongly defined. In this case you have to start with your conception of learning and how it requires you to be able to differentiate between contexts of productive and unproductive learning.

The consequences of the 1954 desegregation decision are helpful here. It was not a legislative but a long, long overdue judicial decision. However, it contained a phrase which would lead to legislative actions. That phrase was that the decision should be implemented with "all deliberate speed." The justices of the Supreme Court are not social scientists or knowledgeable about education, and they were presumably unaware that phrase was wildly impractical. If I can excuse the naïveté of the court, I cannot excuse the social scientists who should not have been so unprepared or offered advice that confirmed Mencken's caveat. And that was no less true for educators responsible for governmental policy. I did not hear any of them say the problem had no solution in the sense that four divided by two is a solution, that the problem was predictably and horribly complicated and that a quick-fix mentality would be a disaster. Nor did I hear anyone even suggest the possibility that the quality of contexts of learning in *nonsegregated* school systems was not a cause for satisfaction and complacency, and whatever we did to desegregate schools had to deal with the question: What do we mean by learning, productive or unproductive? If we do not gain clarity and consensus on answers to those questions, why should we expect better educational outcomes for students generally? A half-century after the 1954 decision those questions are still not being posed and discussed and our schools, urban and suburban, are lamentably what they have always been and will, I predict, remain so or get worse as a result of the recent shape-up-or-ship-out legislation.

I said that the problem is horribly complicated, by which I mean that by virtue of history and tradition its tentacles run through our entire society. But one of those tentacles is as important as it is obvious: the selection and preparation of educators. Even though these programs have been the object of criticism and derision in the post–World War II era, their response has been a self-defeating one; they have buried deeper the basic questions and rivet on requiring teachers to have a firmer grasp of subject matter. I have never met anyone who denied the importance of subject matter. *But what evidence is there that if you truly know your subject matter, you will better be able to create a classroom context in which students are motivated and interested in learning, respecting, and utilizing that subject matter?*

At the beginning of this chapter I said that a practical person is one who, when asked to advise about a particular problem, comes up with an answer or suggestion that in some significant way has positive consequences in the short term. He is not a seer or a theorist. He is considered practical because *in practice* his advice works far more often than not. The impractical person is one whose advice *in practice* does not work in the short or long term or, not infrequently, one whose advice is not taken because it is regarded as utopian or unpersuasive, or obviously unrealistic.

I know, because I have met and talked with them, that there are people familiar with my writings who regard me as single focused, uncompromising, and overly critical, someone who refuses to take the long view, who zeroes in on what can be done now, what is "practical" now. Depending on when in the last four decades I talked with them they were referring to my lack of any enthusiasm for the new curricula, open classrooms, the selection and preparation of educators, site-based management, President Nixon's Experimental Schools Program, block scheduling of classes, inservice training and staff development, charter schools, and to my assertion that the belief that increased expenditures for schooling were or would be correlated with improved educational outcomes courted disillusionment. I deliberately left out Head Start for two reasons. The first is that when Head Start legislation was enacted I gave a public lecture at Boston University where I said (a) if I were a member of Congress I would have voted for passage and (b) I would have done so at the same time that I believed that Head Start would by no means be as successful as claimed because it was based on the assumption that Head Start would, so to speak, innoculate the preschooler from catching the virus of low motivation and disinterest in the classrooms of the school they would later attend, an assumption that even some of the child development advisors to the program feared was at best questionable. The program they envisioned was not the program the legislation contained; political and fiscal considerations trumped their advice. Head Start accomplishments have been small. The administration and Congress in essence told the public that the legislation was a very practical response that in a few years would pay high dividends. From my way of thinking, from my experience in inner-city schools, it was a very impractical response.

Most of the reform efforts I have criticized had worthy goals but they were rendered impractical and unworthy because they would founder on the rocks of a narrow and superficial conception of learning in the classroom. I am not saying that we should stop whatever we are doing about these problems. But whether their potential for improvement is realized depends on changing the context of learning in the modal American classroom. And from what I have said are the features of a context of productive learning, it should be clear that predictably there will be potholes, obstacles, and resistance. Changing the context of learning will require national leadership, by which I do not mean issuing manifestos, fiats, hype, and using a short time perspective. Such leadership will confront, accept, and have the courage to say out loud that of the many things we have tried to improve the outcomes of our schools none of them has come anywhere near to what we hoped and predicted they would accomplish.

Readers of this book, especially if they are educators, may have come to this conclusion: in light of what I have said about the skills, interpersonal style, knowledge, and obligations of a teacher in a context of productive learning, some researchers may have concluded I am not in touch with the reality of the time pressures under which teachers operate. As more than a few teachers have bluntly said to me (I paraphrase), "We do not have the time to accomplish what is expected of us. And yet, you are describing a teacher as a combination of a psychologist, psychotherapist, a specialist in the formation and dynamics of groups, and someone who respects the individuality of students. We do not have enough time now to do what we are supposed to do. What you are describing is a fantasy in which saintly, all-knowing teachers have and can control how time is allocated in the school day." I am reminded here of a conversation with a small group of school principals. I had said something about the indubitable superiority of the preventive orientation over repair. One of them interrupted me and said (not unkindly), "It really bothers us when someone from the outside like you sings the praises of prevention when our problem is that we do not have time to repair the things we know are broken. Time is our problem. We are firemen putting out fires."

My response to these criticisms by teachers and administrators goes like this: "I would be astounded if you told me that time was not a major problem in your roles. I am well aware that you feel you are on a high-speed treadmill and you do not know if you can get off it. As a result you literally cannot even think about alternatives you might consider that would slow down the treadmill. You describe yourselves as prisoners serving a life sentence in a maximum-security system. That was precisely how teachers felt up until the 1950s, when they learned there is power in numbers and they joined a union. They had been peons, paid like peons, and had no voice in any policy decision. But a labor union is about bread and butter, what is euphemistically called 'working conditions.' It got you more pay, for which it deserves high marks, but it has done little or nothing about the treadmill and time. Are you really so helpless as a group that you cannot even consider, let alone advocate for, ideas and steps that should gain currency with an uninformed public and a public officialdom that recycles failed policies every five years or so? There was a time when you and most everyone else blamed underfunding of schools as the culprit. You know—and many of you have told me—that in the quiet of the night you conclude that money is a small part of the problem. You probably will not agree with my conclusion that in a basic sense money is not at all the problem because if you double the expenditures on schools, classrooms will remain contexts of unproductive learning. It took a long time for people finally to accept the argument of Copernicus that the sun and not the earth was the center of the universe. It will take as much or more time for people to confront the possibility that the basic problem in education today is a ridiculously narrow and misleading conception of productive learning. You have taken the most important first step to a new vision. It is no sin to fall short of the mark that vision represents. We always will fall short of the mark in human affairs. What is sinful and, therefore, totally impractical is not to have a mark at all."

I never, of course, delivered the above sermon to the teachers or administrators who directly said to me that I was impractical and unrealistic. I did not want to terminate the conversations. Besides, in a context of productive learning you start where the learner is, you do not assault them with arguments, facts, and ideas the learner cannot assimilate.

In the next chapter I will discuss the criticism that what I have said about the context of productive learning describes a teacher who among other things should be a combination psychologist, psychotherapist, parent substitute, and more. I regard it less as criticism and far more as an unintended seminal question: Who should be a teacher? As we shall see, we too frequently use conventional labels in ways that mightily impoverish our understanding of what they may have in common. That is certainly the case with the label *teacher*. If you doubt that, you should observe a classroom for one or two days. It will be far more persuasive than the words I write. One of my uses of fantasy is to come up with legislation which I think would make the world better. One of those fantasies is that no one seeking public office, from the president on down, can be on an election ballot unless he or she has spent one day observing a classroom in urban and suburban elementary, middle, and high schools. Six days of observing is not too much to ask of people who will be in a position that mightily influences the lives of students, educators, parents, and the course of our national life. Is that asking too much? Is it obviously impractical? Not so incidentally, my experience indicates that fewer than 1 percent of all members of a board of education have done what I fantasized. I would have to confess that 1 percent is high.

Chapter Eight

Creativity and Classrooms

If someone unfamiliar with such fields as physics or molecular biology or genetics asked a random sample of their theoreticians and researchers, What are the three or four or five puzzling problems which if better understood, let alone solved, would have direct and positive effects on human existence and welfare, thus justifying support for these fields? Although the answers by those in each of these fields would vary, there would be a lot of overlap. It is unlikely, for example, that if biochemist X did not include a problem contained in the list of biochemist Y, X would not say that that problem is not an important one and does not deserve serious study. Posterity may tell us that X was wrong, or Y was wrong, or neither was right. The point is that in any era there would be a significant degree of agreement about what was an important puzzle that if clarified would make a big difference in the human world. Now, if that stranger were to ask that question about American psychology, it is highly unlikely that any of these theoreticians and researchers would have human creativity on their list. If asked, they would not deny that human creativity is quite an important problem we are far from understanding. But what if we pressed on, as I have on numerous occasions, and asked, If it is an important problem, why is it so far from the mainstream of American psychology, a semidry tributary that every now and then becomes what may be called a trickle? There is an articulated and unarticulated answer, each reinforcing the other. The unarticulated answer is that in their education and training, issues surrounding the nature and contexts of creativity were rarely or never discussed. The articulated

answer is that creativity is by no means a universal human characteristic; it is a characteristic of relatively few people and, therefore, not
one of much interest to the development of a general theory of human potential and behavior.

The articulated answer has long interested me. Before going on let
me acknowledge that the concept of creativity is defined differently by
different people; the contexts in which and the psychological processes by which creativity is deemed to be manifested are not clear.
Nevertheless, there is one characteristic about which there is clarity
and agreement: It involves the recognition or discovery by the
individual's covert (internal) or overt actions that things or ideas heretofore unconnected can be productively brought into relationship
with each other and that the newly discerned connection opens new
vistas of possibilities. The creative act produces what for the discoverer
is a novel rearrangement of an existing state of affairs. Why, how, and
when the creative process occurs is a source of dispute. The concept of
intuition or a phrase like "unmotivated surprise" are often invoked. In
either case (or their variants) the creative process begins with a sense
of some unsolved problem or puzzle. The phrase "unmotivated surprise" refers to the end points (the solution), not to the initial troubling problem. Striving and motivation are always in the picture. That
raises a question very relevant to this book: Is there a learning compo-
nent in the creative process?

Is the process of creativity an unusual instance of learning in general? To the extent that the creative process so often requires persistence and motivation in the face of a troubling problem that is
important to the individual, we can say that the learner has to stay
with the problem, however frustrating it may be. But staying with a
problem is no guarantee that it will culminate in a solution, let alone a
creative one. But, it must be added, that does not mean that the individual will be unsuccessful with other puzzling problems. We hardly
know why that is the case and saying that it reflects an individual's
learning history is tantamount to restating or begging the question.
The glaring inadequacy of learning theories in American psychology
has been that it took for granted that contexts are crucial and at the
same time ignored studying them, paying it respect by considering it
composed of discrete stimuli differentially evoking a discrete response.
If context was not "noise," it certainly was not a patterned gestalt, a
complicated one. Creativity almost never occurs in contexts which do
not in one or another way stimulate, or encourage, or support, or recognize it, be that context in the home, classroom, or work setting. Unlike Athena springing full-blown from the head of Zeus, creativity
requires recognition and support and that assumes respect for the individual even when the individual's behavior and products seem

strange to you. That does not mean, of course, that you accept and support anything or everything about a person's thinking and products but rather that you are alert to the possibility that what seems strange to you derives from the fact that by its very nature the creative process and its outcomes are a novelty, a new or different way of thinking and doing.

Before going on to the problematics of the creativity, it is important to point out why I am so puzzled that American psychology pays so little attention in theory, research, and practice to creativity. No one will deny that one obvious way, perhaps the most obvious way, that humans differ from all other animals is in the degree to which they can learn and use language. I say degree because there is now abundant evidence that other animals (e.g., birds, monkeys, whales) can communicate with others through a language of distinctive sounds. But our language is incomparably more nuanced and complicated than theirs, a difference that is literally impossible to overestimate. And the same is the case with creativity. It could be argued that creativity, unlike language, is an attribute of relatively few people and explains why creativity does not receive or perhaps deserve as much attention as language. (I shall quarrel with that view a bit later.) But how did it come about that a true language was created that allowed totally deaf people to communicate with other people? Creating that language was an amazing achievement and I mention it here because human history is replete with such examples. Creativity no less than language has transformed the human race and will continue to do so. So even if one conventionally assumes that creativity is a characteristic of relatively few people, it is puzzling why the recognition and nurturing of creativity so little occupies American psychologists. Earlier I asked: By what scale of values should the significance of what a field considers its most important problems deserve serious study because those problems will, when "solved," contribute knowledge that will enhance people's capacity for more effective and socially satisfying use of their potential? What I have been suggesting is this criterion: a human capacity that has altered the course of human history but is a capacity we hardly know how to recognize and nurture. Creativity meets that criterion.

Is creativity a universal attribute or one that only a few have? Humans are not born being able to walk or talk. We say that they have to learn to talk and walk and we have a pretty good idea of how those capacities can or should be nurtured. Whatever stand you take on the nature-nurture issues or on whether creativity is a universal attribute, you take for granted that the appearances of these attributes were preceded by contexts which can vary considerably in influencing when and how they appear. Those contexts are never affectively neutral for child and parents; both sides live in a context in which, for example, a noncognitive factor like temperament may be compatible or noncompatible; and the same is true for frustration tolerance and more. And let us not gloss over the fact that contexts vary depending on the gender of the young child. So, when we use concepts such as learning, ability, and creativity, we should not make the mistake of regarding them as platonic essences encapsulated and not suffused with a host of noncognitive factors. That is what makes the study of cognitive and noncognitive variables as complicated as it is fascinating. We hear much today about the mapping of the human genome, and one of the predictable findings is that the manifestations of one gene rarely, if ever, arise independent of all other genes; those manifestations depend on context, and when that mapping is completed and employed in future research, it is highly likely that that context will be found to be more complicated than is now believed. There is an old maxim that states that the more you know the more you have to know. The wisdom in that statement is too often overlooked by those who talk about learning, ability, and creativity as if we have a relatively firm grasp and understanding of the parameters of those concepts. We do not, but we have learned some things. Modesty and a stance of tentativeness should be the order of the day. That may not satisfy the need for certainty but it may serve to prevent or dilute the predictable severity of posterity's harsh judgments, as I said elsewhere in regard to American psychology: Posterity is the cruelest of critics.

Let us focus on creativity by imagining that we have spent the next six months observing classrooms. And since we are imagining, we also videotape the classrooms so that we have a record which we can study and upon which we can reflect. For each grade we select a random sample within each of the country's major geographical areas. We spend one full day in each classroom, and at the end of the day we select, again at random, several students to interview as well as their teachers. And, finally, let us assume agreement that a major feature of the creative process is that it brings together ideas or things in a distinctively novel way, a way that may be literally unique among all other students in that classroom. (Research done in our imagination goes smoothly; in "real life," however, what I have just outlined is by no means complete and I have said nothing about the obstacles, conceptual and practical, that would be encountered.)

Since the imaginary "we" have no data, the palpable me will draw on personal experience. That experience had a beginning in an institution for mentally retarded people. That is where I met Henry Schaefer-Simmern, a political refugee from Nazi Germany. He was an artist, art educator, and art theorist. I have discussed him and his work in previous books (Sarason 1988, 1999) and I will not repeat here the substance of what I have said. The interested reader should consult his book *The Unfolding of Artistic Activity* (1948). One of the last things John Dewey wrote was the introduction to that book.

For my present purposes there are several things that the reader should be told. First and most basic was Schaefer's belief that artistic process—by which he meant a creative process—was a universal feature of people; it was not a special feature of special people, although the quality of the end product varied considerably and dramatically among people. Second, what interfered with, inhibited, or extinguished such activity was the widespread and insidious notion that the purpose of that activity was faithfully to replicate something in the external world. Third, for artistic activity to become manifest required a context that would facilitate overcoming the conventional view of what was art and also would support the person's use of his or her personal imagery for the content of the end product. Fourth, the obligation of the teacher is *not* to tell or show a student what she had to draw but rather to encourage her to study what she had done and to identify those aspects that matched or did not satisfy her internal imagery.

These four features will, I am sure, raise more questions than answers in the minds of readers. I had been asked by the superintendent to select a dozen or so individuals, and Schaefer would decide with which of them he would work on the two days each week he came to the Southbury Training School. After my initial two-hour meeting with him I came to several conclusions: He was a dedicated, passionate person; he was abysmally ignorant of mentally retarded individuals; his "theory" or beliefs were at best murky and at worst grandiose in their expectations; and his rigid and authoritarian manner were the opposite of the characteristics of the nondirective teacher he described to me. Several things tempered my pessimistic judgments. I was sympathetic to anyone who challenged conventional conceptions of human potential; my disenchantment with those regnant conceptions in American psychology had already begun. He showed me the artistic development of adult individuals who had regarded themselves as totally devoid of creativity, whose initial efforts were to them pathetically primitive but whose productions over months and years were of a quality and compellingness that would add grace if hung on the walls of your home. And, finally, that initial discussion brought back to me a traumatic experience I had in the fifth grade with an art teacher, an experience that was proof positive to me that artistic activity was something to be avoided at all costs. Nevertheless, I came away from that initial meeting feeling sorry that this self-absorbed political refugee was doomed to be disappointed. I was also sorry for myself because I had been given the responsibility to keep tabs on what he was doing and how things were going.

I spent hours, and soon days, observing what was going on. I was dumbfounded and entranced. From what I have written elsewhere I single out the following:

1. Schaefer was amazingly nondirective. What he always did when an individual showed him a completed work was to ask: "Do you like it? Is it like you wanted it to look? Is there anything about it you want to change or do better?" There was never group instruction. Each individual worked alone.

2. He was with the class for three consecutive hours each time he came to Southbury. They would come in, go to their individual tables, and start to work. There was no horsing around. The degree of absorption in their work is hard to exaggerate. Their struggle was frequently expressed in facial expression and body language. Not infrequently, they would crumple up what they had done, get a new piece of paper, and go to work.

3. All of them had been institutionalized for years (even decades). This was the first time that an authority figure had asked them to engage in a process and task for which the substance and end product was their choosing and responsibility. It was also the first time that such a figure had treated them with respect, encouragement, and with the kind of friendship that it would not be an exaggeration to say bordered on love.

Did it raise their IQ? It never occurred to me to retest these individuals, whose IQs ranged from 50 to 68. It was those same test scores which to my way of thinking in 1942 convinced me that what Schaefer said he would demonstrate was pathetically unrealistic. Those scores said nothing about creativity in any or all contexts in which creativity might become manifest.[1] The tests tell us something important and useful but we should never confuse that statement

---

1. My longtime Yale colleague and dear friend Dr. Edward Zigler has spent over four decades in research with mentally retarded individuals. He never has challenged the conclusion that they had cognitive deficits (and never have I). For Dr. Zigler the theoretical and practical question was identical to that we should ask about any human being: In what altered contexts engendering high motivation and stimulating opportunity could they develop attitudes and skills that were adaptive and personally and socially satisfying? In 1999 he and Bennet-Gates edited a book called *Personality Development in Individuals with Mental Retardation*. Everything in that book is consistent with what I have written in the pages of this book. Dr. Zigler's chapter is a succinct and yet masterful exposition of what he has demonstrated and learned. He always looked beyond test scores for the role of other variables, and he did this in ways that gave substance to the usual empty and superficial use of the concept of the "whole personality."

with one that even suggests that we know all we need to know when we make judgments or decisions that influence people's lives. So, for example, when a twelve-year-old boy strangles a neighbor's cat to death and we learn that he has an IQ of 160 we do not say he did it *because* he has such a high IQ. But if the boy has an IQ of 60 we think we know where to place the blame. Clearly, we would not say that Schaefer's group did what they did because they had low IQs. What would we say? That by a stroke of luck or divine providence he selected those who had some creative spark? Or would we, should we, say formal tests of cognition and cognitive activity were not developed to tell us anything about creativity and the contexts in which it is extinguished or stimulated?

But, the reader may ask, on what basis do I conclude Schaefer's pupils were creative? The only basis I have provided is that closely watching them at work, observing them struggle to make the external object reflect their internal imagery, seeing that look of glee and surprise when *now* they knew how to overcome the problem with which they were struggling—these have been the evidence I provided and it clearly can be deemed insufficient and subjective. But in the instance of artistic creativity there is another kind of evidence, which in the case of indubitably creative artists is so closely studied. I refer to the preliminary sketches and drawings these artists make as a way to clarify their internal imagery, e.g., to sense what the problems of spatial composition may be, to leave the self open to new spatial relationships. Those sketches and drawings can be numerous as the artist struggles to put it all together, a kind of playing around that hopefully will satisfactorily integrate ideas and imagery, to arrive at the point when he or she says, "*Now* I understand how to do it; this is an understanding I did not have before."

The above is by way of telling the reader that in his book Schaefer presents to the reader in a longitudinal fashion the artistic development of retarded individuals from their initial efforts to their final products. I ask the reader to make an independent judgment about the presence or absence of creativity. Are those end products great or middling works of art? Of course not. In the pantheon of artists creativity is taken for granted at the same time it is recognized (judged) that some artists have displayed different degrees of creativity. The question one should ask about Schaefer's retarded individuals is not whether they displayed this or that level of creativity but whether they showed *any* creativity; that was the question Schaefer sought to answer to buttress his belief that creativity was a universal feature of people. And if you read his book, do not fail to study his chapters on "ordinary" individuals whose initial efforts were strikingly similar (e.g., stick figures) to those of the retarded individuals but whose end products I am certain the reader will say are very creative. The frontispiece in his book shows the painting "Negro Boy in Central Park." After looking at it, then study this woman's development in a later chapter, in which this self-deprecating social worker falteringly and even ashamedly drew primitive stick figures when she first began creating. It will not occur to the reader to ask if her IQ was raised. I hope it would occur to the reader to question whether our conventional conceptions of learning and ability have for too long been derived on a grossly inadequate conception of context. I shall have more to say about this later.

A second experience came years later. It did not involve me in any direct way because it came from reading two books by the well-known poet, Kenneth Koch (1970, 1977). He, like Schaefer, believed that creativity was not a special feature of special people. In his 1970 book *Wishes, Lies, and Dreams* Koch describes his initial effort to teach poetry in a New York City elementary school (P. S. 61) made up largely of black and Hispanic children. "I was curious to see what could be done for children's poetry," he writes. "I knew some things about teaching adults to write. . . . But I didn't know about children. Adult writers had read a lot, wanted to be writers, and were driven by all the usual forces writers are driven by. I knew how to talk to them, how to inspire them, how to criticize their work. What to say to an eight-year-old with no commitment to literature?" (p. 2). Not only what to say but what to do to gain that *willing* commitment without which having an artistic experience is nearly impossible. Koch's book contains more than three hundred pages, most of which are devoted to the works of these children, from their earliest to their latest efforts. I must leave it to the interested reader to examine and judge what Koch and these children accomplished over a period of several months. "I usually went to the school two or three afternoons a week and taught three forty-minute classes. Toward the end I taught more often, because I had become so interested and because I knew I was going to write about it and wanted as much experience as possible." (p. 2). Let me summarize the major points with which I think any reader of Koch's book would agree:

1. Koch came to his task already impressed with "how playful and inventive children's talk sometimes was. They said true things in fresh and surprising ways. . . . Some children's poetry was marvelous but most seemed uncomfortably imitative of adult poetry or else childishly cute. It seemed restricted somehow, and it obviously lacked the happy, creative energy of children's art. I wanted to find, if I could, a way for children to get as much from poetry as they did from painting." (pp. 2–3).

2. Two things needed to be avoided: (a) requiring the child to use forms of verbal relationships (like rhyming) that are difficult and confining, and (b) suggesting content of no personal significance to him or her. No less than Schaefer-Simmern, Koch understood the negative consequences of imitation.

3. One should not judge the poetry of children by its obvious differences from that of recognized adult poets. But Koch found early on that their poetry was similar in one crucial respect: both possessed form. The children's poems "were all innocence, elation, and intelligence. They were unified poems: it made sense where they started and where they stopped. And they had a lovely music" (p. 6). The children *were* poets. The seeds of artistry were there.

4. What occupied Koch in the earliest days, what required him to experiment, was not only how to interest children in constructing poems but also how to help them overcome the mind-set that there were "right and wrong" ways of proceeding, a set that short circuited imaginativeness. If anything is obvious in Koch's account, it is (again as in Schaefer-Simmern) the respect he had for what the children could do and his support and acceptance of what they did. He liberated their imaginativeness, not fearful what they would write would be an amorphous, verbal glob. "Children have a natural talent for writing poetry and anyone who teaches them should know that. Teaching really is not the right word for what takes place; it is more like permitting the children to discover something they already have. I helped them to do this by removing obstacles, such as the need to rhyme, and by encouraging them in various ways to get tuned in to their own strong feelings, to their spontaneity, their sensitivity, and their carefree inventiveness. At first I was amazed at how well the children wrote, because there was obviously not enough in what I had told them to begin to account for it."

5. "I was, as I said, amazed, because I hadn't expected any grade-school children, much less fourth graders, to write so well so soon. I thought I might have some success with sixth graders, but even there I felt it would be best to begin with a small group who volunteered for a poetry workshop. After the fourth-grade Wish Poems, however, and after the Wish and Comparison Poems from the other grades, I realized my mistake. The children in all the grades, primary through sixth, wrote poems which they enjoyed and I enjoyed. Treating them like poets was not a case of humorous but effective diplomacy, as I had first thought; it was the right way to treat them because it corresponded to the truth. A little humor, of course, I left in. Poetry was serious, but we joked and

laughed a good deal; it was serious because it was such a pleasure to write. Treating them as poets enabled me to encourage them and egg them on in a non-teacher-ish way—as an admirer and fellow worker rather than as a boss. It shouldn't be difficult for a teacher to share this attitude once it is plain how happily and naturally the students take to writing." (p. 24)

That young children happily and naturally take to writing will sound odd to those who have been frustrated in their attempts to improve educational outcomes and who end up blaming the victims—the students—for lack of interest and motivation.

The atmosphere in the classrooms during the few hours a week Koch was there contrasted dramatically with that in the modal classroom with which we are all too familiar. The children were buoyant, eager, hardworking, *and* productive. Koch set the stage, he was the director, but he had no script. He knew what the ending of the drama should be, could be. The children were like actors seeking an author in a Pirandello play. They became the authors.

The force of Koch's book derives from the fact that the children were not "ordinary." They were black and Hispanic children in an inner-city school, not the usual setting for a project like his. The parallels with Schaefer-Simmern's work with mentally retarded individuals at the Southbury Training School are noteworthy.

Wishes, Lies, and Dreams was published in 1970. In 1977 Koch published *I Never Told Anybody*, more telling, poignant, and upsetting than the previous book. Chapter 1 begins with a poem by one of Koch's "students":

AUTUMN
Your leaves were yellow
And some of them were darker
And I picked them up
And carried them in the house
And put them in different vases
Your leaves sound different
I couldn't understand why
The leaves at that time of year
Had a rustle about them
And they would drop
At the least little thing
And I would listen
And pick up some of them.
                    —*Nadyl Catalfano*

That book is about teaching poetry writing to residents of a nursing home on Manhattan's Lower East Side. It was a run-of-the-mill nursing home with its usual features: infrequently punctuated silence, residents lost in their private worlds, little or no give-and-take between residents or between residents and staff, passivity of residents their most obvious feature. Most were from the working class and had a limited education. They had worked as dry cleaners, messengers, short-order cooks, and domestic servants. A few had worked in offices, and one had been an actress. Almost all of them were unable to use their hands to write—either because of muscular difficulties or blindness.

One aspect of change has yet to receive the attention it deserves. It is wrapped up in what I call the one-life, one-career imperative. What society had said, so to speak, to young people was: "Here is a smorgasbord of career opportunities, choose the one 'task' you will work at in your lifetime; you can be A or B, but you cannot be both." That is a message to which young people in the post–World War II era began to react negatively. The one-life, one-career imperative was on a collision course with "Be all that you can be." As our studies reported in *Work, Aging, and Social Change* (Sarason 1997) suggest, young people resented and resisted the idea that they could be only one thing in life. There was more to them than that! They feared being "slotted," socialized into a narrow career path, unable seriously to exploit and test their diverse interests and capacities. They wanted to avoid what they perceived to be the straitjacket in which their parents found themselves.

Although they did not verbalize it in this way, our interviewees feared being unable to give creative expression to what was in them—to put their unique mark in and on something. Career change has escalated markedly in the post–World War II era. The individual and social dynamics powering that escalation are very similar to those powering the increase in the number of people actively engaged in some form of artistic activity. When John Dewey spoke about the need for artistic activity, he was referring to the bedrock importance of ordered, creative expression in whatever one does, of being able to claim psychological ownership of an activity because it bears the unique stamp of the individual. No one who reads Dewey's *Art as Experience* (1934) will find it easy to regard artistic activity in the customary narrow, segregated, special way. Dewey wrote that book in the 1930s. If he did not predict the changes in worldview that would be wrought by World War II, his book contained a message that people born after the war began to take seriously, although many were completely unaware of what Dewey wrote.

But more than young people heard and responded to Dewey's message. Unless my observations are grossly atypical, there has been a startling increase in the number of older people who seek and decide to engage in some form of artistic activity, especially women. I have spoken to scores of such people, and one theme runs through their responses: "I have *always* wanted to do something creative, to *make* something that was *me, mine.* But I always saw myself as *uncreative.* Who was I to regard myself as an artist? As the years went by, as I began to ask what I wanted to do with my time and myself, I knew I had to do something about that empty feeling, that sense of unfulfillment." In most of these instances the decision to act was facilitated by a friend's action or by receiving a brochure of adult education courses offered in local schools or at a local "creative arts workshop." If their responses to my queries varied somewhat, there was no variation in the degree of satisfaction they voiced about engaging in artistic activity. In that respect they were no different from Koch's people, who had been languishing and slowly dying in a nursing home.

The title of Koch's book, *I Never Told Anybody,* in a way says it all: our need to express—literally, to press out of ourselves—in some ordered, configured way our imagery, thoughts, feelings is early on inhibited and degraded. It is a need that then goes underground but is never completely extinguished, as Koch's book so poignantly demonstrates. It is inescapable that in children that need hits us, so to speak, in the face. After early childhood it begins to disappear, and to reappear only in a few specially gifted adolescents, which says far less about artistic activity than it does about the force of culture and tradition and about a narrow, acultural psychology. A psychology that begins and ends with what people are, with what they appear to be, and only minimally and unimaginatively faces up to what people *can* be is at best an unproductive psychology and at worst an unwitting collaborator with other forces in the underestimation of human potential. Artistic activity is special because of the challenge it represents to our conception of how human nature and nurture transact.

So what would we observe and learn if we did the study of classrooms I outlined earlier in this chapter and for which the experiences that followed were one form of answer? That answer has several parts.

1. Identifying and nurturing signs or products of creative activity are not on the lists of teachers' purposes except in the usual minuscule number of instances. There are always these exceptions which serve to remind us that what we usually see is not what we should or want to see.

2. For most and frequently for all of the day, the classroom is structured and organized in a way in which the creativity of students is

not stimulated, encouraged, or supported. This is *not*, I hasten to add, to suggest that such activity should be the major, let alone sole, purpose of the teacher but rather that its manifestations, direct or indirect, should not be as unrecognized or ignored to the degree they are.

3. Many schools have no periods for artistic or musical or literary activity. Some schools may have one or two on one day. Where there are such periods, the justification by the school is that it gives the student an opportunity for creative personal expression, a justification that clearly implies that the bulk of the curriculum has little or nothing to do with creativity.

4. The context of the classroom is an overwhelming one in which the task of the students is to get the right answers to the problems the teacher has presented to them.

I am reminded here of Max Wertheimer's (1945) famous study of the way that children solve the parallelogram problem. When Wertheimer demonstrated to the children that there was more than one way of arriving at a proof, they categorically denied that these alternative ways were right because they conflicted with what they had been taught. How children are taught to regard their art products or those of others is no different. To expect children to like to engage in artistic activity, to "appreciate" art appreciation, is to expose one's ignorance of the modal classroom in the school culture. What would be mystifying is if children had more positive attitudes—that would really require explanation! If the spontaneous creative artistic activity of preschoolers is not in evidence during formal schooling, this says a good deal more about the school culture than about the interests and capabilities of children generally. As I have said before, with rare exceptions schools make no serious attempt to stimulate and guide artistic development. Today we hear much about "scientific illiteracy" and how schools must do a better job of making science as knowledge *and* process more interesting and relevant for students. We want students to like science, to see it as important for their intellectual development. Indeed, there are those who insist that students should begin in the earliest grades to engage in the scientific process at a level appropriate to their personal experience and cognitive level. And engaging means far more than acquiring important knowledge. This is no less the case with artistic activity.

No one more than Piaget has studied and illuminated how scientific thinking develops and unfolds in children (in preschool and beyond), just as no one more than Schaefer-Simmern has done the same for the unfolding of artistic activity. Piaget wrote the preface to a book by Kamii and De Vries (1978), to my knowledge the only time he agreed to do that for a book on pedagogy. His reluctance is alluded to in the first sentence of his preface, a part of which follows:

> Many educators have used our operatory tasks by transforming them into kinds of standardized "tests," as if their purposes were to diagnose the performances a child is capable of in a given situation. Our method of asking questions with free conversations, as well as the theory of the formation of structures which we have studied stage by stage, permits a much more nuanced use of these tasks—to know how a child reasons and what kinds of new constructions he is capable of when we encourage his spontaneity to a maximum. In this case the double advantage which can be obtained is: (1) from the standpoint of psychological diagnosis, to foresee in part the progress the child will be able to make later; and (2) from the pedagogical point of view, to reinforce his constructivity and thus find a method of teaching in accordance with "constructivism" which is the fundamental principle of our interpretation of intellectual development.
>
> This is what the authors of this book have well understood. I had already visited with great pleasure in 1967 the Ypsilanti Public Schools (Michigan) and observed the efforts made there to develop the pupils' creativity. The new experiments done by the authors at the University of Illinois at Chicago Circle are inspired by the same principles: Focusing on physical knowledge more than on logico-mathematical knowledge, they centered their effort on inventing activities to permit children to act on objects and observe the reactions or transformations of these objects (which is the essence of physical knowledge, where the role of the subject's actions is indispensable for understanding the nature of the phenomena involved). (p. vii)

For Piaget and Schaefer-Simmern engagement is a constructive process: acting on and in turn being acted on, an ongoing transformation between "in there" and "out there," a willing pursuit powered by curiosity, interest, and the desire to master. It is knowledge acquired by action, not passive receptivity, knowledge about self and the world, and what the self can *effect*.

Creativity, its manifestations or absence, is not understandable apart from context. And creativity is not a process or characteristic that we display from the time we get up in the morning until we go to bed at night. By conventional standards I am intelligent but by conventional standards I can be quite stupid. Creativity is not a now-you-have-it-and-now-you-don't characteristic; it is rather a now in which you can indulge or display its characteristics, mightily depending on context. If it is displayed, it does not follow that the person or observer will characterize it as creative, a not infrequent occurrence in classrooms. Let me conclude this chapter by elaborating on that point.

I shall describe one of three similar experiences that I found very instructive. Some friends of ours bought a house. After living in it for a couple of months they invited us over for dinner. Having been in their previous home we knew that Mrs. X would have been a very good interior decorator, if she had chosen a career. She had an eye, as they say, for what goes with what. When we entered their new home, far more spacious than the previous one, my wife exclaimed, "This is a work of art. You brought everything together so beautifully. You really have artistic talent." Mrs. X laughed and said, "I'm no artist but I can say that furnishing this house sent me up a wall. The living room drove me nuts. I tried this and that but nothing seemed to work. At first I thought the colors in the paintings on the wall did not go together, they clashed. So I took a couple off and substituted others I thought would integrate better with the others. That didn't work. I rearranged the furniture I don't know how many times and nothing worked. I was obsessed and frustrated. I went to bed one evening and just when I was falling asleep, it hit me: The coffee table in this large living room made everything else in the room look too large. In the upstairs study we had a much larger coffee table, more like a bench, and so I got up, we brought the table down and that did the trick. We went the next day and bought a larger table of the color that would fit in."

We are not used to describing what she did as creative, and she refused to regard what she did in that way. But that is my point: we are schooled to apply the concepts of artistic and creativity to individuals who the larger society (or segments of it) say are creative or artistic, and we are not set to look for their manifestations in "ordinary" individuals. The instance I have described took place thirty years ago at a time when the nature of creativity played a minor role in my thinking. I found what she said more amusing than significant, a reflection of what I then thought was her perfectionist makeup. But that and two other comparable instances stuck with me so that when I much later became interested in creativity, it popped into my head. And it was then that I realized that the relatively small amounts of research on creativity in American psychology was primarily on individuals or groups of individuals (e.g., architects) who their peers agreed were creative, reinforcing the view that "real" creativity is a characteristic of specially gifted people. I have no difficulty in this case accepting the fact that some people display more creativity than others and even display it more often, although variation in frequency is considerable. But accepting that in no way justifies the conclusion that creativity is a special feature of special people. If that conclusion is wrong, one must then raise two questions which have enormous relevance for schooling and psychology's quest to understand human ability and performance. Has the narrow view of ability and performance held by American psychology been an obstacle to recognizing creativity in people and contexts where we assume creativity is not to be observed? Do we not have to know far more than we do about contexts, like schools, where creativity is never totally absent?

We hear a good deal today about the failure of schools to instill critical thinking in students. No one opposes such a policy. But critical thinking is not a process or set of attitudes with which we are born. It is not a characteristic learned and displayed in any or all contexts. It is only somewhat of an exaggeration to say that the modal classroom is a place where students are required and judged to accept uncritically what they are taught, that contrary personal opinion and expression are not encouraged. In an earlier book (1996b) I describe and discuss how the constitution of the classroom is forged, how the rules governing relationships among students and between students are formulated. I was not interested in subject matter but about rules, obligations, and expectations governing interpersonal relationships. We observed a number of classrooms for a month starting on the first day of school. We were to note and briefly describe any instance of rule formation, by and with whom. We hardly used our pencils because the constitution was formulated by the teacher, period. No explanations, no discussion, no invitation to students to voice any contrary opinions. Teachers know best, they are the authority figures, you do not mess with them, you may think critically but you had better not voice your thoughts. That is beautifully portrayed in the first half of the film *Mr. Holland's Opus*. Classrooms are not contexts for critical thinking or the manifestations of creativity.

One final point. The end product of the creative process may not be to your liking but that should not blind you to the possibility that the process had taken place. For example, as I write these words Edmund Morris' book on Ronald Reagan has created a storm because what Morris did was to create a fictional character named Edmund Morris who knew or observed Reagan when they both were quite young and who interacted or observed him thereafter at intervals. Most critics took a very negative view of what he had done; a minority of critics reacted if not with high praise then with muted approval. Why did Morris not write in the form of a conventional biography as he did to wide acclaim in his biography of Theodore Roosevelt? Morris' answer is quite clear. After several years writing the biography in the conventional way he was totally frustrated and dissatisfied with his attempt to explain the enigmas that the personality of the president presented. And then one day he had an "aha" experience in which he hit upon the clarifying role a fictional character could play. He scrapped several years of writing and started afresh. From the time the president authorized Morris to do the biography until it was published, fourteen years passed. From my standpoint, disliking the book is one thing, failing to give him credit for creatively resolving *his* problem is quite another thing.

Chapter Nine

The Disconnect Between Administrators and Classroom Learning

Up to this point I have been talking about learning in the classroom and I have indicated that in my experience all but a small percentage of classrooms are contexts of unproductive learning. Leaving the personal aside, my opinion is deducible from studies (e.g., Steinberg et al., 1996) that as students go from elementary to middle to high school their interest in school and learning steadily decrease, although why that happens is not totally attributable to school experience. The researchers who did those studies were, like me, external to the schools; they were not formally trained classroom teachers. This raises the accountability question: Why does it take outsiders to point out how students regard their schools and learning? Is it unreasonable to expect that those who administer schools would have and discharge the obligation, the self-interest, to have or develop the means to ascertain the attitudes of students toward learning and schooling? *These are questions in principle no different than what a teacher has to ask and get answers to in regard to students if the context of learning is to be a productive one.* When we say that a teacher has to get to know her students we mean a relationship of trust and safety which makes possible discussion of heretofore unverbalized attitudes and motivations always present in the learning context. The maxim "from your students you are taught" is more than rhetoric or an insincere expression of humility but rather an obligation to create the conditions in which that maxim is taken seriously; it is the vehicle for mutual learning. But having said that, a question arises that phenomenologically starts in the classroom but very quickly involves the school and the school system. *Can a teacher create and sustain a context of productive learning if those conditions do not exist for his or her growth as a teacher?* One of the defining features of burnout among teachers (and others in the helping professions) is a large discrepancy between what they are giving of themselves to others and the lack of personal rewards and recognition they get from those who administer the school and/or school system. One young woman who had been teaching for three years in an inner-city school put it this way: "I work my butt off for my kids. I get home at night, and in the wintertime it is night. I'm exhausted. There are times I get to school at seven in the morning to grade papers and work out my plan for the day. The janitor thinks I'm nuts. He brings me coffee. On the state's achievement tests my kids are a little below norms, which I consider a real achievement on my part. But who in the system cares, who pats me on the back, who says thanks for what I am doing, who asks me if I have any ideas about the curriculum we are told we must follow? If my kids were really doing poorly, I would hear from them. They might, God help me, even come to see what goes on in my classroom. That will be the day. They are not interested in me, they are interested in test scores. And to be completely honest, I'm not sure they are interested in the kids." This young woman also told me she was going to be married and she would have to decide whether to stay on, or leave teaching.

The first book that came from the staff of the Yale Psycho-Educational Clinic in 1966 (Sarason, et al.) contained a chapter by Dr. Murray Levine titled "Teaching Is a Lonely Profession." Although a school is a densely populated place, many teachers feel not only alone but lonely, and that is especially true for new teachers. We received more spontaneous letters of commendation from teachers about that chapter than any other part of that book. That was in 1966. The situation today has changed and not for the better as teachers see it. In an era when the pressures to improve test scores are enormous and failure to do so comes with penalties, teachers resent (too weak a word) feeling like servants who must do what their administrative masters tell them to do and do it in a prescribed way. Education is a big business and it is flooded by entrepreneurs who have developed and marketed this or that silver bullet or vitamin that will elevate test scores. School administrators are eager consumers in this market and what they buy is fed to teachers without any thought that teachers may regard it as a form of educational castor oil which they see as irrelevant to the illness they have, a case where Father thinks he knows best but Father is wrong again. I say "again" because those who have been teaching for, say, more than five years view what is happening from a "here we go again" stance. The more things change the more they remain the same.

I am being descriptive, not judgmental. I have gone to pains in previous books to explain why I regard both administrators and teachers as unwitting victims of a longstanding state of affairs in which, among other things, a basic question has been *assumed* to have been clarified and answered. What do we mean by learning? How can we get to the point where we can credibly establish the differences between contexts of productive and unproductive learning? Absent discussion, clarification, and demonstration of those differences, educational reform is doomed. So, when I say that what I am doing is describing a state of affairs, I am doing it because that state of affairs has not confronted what I consider a truly basic question. The reader may disagree with me. In defense I can only say that for over fifty years my public predictions of failure of educational reform have been on target. It may be that I have been right for the wrong reasons but no one has seen fit to criticize me on those grounds. I know that silence is not to be confused with agreement.

On the day I finished the paragraphs above I received a letter from a friend, Dr. Dale Brubaker of the University of North Carolina at Greensboro. In it he says:

> I'm enclosing a paper by a very bright African-American doctoral student in her mid-twenties. Her story reminded me of much that you write about in your books—an idealistic young public-school teacher does her best but is beaten down by the system and flees to the university for doctoral study.

I have received more than a few such letters and enclosures, to one of which I felt compelled to devote a chapter in my 1999 book *Teaching as a Performing Art*. I feel compelled again to give excerpts here from the paper Ms. Danyell Roseboro wrote. I'm grateful for her permission to do so.

> On one particular day, after a meeting of Future Teachers of America, our advisor handed me an application for a North Carolina Teaching Fellows Scholarship. I accepted it, rather awkwardly. So I had been president of FTA, tutored countless elementary children, and had a mom who was a teacher. The idea of teaching fell unwanted at my feet. I had watched my mom work seemingly fruitless hours grading papers, make lesson plans, worry about other people's children. I could not possibly relish the idea. But . . . it hung out there at the periphery of my imagination . . . always waiting for me to take that first tentative grasp. Teaching offered little monetary gain, but it had meaning. I could still excite, infuriate and enlighten people. In this case, my students would listen as a captive audience. The novelty of the idea struck me. And so I decided . . . I would teach.

"Ok . . . so how am I supposed to code this attendance sheet . . . did you say use the red pen if they are absent or only use the red pen if they show up on the first day? Where do I send the child if she's tardy? Let me get this right, if she's tardy on the first four days, I don't send her anywhere, but if she's tardy on day five I send her to ISS? And where is ISS exactly? So Level II, III and IV offenses go on the D1 form, but for Level 1 offenses I handle the disciplinary action. And I send the D1 form to the appropriate administrator for the child based on the student's last name? Do I send the study with the D1 form or do I bring it up to the office later? And then I have to find the time to go to the Guidance office, look through every child's individual folder and make note of any special modifications. What do you mean we don't have the freshmen IEP's yet? Did they get lost? Why does it seem that those of you in charge have no more of an idea what's going on than me and I'm new?"

On day one of teaching, there I stood, with what I hoped was not a smile (no smiling on the first day . . . you have to look tough) and some semblance of confidence. Realizing with perfect clarity that I had just been thrown to the wolves, I watched them as they watched me. Swiftly, they sized me up and began what would become a daily ritual of testing the new teacher. I scrambled from day to day to create challenging and interesting lesson plans, but barely had enough time to photocopy worksheets. Discipline issues dominated my thinking. How do you discipline a child with love and care after they have disrupted an entire classroom and seemed to relish in the act? How do you teach a child who comes to school just to get two meals a day, already has two children at the age of fifteen and has no hope? Painfully I realized that education had come to mean little more than following the state mandated curriculum and maintaining order. As Gloria Steinem suggests, "it had separated what we studied from how we lived." With teaching, I found little personal meaning in curriculum and I empathized with my students who questioned the purpose of education in a system that ignored all of us as participants.

Apart from teaching, I found myself coerced into coaching cheerleading and track while also sponsoring a girls' step team. The fact that I had never cheered before in my life seemed unimportant to my principal. When I found myself battling with administration for uniform money, I was told that the cheerleaders always raised their own money for uniforms. I realized that by giving the cheerleaders a coach with no experience and ignoring our request for uniforms (though they routinely purchased uniforms for the boys' teams), administration placed no value on girls' athletics. Infuriated, I posed this question to my principal. He responded by saying that as a non-revenue sport, we had no claim to school money to purchase uniforms. Refusing to retreat, I pressed the issue and finally elicited a promise that the cheerleaders would be placed on the regular three year rotation for the school purchase of uniforms. Somehow, I knew he had no intention of fulfilling this promise, but I had to move on and trust that he would. Curiously, I found myself becoming a champion of women's rights, not identifying with feminism, but definitely demanding equality.

By the end of my second year, I found myself disenchanted and exhausted. With no time for myself, I realized that I had never enjoyed going to work. Like my students who had lost hope, so I had lost my dream. This dream to educate my students with excitement and passion—to ultimately transform them from passivity to creativity disappeared in a mass of bureaucratic demands. Having faced failure before, I recognized this, not as failure, but as deliverance. No longer could I disregard my dream for the sake of a profession that, at best seemed confused. At the end of this first two years of teaching, I began to know and accept myself. With this knowledge came power—the power to remove myself from situations that devoured my personality and dreams. So rather than remain in teaching, ignore my identity and negatively impact my students, I decided to leave.

. . . Having received my master's degree from Wake Forest University, I found myself overjoyed, but jobless. Two years had given me time to reflect on my experiences as a teacher and realize that I actually missed the students. Nothing had given me more personal meaning and I had worked many jobs (Sears, Belk, American Express and the Offices of Multicultural Affairs). Still unwilling to face the facts, I reactivated my personnel files with the school system as a "back-up" plan and continued to search for another job. Less than a week after reactivating my file with the school system, I interviewed for a job at Parkland High School, home of the Mustangs. In the interview, my principal (a huge Wake fan) seemed more interested in my experiences at Wake than my ability to teach. He offered me the job, but I hesitated. I needed a sign from God. As I drove away from the school, I realized that I drove a candy apple red Mustang, interestingly enough, the school color and mascot. I took this as my sign.

With more confidence and a clearer sense of identity, I submerged myself within teaching. I lived and breathed Mustang Pride. Under pressure from the state to increase test scores, we pushed our students towards that nebulous realm some call excellence. We embarked on this exhausting journey to "leave no child behind" and maintain our exemplary status. Internally, I despised standardized tests, but externally I became their ardent champion. As the game show host on "Let's Make a Deal" I toyed with students' grades . . . if they scored higher on the test, I raised their semester grade. Once my seminar class reached one hundred percent proficiency, my principal celebrated and inaugurated me as the seminar teacher forever. In the eyes of administration and colleagues, I became an excellent teacher based only on the standardized test scores of my students. Once again, I found myself coaching, cheerleading (this time two squads) and trying to strike some sort of delicate balance between teaching and coaching. This time, though, I loved both. Through teaching, I learned *with* my students and together we struggled. By coaching, I learned *about* my students, their personal struggles and accomplishments. Because I had learned to respect myself, I earned the respect of others by appreciating them for just who they happened to be at the time.

During my third year at Parkland, I began to sense a vague sense of loss and, once again, I searched to redefine the dream that had somehow been deferred. Emotionally drained, I reexamined the success and trial of the past year. In this one year, the football team won the state championship, the boys' basketball team lost in the state championship game (to a team who looked collegiate), two wrestlers placed first and third in the state, the softball team placed second in the conference and the academic team placed third. Our students, traditionally disrespected by other schools, gained an amazing sense of pride that overflowed into the community. Suddenly, we seemed to have achieved our goal of becoming a "community of champions." I had cried and celebrated with them through each victory and loss discovering that teaching was something from which I could never escape. It represented all passion, love, joy and pain in my life. No matter where life took me, I would always *be* a teacher.

Subconsciously, I struggled to bridge the widening separation of my personal dreams from professional reality. Internally, I care more about the process of learning and self-inquiry, but externally, I seemed more concerned with the end product—test results. This clashing of inner and outer curriculum disrupted my sense of purpose. I questioned this purpose (teaching children to question versus teaching the test) and realized, in essence, I lived a lie. Refusing to remain untrue to self, I decided once again to leave teaching. This time, however, I left with a passion for education . . . a dream that learning should have personal meaning for each child.

Unlike my first escape from teaching, this leaving represented an escape from the impersonal and a return to the personal. So I redirected my dream by removing myself from the isolation of the classroom and envisioning the larger picture. For too long, I had floated as an island with no real connection to the world. The idea of leaving this island sparked terrifying thoughts of drowning in the multitude of educational reforms. I had to understand that education represented much more than simply teaching children, it represented an entire process of acculturation. If I remained a part of this system that continued to systematically pacify and desensitize our young people in the name of acculturation, there would soon be nothing left to save. I had to act, immediately. Once again I escaped, but this time I escaped schooling and embraced learning.

With each new class in this Ph.D. program, I piece together an educational puzzle. Through this program at the University of North Carolina at Greensboro, I am able to define the fundamental problems with education and now question the entire road by which I have traveled. While having both blindly accepted and actively rejected this educational system, I understand how we have reached this end, but do not understand how we will reach a new beginning. Thinking back on my educational experiences, I appreciate more each day my *blackness*. As an African American child, I always feared this difference. Beyond these feelings of alienation, I see that this difference has shaped my educational experiences by forcing me to reject much of what we now call schooling. Never had I envisioned learning as rote memorization and regurgitation. Rather, I understood education as a means to revolution, a type of liberation. Only through education had slaves learned to subvert the society of the oppressor. In my community, students before me had continued this struggle for liberation by leading the Civil Rights movement and teachers had given them the tools with which to lead. Thus, my understanding of education came with the belief in change as necessity and not convenience. Ultimately, I will do what my people have always done to effect change, I will teach my students to demand it. Only when students, as the oppressed, demand a fundamental change in the educational system will we see that change. And once we teach them how to demand, they will. By so doing, we shall create a more perfect union of society and education. Therein lies my goal and purpose in life.

Knowing Dr. Brubaker as I do and his conception of learning and its context, I understand why Ms. Roseboro felt safe with and trustful of his reactions to what she wrote, including some personal matters I did not excerpt even though they bear directly on why she became a teacher and reacted as she did to the culture of the school. The educational literature contains many such sagas. It also contains sagas, fewer in number, by teachers whose experience was the opposite of Ms. Roseboro's and illustrate what to me is an obvious but ignored point: Teachers cannot create and sustain contexts of productive learning for students if those conditions do not exist for the teachers. The litmus test for whether schooling has been productive is the degree to which its graduates *want* to and continue to learn more about the world, others, and themselves. Grades, test scores, and diplomas are blatantly incomplete as litmus tests of the overarching purpose of schooling. Is it not mammothly ironic that politicians (I do not use that word pejoratively) seek by surveys and focus groups what their constituents think and feel but educators do literally nothing to find out about how students feel about school learning and how teachers feel about their role of teaching? The methods and formats for obtaining such data (protective of confidentiality), and utilizing built-in measures to identify and control for the limitations of an individual's self-report, are well known and effective. There are no arcane mysteries here. Nor is it a mystery why school administrators, policy gurus, and legislators do not employ such procedures. They assume as if it were a fact that they know what is going on in schools, what students and teachers think and feel. More correctly, they hope they know because they have layers of administrators whose job it is to know what is going on.

Initially, at least, the issue is not an administrative one in the sense that the purposes and quality of administration require the setting of priorities; not all purposes are of equal importance. Would anyone argue that the quality and outcomes of classroom learning should be the top priority? I have yet to meet a school administrator who denied it. If you then ask them how they determined whether that priority is being accomplished, they will tell you about test scores. I have been in many suburban schools in affluent communities. In several of them I got up the courage to pose this question to them: "Your students do well on tests and parents move here because your schools are so highly regarded. But what about research studies and newspaper and other mass media accounts which indicate that middle and high schools in communities like yours contain many students who are bored and uninterested in what they are required to learn in classrooms? Are those accounts a cause for concern to you? How do you feel about those accounts?" I asked that of superintendents whom I had come to know on a superficial level but who had struck me as individuals who would not regard me as a carping academic from a university they knew regarded education and practicing educators with disfavor, to indulge understatement, and had eliminated a department of education from its midst.

Their answers went something like this: "We have the usual bell-shaped curve. Our top students stand out from the crowd; they are highly motivated, some are truly creative, but they all get top grades, they are overachievers. Then we have on the other extreme a larger group, depending on where your cut-off point is, who are underachievers who are content to just get by although most of them have higher than average IQs. Why that is so we don't really know; some are behavior problems but in the main they simply do not seem interested in extending themselves. The large middle of the distribution is not easy to characterize. Let's just say that they are undistinguished. They get passing grades, they present no problems but if again you go by IQ and the families they come from, most of them should be doing better; they are not lost in the crowd, they are the crowd and that bothers many parents who directly or indirectly take pot shots at teachers. It is easy to blame the school because students appear bored and unstimulated, but such blame is too easy and unjustified."

If the quality and outcomes of classroom learning are the top priority of a school's administrators, a question arises: How do administrators know what is going on in the classrooms? What data do they use to answer that question? The conventional answer is that each school has a principal and in middle and high schools they may have one or two assistant principals. (Middle schools are much larger than elementary schools and high schools are much larger than middle schools.) Principals have the most easy and direct access to the classroom and their judgments about quality and outcomes are passed on to higher levels of administration: supervisors of instruction, or curriculum, or pupil personnel, or special education, or staff development; they in turn report to the superintendent or her assistants, ultimately to the superintendent, who reports to the board of education. Why this chain of responsibility? One part of the answer, of course, is that the legendary one-room schoolhouse disappeared because of a steady and dramatic increase in population. The second part of the answer is that the increase brought with it recognition of and dissatisfaction with educational outcomes both from within and beyond the schools. Dissatisfaction was fueled, as it still is today, by different theories and philosophies concerning the nature of human development, the role of schooling in a democratic society, issues centering on social justice and equity, the subject matter of education, and the need for educational specialists whose job it would be to bring to the system the fruits of new ideas and research. What seemed to go unnoticed—it was never explicitly discussed—was that principals were no longer to be expected to possess all the knowledge and skills to ensure the quality and outcomes of classroom learning. He or she needed the guidance of others who possessed special knowledge and skills higher than that of principals. And "higher" was associated with level of authority and power. The principal became an educational leader led by other educational leaders.

What I have described raises an empirical question: How many times in the course of a school month or year should an administrator visit and observe a classroom to make a judgment as to how well a school policy is being appropriately reflected in a classroom? We have no data to answer the question; it literally has not been studied. I must rely on my personal experience, and what teachers and principals have, *without exception*, told me: Those who are above the level of principal visit from zero to one time. No teacher ever was visited by the superintendent. In fact, teachers guffawed when I would ask about the superintendent. Generally speaking, teachers view administrators as conveyors of policies and directives, the choice of curricula, criteria for grading and what is to be contained in report cards, the programs for staff development days, and legal knowledge about student absences, suspensions, and expulsions, etc. The administrators may arrange for workshops and meetings to which teachers come to hear an expert or consultant discuss a new approach for reading or math or social studies. Teachers tend to find these meetings as they do faculty meetings: boring or unstimulating, or at best a good deal less than helpful. In brief, whatever administrators above the level of principal know about quality of classroom teaching and learning is third- and fourth-hand verbal and written reports. They, of course, take notice when the test scores of a school are poor, they are published in the local newspapers, and known by the state department of education. Predictably, they take this up with, and only with, the principal who, it is implied, has been falling down on his or her obligation to monitor what is going on in the classroom; even though it is almost always the case that they had long known that the principal, however well-intentioned and liked, had been unable to improve the situation. They offer advice and increase pressure on the principal and if the crisis and publicity are such as to jeopardize the administrators' jobs and reputations, they may remove him or her. But as long as a school's test scores meet a minimal standard or better they have no cause for concern and action. Students are learning, aren't they? The principal and teachers are doing something right, aren't they? What more do you want? That is akin to going to a doctor who only takes your temperature and assures you that you are in good health. It is also like the stock market analyst who tells you that the Dow Jones average is rising, your investments are safe, you have no cause for worry, even if the chairman of the Federal Reserve Board has gone out of his way to inform the public that the stock market is suffering from "irrational exuberance." Test scores, like the Dow Jones, tell you all you need to know! And if you disagree, you are a complaining, carping critic who will be satisfied with nothing less than perfection.

Administrators above the level of principal have a ready answer to what I have said. The first, of course, is that compared to the number of classrooms their numbers are minuscule, and that is an understatement. Even if they were restricted to overseeing schools and not classrooms, in a moderately sized school system the number of schools is too large to permit spending much time in any of them. Besides, the public underestimates that each administrator's specialty involves the collection of data and report writing for the superintendent who has to deal with rules and regulations laid down by the board of education, the state department of education, and local, state, and federal agencies to whom yearly reports have to be submitted to demonstrate that the school system is following their guidelines for civil rights, the hiring of certified teachers, special education, and use of state and federal funds for targeted, special programs. Just preparing the budget takes a huge amount of time and planning and when they have to construct a new school they need to collect and organize data to get state funding; in addition they have to decide where a school is needed, work with the community, and decide how they will staff it consistent with its purposes. The amount of time spent in meetings, on planning, on proposed and necessary changes, writing reports, arranging meetings, dealing with collective bargaining issues—the amount of time these take is enormous. From an administrator's standpoint a school system and its tentacles to the outside world can devour you. At the end of the school day a teacher can be home by three in the afternoon. Administrators do not have that luxury. They depend on the school principal to oversee and advise teachers in the ways that will do justice to the abilities of students. That is their area of expertise and they are expected to know what is going on in the classrooms. Administrators sometimes make mistakes in selecting a principal. To a principal who is new to the game the first year or so can be rough as he or she comes to realize that having power and authority does not equate with being influential in getting teachers to go along with new ideas.

Administrators do not talk about learning and what they mean by it. More correctly, they regard scores on mandated achievement tests as the best indication of how much a child has learned. If, say, the test scores in a school are acceptable by standards set by the school system (or in the coming years the federal government), the school system has done a good job getting students to learn. School personnel are discernibly concerned, really anxious, as the day approaches when test scores are made public. They breathe a sigh of relief when the scores are "good"; they have done their job, this despite the fact that they disapprove of having to teach to the test and little else. They offer no alternative way for ascertaining what students have learned. When test scores reveal that a large number of students are far from meeting standards, they can ask, "What can we do now?" but they cannot provide an answer. That their thinking about learning may be part of the problem does not occur to them. With very rare exceptions there are well-documented accounts of failing students and schools who were

turned around by individuals who began with a conception of learning that led to contexts of productive learning in which students came
alive and flourished.

Let me turn now to the principal in regard to classroom learning.
The first thing that has to be recognized is that principals had been
teachers whose preparation for teaching did not include examination
of what was meant by learning. When they become teachers, it does
not take long before they can be categorized into several groups:
Those who are content to remain teachers because it is satisfying despite many criticisms they have about colleagues, the school, the
school system, criticisms of situations that are tolerable as long as the
teacher can continue to do what she considers to be good practice in
his or her classroom. They do not seek an administrative position. The
second group consists of those whose criticisms are festering sources of
discontent and they resign themselves to a career in which their
dreams of influencing positively the development of their students
lose motivating power. They stay on, it's a job, the future will be like
the present, there will be few kicks, you roll with the punch, nothing
will change. The third group is small and consists of those who because of personality makeup, background, and God knows what else
have and sustain the stance that you do not succumb to the organizational craziness and mediocrity surrounding you, that in your encapsulated room you do your best to bring out the best in your students,
that when you close the door to your classroom the rest of the school
world does not exist. Unlike the first group, those in this small third
group know they are regarded by others in officialdom as outstanding,
not ones who need advice and help. The fourth group are those teachers who early on decide that life as a teacher is a kind of dead end in
that the frustrations are many, teachers have no voice, they are pawns
in an educational chess game, it is administrators who have the power
to change things but too few of them have vision and courage, and, of
course, administrators are paid significantly more than teachers.
Teachers in this group seek to become principals.

No one who seeks to become a principal sees his or her responsibility to be to maintain the status quo. In small or large ways the principal wants his or her imprimatur to mark that school. In recent
decades new principals have been appointed with the most clear message that he or she should change an unacceptable state of affairs.
Change, let us not forget, is one of the most prevalent elements in the
educational air, and in administration offices it is as if it is the only element. Principals early on in their career learn several things. The first
is that teachers are resistant to change which explicitly or implicitly
implies that what they learned and do is misguided, wrong, and inimi-

cal to student learning. That, the principal finds, is especially true of teachers who have taught more than five years. Whether this resistance results in open warfare depends on the personal style and resolve of the principal. In the modal instance, it results in a silent civil war ended when the principal concludes that only a few of his teachers are rescuable by his lights. The second thing the principals learn is that they have limited means they can utilize for change. If in the yearly written evaluation of each teacher they would say what they truly think, they will increase the strength of negative feelings teachers have about them, the teacher may ask the union to file a grievance, their superiors will remind them how long and hard it is to prove incompetence or an inability to adapt to school policies for change, and there is always the possibility that their superiors may begin to question their leadership qualities. *The irony in all this is that principals know most of what I have described from their experience as teachers.* Now, however, their relationship to teachers requires them to carry out mandates for change in which teachers had no voice and which require that teachers have to change, not the administrators of the school system. As a teacher the principal knew that his colleagues preferred that their principal visit and observe their classrooms very infrequently, that teachers do not see their principal as an educational leader, let alone a gung-ho one, but rather as a manager who gets for them the resources they need, supports them in disciplinary action of unruly students, and who supports them in dealing with this or that parental complaint, makes sure the buses are on time, there is law and order in the cafeteria, and that when needed gets for students the services of the school psychologist, social workers, speech therapist, etc.[1]

If you, as I have, asked teachers why they appear not to regard the principal as an educational leader, you get an initial reaction in the form of a facial expression of indecision or puzzlement, as if they do not know whether to agree or disagree with what I asserted in the question. The reaction is the following paraphrase: "How can he be an educational leader when he comes to my classroom no more than twice a year specifically to observe my classroom, and then never for more than a half hour. I talk with him for longer periods many more times. Most of us are experienced teachers, we know what we are doing and why. It may be different with a new teacher who really needs

---

1. The teacher-principal relationship is both complex and fascinating as it usually is between people of unequal power and authority. It has hardly been described and discussed in detail and with the necessary candor which would require not only candor about what is personal but also how its sources are systemic in that it has to be seen as embedded in the school system and preparatory programs. What I have said here about that relationship does not do justice to that relationship.

help and asks for it or the principal correctly believes he should know what is going on in her classroom. I am not saying that I know it all, that there is no more I can learn, but I want it to come from somebody who has been at least a couple of hours in the classroom and whose suggestions or criticisms are not trivial or too general or simply unhelpful. Maybe it's as simple as the fact that most of our students are doing okay, so why waste time coming to the classroom?"

Why is it a waste of time? And again the answer is, look at the test scores and if they are okay, there is no problem. That's like saying that it is gratifying and an accomplishment that students graduating from high school have met requirements for reading many books of literature, history, social studies, and science but have little or no interest in reading a newspaper, going to a library to get books that interest them, watching TV programs about history, or learning about social-political issues, and go on to college more because their parents expect or demand it and less because they eagerly look forward to intellectual stimulation and learning, and do not think to register to vote. (Let us not gloss over the fact the national average for dropouts from college is well above 30 percent.)

It would be egregiously oversimple and obfuscating to blame students, or their parents, or social change, or schools as if any or all of them willed this state of affairs, a state which has existed from the time when schooling became compulsory. In the modern era that state of affairs was mightily exacerbated by the societal consequences of World War II, most clearly evident in the decades between 1950 and 1970 (Sarason 1996a). In those two decades every major societal institution was under attack and pressured to change. And change was reflected in a cascade of legislation about the status and rights of women; race and ethnic discrimination; discrimination because of age and physical or mental handicap; Medicare and Medicaid entitlements; environmental protection legislation. If the different legislative actions have not achieved all that one had hoped, it cannot be denied that they achieved a discernible degree of intended change and in some instances a dramatic change.

But what about schools, which were also under attack from all sides, especially after the 1954 desegregation decision? Expenditures for schools steadily increased. From federal, state, and local governments, and from foundations, the total amount of money for schools, score upon score of billions of dollars, poured into schools in the effort to improve educational outcomes. There were more new initiatives and programs than you can list or shake a stick at. And that is true today, especially in regard to urban schools. Test scores drifted downhill and then flattened and there is no good evidence they are on the way up.

School violence has increased, teachers are retiring or leaving the field in large numbers, for the first time schools have difficulty filling openings for principals, superintendents leave their positions or are pushed out within five years, controversy continues to rage about who or what is to blame. One thing is for sure: the goal of improving test scores is as elusive as eliminating wars. Another thing that is for sure is that money has not provided us answers and will not.

What does this have to do with administration and classroom learning? My answer is in several parts. First, school administrators have little or no direct knowledge of what goes on in classrooms. They formulate policies, they exhort (sometimes they threaten) teachers to implement those policies but they have no basis for explaining why test scores have not improved. They are like absentee landlords who tell the occupants of their buildings what the rent is or will be and do not want to hear "excuses" for being unable to comply. They can get rid of occupants (= teachers) but the occupants cannot get rid of the landlord (= administrators). That they do not like each other, to put it mildly, requires no further explanation. The third part of my answer is the most crucial one: There is an appalling lack of anything resembling serious discussion of what is meant by learning, the meanings that word or concept has for them. More correctly, what is there to discuss when no one denies that test scores tell us what students have or have not learned? So let me quote some excerpts from Brody (*New York Times*, November 12, 2002). The italics are mine.

No Proof of Value

I will start with the bottom line, neatly summarized by Dr. Mary Hufty, who leads a committee on prevention guidelines for the Palo Alto Medical Foundation: "A negative total body C.T. scan does not provide reason to feel reassured, and a positive C.T. scan does not provide information that has been shown to improve life expectancy or quality of life."

. . . What if the findings of a body scan are negative? Doesn't this mean a clean bill of health? Not necessarily, say many experts. "Many things can be amiss that are not shown on a C.T. scan, such as infectious, hematological, metabolic or endocrine abnormalities," Dr. Hufty said.

Test scores are not X-rays which give at best a picture of your body. Test scores are numbers the significance of which may or may not be positive or negative regardless of whether it is a high, average, or low score. Individuality is a fact and respect for it carries with it the obligation, the moral and professional obligation, to know and understand a student in a way that allows you to determine how and why a test score takes on meanings when related to the features

present in the learning process. Administrators are literally not interested in individuality, they are interested in the average scores of
classrooms and schools. Teachers do recognize the fact of individuality, just as parents recognize it. But neither by their preparatory program or by the educational "leaders" are they helped to grasp what
that means in practice. They are alone in the classroom in an educational community for which the label "learning community" is, unfortunately, laughably inappropriate.

Schools and school systems are anti–contexts of productive learning, certainly not by conscious design. The most extreme instance is
New York City, where the chancellor of the school system is responsible for 1,100 schools and over one million students. How knowledgeable or wise a sage do you have to be to predict that the
chancellor and his many scores of administrators will have no direct
knowledge of what is happening in classrooms until, of course, they
read the test scores of their schools, are galvanized to take actions they
pray will have at least a smidgeon of positive effect at the same time
they know they are dealing with the latest manifestation of an impossible situation? Who has time to think? Who has the time to think
about kooky ideas of alternative conceptions of learning and its contexts, which may work in heaven but not on earth? The administrators know the game and the score. The game is putting out fires. The
score is the latest test scores. Understandably—and I mean that sincerely—administrators will not give public voice to these feelings if
only because they do not know what else might be done, an admission of which would not sit well with the community which pays
them much more than a living wage. They are locked in the system in
which the more things change the more they remain the same.

In the next chapter I describe a less depressing feature of the
New York City school system. From the standpoint of contexts of
learning I have discussed in these pages, it is an inspiring one. That
the New York City school administration does not capitalize on this
feature does not rob these instances of their importance; it is par for
the course in other urban school systems far smaller than New York.

Chapter Ten

What Do Administrators Know About Contexts of Learning?

I have known several schools in New York, each in one or another of the city's stereotypical poor "ghettos," where a new principal started and accomplished a transformation that was surprising and gratifying. Test scores had always been on the poor side but not scandalously so. They had not been what is called "troubled" schools, they were undistinguished, unimaginative, uninteresting, boring enclaves. Because their test scores were not blatantly poor, the administrative powers that be were grateful and in their view could leave well enough alone. When a new principal was appointed, I have no reason to believe they expected him or her to shake things up, to depart from custom. These new principals were ambitious people. Now, ambition is inherently neither a virtue nor a vice. If you are ambitious to obtain and wield power, to enjoy, it can be very problematic in its consequences. These new principal's ambitions were powered by assumptions or beliefs. The first was that the students were capable of more than they were demonstrating. The second assumption was that teachers, parents, and students had to know each other, and work with each other, and that included learning how to get resources from outside the school (for example, musicians, actors, writers) to have a stake and interest in expanding the horizons of students.

My use of the word *assumption* may be misleading because it suggests that these individuals had a formulated theory or conceptualization of why and how you proceed. There may have been some of that but what most impressed me on the basis of talking with them, observing in classrooms, and talking with parents, the starting point of these principals was what students thought and felt about what they were learning, what interested them, what they were curious about. They never talked about the curriculum or the lack of resources, or the problems these students may be experiencing at home or in their neighborhoods. When I asked one parent how she felt about the school, she laughed and said, "My two older kids went to this school and I never expected that a child of mine would get up on a Saturday and say he is sorry there is no school on Saturdays." In the classroom students were relaxed, worked diligently on their assignments, would occasionally and spontaneously "visit" with another student or group or to talk with the teacher for varying lengths of time (but I could not tell about what they were talking).

I never inquired about test scores. I did not want to give the impression that my judgment of the school would be largely determined by the academic Dow Jones.[1] That does not mean it is without value, it means you have to know more than is given by a score, especially if you are going to take action which will affect a student or students. The principals at some point volunteered the information. Each in her or his way said, "They are doing better on the tests but there is so much they have learned that the tests don't reflect. They are a live bunch of kids who are going to make it."

I assumed that each of these principals did not have an easy time creating the kind of classroom and school atmosphere they did. Early on in my involvement in educational reform I learned to get at it (at least try to) indirectly by casually asking what teacher turnover had been after taking over. The number was startlingly low and my face must have registered it. Each principal explained the low turnover in different ways and styles. What they said became clearer to me after I met alone with the teachers: the principal was no bull in a china shop, no pressurer, and from day one had made it clear that the school had to be an interesting place for students and teachers and together the principal and teachers would meet and plan. There would be no unilateral

---

1. At least with the Dow Jones we know the companies that comprise it, their histories, why and when they were included, and we can determine what risks we may be taking if we use it for this or that action we are contemplating. Attributing meaning to the Dow Jones number and ignoring a host of other indicators which very much are related to and affect the Dow Jones is foolhardy. Like test scores the Dow Jones is a very narrow measure of many other economic indicators which it does not take into account. Similarly, test scores tell us nothing about factors very much a part of the learning process.

decisions, and they would not judge themselves only by test scores but by "the changes we see in our students that tell us they like learning."

A question: Would you not hope and expect that someone somewhere in the administration would have made public, in speech or in writing, their appreciation of the efforts and accomplishments of the principal, teachers, and *parents*? It is very likely that the administrator to whom the principal was directly responsible had said something positive in the infrequent meetings (not one-on-one meetings) they attended. It would not surprise me if that administrator spent any length of time there on more than one occasion. Is it outlandishly unreasonable to say that the administrator should have requested a meeting when he or she could express that appreciation personally? Has the idea of reinforcement of a job well done been disproved? Is it only a good idea when teachers employ it with students, but is it not as important for administrators in relation to the principal, teachers, and parents? Are the rules of the spirit of the obligation of courtesy off limits? The sad diagnostic fact is that teachers and parents do not expect such personal reinforcement for the same reason they do not believe in miracles. And what I am saying here is not peculiar to the New York school system, which is an extreme instance of what is also a feature of smaller systems.

There are more troubling aspects to the situation. Engineers, especially in manufacturing companies, employ a process called reverse engineering: When a product is not performing as expected, customers complain, sales decline, competitors gain more market share, so you go back step by step in its manufacture and try to determine where the problem or problems may be. They knew the product should have performed well, but it has not and they had better find out why and make appropriate changes. Not cosmetic changes but real ones that will last and allow the company to be competitive. It was, I think, Samuel Johnson who said that nothing focuses the mind more than the knowledge that you will be hanged tomorrow. Well, nothing sharpens the mind of company administrators more than the knowledge that their product has serious deficits which if not corrected as promptly as possible could cause the demise or sale of the company, or cause it to go bankrupt. They ask and study specific questions. Are some of the materials faulty? The design? Since many products are made or finished in different departments, is the failure a result of lower quality control among one or more of the departments? Do we have any data that suggests that this or that manager is not as careful in checking the product or supervising his workers? We should talk to workers to find out what they think may be the problem and what might be done to correct it. Responsibility for getting answers is that of those who have the most direct knowledge of the steps of the manufacturing process.

The spirit and letter of the reverse engineering process are absent in school systems. Reverse engineering is an alien concept. A problem is not identified—at least recognized—until, so to speak, it explodes, even though when it does explode there is a principal or some teachers who are not surprised. Administrators are surprised, and they are pressured to correct the situation by higher powers who have very little direct knowledge of the school. The administrator feels compelled to act and that almost always results in one or even all of several things: changing principals, seeking to remove inadequate teachers, providing new services by experts from within or outside the system to the school's principal and teachers. (In the case of the killings at Columbine High School in Colorado by two psychologically disturbed boys, there were students who knew the two boys were strange but no teacher or administrator had such knowledge either directly or indirectly.) When a state board of education provides a city with a list of its failing schools and threatens to close them if the situation does not improve, the administration of the system is galvanized into action even though it long knew the schools were educationally inadequate. What they long knew was that the test scores of these schools were scandalously low and little more.

What I have described is the polar opposite of the spirit, letter, and seriousness of the process of reverse engineering. Some readers may have difficulty believing me to be sincere when I say that administrators are intellectually bright and truly desire to provide students a quality education. All that I have said is descriptive and illustrative of several points. First, whatever the reasons, the higher up in the administrative hierarchy you go, the less the administrators have direct knowledge of classrooms and schools, so that the superintendent's direct knowledge of classrooms and schools is a teeny bit above zero. For the board of education it is zero. Second, schools do have a "product" in which their "customers" are more than interested: test scores. When that product is at or above an arbitrary standard, they are gratified, satisfied, and buy the product. They do not shop elsewhere for a better product. It is different, of course, in the case of poor or failing schools.

Why do I make so much fuss about direct knowledge? *Because the more direct knowledge you have of classrooms the better able you are to answer what I consider to be the most important question that should determine the actions (if any) you should take: Am I observing a context of productive or unproductive learning regardless of the test scores of students?* But that question assumes that you have criteria for distinguishing between the two contexts, that at the least you know that test scores are not the be-all-and-end-all of the learning process and context. In fact, and generally speaking, administrators can tell you that there are schools in the same geographic area with similar students who are as different from each other as day is from night but school X is a delight to be in and school Y is a sealed-over mess or simply a dull, boring, quiet place. That is why I discussed at the beginning of this chapter several inner-city schools that impressed me as reflecting some of the features of a context of productive learning; they were so different from inner-city schools I had known.[2] Let me turn to another reason these and other schools I will discuss are important in regard to administrators and innovations.

Put most briefly: Innovations do not spread, they are and remain encapsulated exceptions. The administration has no means whereby the possibility of spreading the innovation is taken seriously. That assumes, of course, that the leadership knows about these exceptions, which is frequently not the case. But even where it is the case no spread takes place. Why? One reason, which the reader may find surprising, is that despite the satisfaction and even pride they may have about these exceptions, it does not occur to them to consider ways by which they can have impact on other schools. If your days are spent putting out fires, spreading credible and important instances illustrative of productive learning is not a welcome obligation. Spread is not a matter of saying "come see what they do" or "you may find what they do interesting and helpful," as if watching actions does not require grasping the rationale for learning, which preceded and undergirds what you see. For example, when a preparatory program places a student for the purpose of practice teaching in the classroom of a highly regarded teacher, is it primarily for the purpose to learn to do what that teacher does and only secondarily to learn how and why that teacher thinks about children who learn or do not learn, what constitutes a context of productive or unproductive learning, that imitation may be the highest form of flattery but it can also be a mindless one, that teaching is not about filling

---

2. My visits to each of these schools were for a day and I cannot say that if I had spent more time in them my favorable, global impression would have been sustained or not. These visits were at a time in my career when the difference between the two learning contexts was beginning to take shape in my mind. However, in light of what I shall soon present in this chapter I felt justified in using those schools for introductory purposes.

empty vessels but lighting fires, that it takes time, persistence, courage, and failures or mistakes to feel secure that you forged a satisfactory marriage between your conception of learning and actions by which that conception is overtly manifested. *Please note that the relation between the student and experienced teacher raises all of the questions about how one distinguishes between contexts of productive and unproductive learning.* I must add that in that relationship the burden is on the teacher never to gloss over the tendency *that in a relationship of unequal power and status "doing" too easily trumps thinking.* In the case of the process of spread, I have yet to meet an administrator who started the process by confronting this question: "Because what I want to see spread to certain other schools will be interpreted by them as implying that they have something to unlearn and learn, something that has been accomplished elsewhere, how should I think about how to make it less likely that their anger will result in nothing other than taking actions they think will satisfy or pacify me?" I am sure there are administrators who have more than a superficial conception of the features of *classroom* contexts of productive learning. Nevertheless, in my experience I have not known an administrator who took that conception seriously in regard to his or her efforts to encourage and support certain schools to unlearn and learn from a particular school. You can say that I am using too many words to say that the administrator has to be better skilled in the arts of diplomacy. I would not object as long as I knew that you knew that a bedrock obligation of a diplomat is to acquire and appropriately utilize as much knowledge and understanding as possible of the diplomats and the country with which he or she is dealing. Skill is the happy marriage between knowledge and understanding, on the one hand, and action, on the other hand. When Chamberlain left his meeting in Munich with Hitler in 1939 waving a sheet of paper and smilingly proclaimed that "there will be peace in our time," and shortly after that Hitler took military actions that compelled England to declare war, Chamberlain was exposed as an egregiously sad example of a poor diplomat.

Let me turn to a new middle school in New York with which I was intimately associated for several years beginning with its opening. It is the Louis Armstrong, I.S. 227 in Queens, where Louis had long been a resident. (If memory serves me correctly, his trumpet was hanging on one of the walls.) The school was ready to open two years before it did open. That was because some community groups had obtained a court order that the school would not open until a plan was approved ensuring that at least half of the students were minority students who could apply from wherever they lived in the city. Shortly before the school opened, Dr. Saul Cohen, who had been at Clark University, was appointed president of Queens College. Besides being director of Clark's prestigious school of geography—his special field of interest was geopolitics and his writings internationally respected—Dr. Cohen had played an influential role during the turbulent 1960s in the development of several major educational reform efforts. His appointment as president of Queens College coincided with New York City's struggle to avoid bankruptcy and the city colleges' severe budget cuts. As one might have predicted, schools of education had the largest cuts and the faculty was thoroughly demoralized. At the top of Dr. Cohen's priorities was the reinvigoration of the school of education. Basically his plan was to give faculty opportunity to become active in I.S. 227 through the provision of services to school personnel or conducting research directly relevant to the school, or by providing students in education with responsibilities that would be seen as helpful in the daily activities of teachers and their students. The Queens personnel would have no formal authority or power. Whatever they would accomplish would only be achieved with the permission and cooperation of the school's personnel. Dr. Cohen asked Professor Sidney Trubowitz, who had been a classroom teacher and principal, to take the leadership role. For the first three years of the school I spent a minimum of at least one day a week, sometimes including an evening, at I.S. 227 in a variety of meetings and activities, including classroom observations. They were inspiring, exciting, instructive years. It is not my purpose here to describe what went on and why at I.S. 227. The interested reader should read the book of the first seven years by Trubowitz, et al., in 1984, and a second book by Trubowitz and Longo in 1997, years after the school opened. Let me just say that if you read the two books you understand why as time went on the spirit and accomplishments of the school–Queens collaborative were steadily diluted, although by conventional standards it is considered a "good" school which cannot accommodate the many students whose parents want them to go there. Indeed, it was in a way a victim of its success because of administrative pressure (fiat, really) from "downtown" to take in more students in numbers beyond what had been a strict upper limit, a pressure the school was powerless to withstand. That is by no means unique to New York City, whose teaching personnel view administrators as people who spend their days making decisions which affect teachers, classrooms, and schools, decisions in which teaching personnel had absolutely no voice. It is no different in Chicago, Philadelphia, Los Angeles, and other cities, as well as in smaller systems. How can groups understand each other if they do not know each other? Here are the points I wish to make.

1. In the early years there were, predictably, issues and problems in the collaboration. After all, the two groups of collaborators were each embedded in institutions with different histories, traditions, values, working life-styles, allegiances, and criteria for membership. In the abstract, school personnel have respect for the university but in the case of a school education in the concrete, many regard their faculty either as out of touch with the realities and problems of "real" schools or as those who use schools for research that furthers their careers and from which schools derive at best little and at worst no benefit. It is not infrequently the case that school personnel resent college faculty who wittingly or unwittingly, directly or indirectly, convey the message "we are the experts bringing culture and understanding to the deserving poor." It took at least a year for the Queens faculty to demonstrate by word and action that they were there to be helpful as the principal and the teachers defined helpful. The Queens faculty might have ideas and suggestions that school personnel might not have thought of and, if so, they might give voice to them for discussion. Decisions were the province of school personnel. Dr. Trubowitz chose colleagues who respected the spirit and letter of the arrangement; on the surface they varied in many ways but there was (to me at least) one thing about which they were in total agreement: whatever they had to contribute or do had to make for stimulating contexts of classroom learning. Keep in mind that the Queens faculty, numbering around seven, were not occasional visitors; they spent upwards of five days a week in the school (as Dr. Trubowitz did) but no fewer than two. That does not include Queens students who also engaged in some helping capacity.

If you spent a day in the school but knew nothing about the collaboration, you would be hard put to distinguish between school and Queens personnel. What initially seemed like it might be a problem was the principal, who was a veteran of the school system, had held a higher administrative post, was bright, articulate, and a friendly person who left no one in doubt about who made final decisions. He liked to argue about ideas with the Queens people, individually and in a group, but it was our conclusion that although he wanted us in his school there would be definite boundaries we would do well to respect. We were wrong in our conclusion in that over a period of a few months he came to truly like us as people, as we did him, and, so to speak, talking about ideas was seamlessly replaced with planning actions, services, and programs. We had had a foot in the door and now the door opened wide. I mention this because by the end of the year the Queens group would occasionally discuss two questions. Did this unusual person who did not lack ambition have his sights set on a coveted higher post in the next two or three years? If so, would we be asked to be part of the selection process? According to our knowledge of how the system works, especially Drs. Trubowitz and Longo who had been in the system, selecting a principal was an internal affair in which internal politics played a significant role, and consideration of outsiders with vested interests in an appointment was either unwise or potentially dangerous or internally divisive. I take this up in point 3 below. Chronologically, a variant of this feature became apparent in the first year, hence point 2 first.

2. Toward the end of the first year it became apparent that the upper limit of the student population would be reached much sooner than expected, largely because of glowing word-of-mouth parental reports. New teachers would have to come on board. Also, more than a few teachers from other schools put in for transfer to I.S. 227. Who would select new teachers for a school which already had become distinctive in numerous ways and in which everyone new in it (including the Queens contingent) enjoyed a truly surprising degree of intellectual collegiality, openness to new ideas, and a sense of parity with and respect for the Queens people, who were demonstrably and strangely willing to be helpful as defined by school personnel? The principal was the only person in the school who had a formal connection to teacher selection but it was by no means a decisive one; the final decision was made at higher levels by criteria which for all practical purposes were top secret, assuming of course they had clear criteria, which is quite an assumption. The one fact that was valid was that those who would make the final decision did not know I.S. 227 except to know that teaching there was regarded as a plum. Now, there were teachers who wanted to transfer to I.S. 227 and applied to transfer but did not simply apply and pray; they used whatever connections they had in the system to seek support, which meant "How do I get someone in the administration to make sure that my application does not get lost in the shuffle?" That is an understandable thing to do and I am not critical of those who use their personal networks. The fact is that every administrator in the course of a year gets many such requests which he is unable to satisfy even though he or she would like to, because the number of openings is far less than the number of applicants, or one transfer sets in motion a series of transfers, or he seeks to satisfy an administrative colleague on a quid pro quo basis. What we call politics is predictably endemic in all human institutions, and the larger they are the more the political dynamics come into play, dynamics not even hinted at in organizational charts

and administrative reports. Administrators know this, teachers intuit it. Finally, there is the union-school contract and its spelled-out provisions about how and to what extent seniority must play a role in a matter of teacher selection for job openings. Union-school contracts are often interpreted differently by each side.

Now, what does all this have to do with learning? The answer, of course, is precious little, really zero. It never gets discussed. It is as if the unverbalized assumption is "Of course we know who a good teacher is even if we have never met these good teachers. If their students get acceptable scores on the tests, we regard such teachers as good.[3] What more do you need to know?" There was a time when I would reply, "There is another way of thinking about learning that demonstrates, and I mean demonstrates in actions in the classroom, that you need to know more than what a test score can give you, and if you take that seriously, it opens up new vistas about the process we call learning and what we mean by a good teacher." When I would expand on my reply, they would not disagree with my conception of learning. They would say I was impractical, implying that academic me was not well acquainted with the real world. In any event, of the new teachers who were transferred, two of the five were mismatched for I.S. 227. Two mismatches would not jeopardize what was being developed at the school. But if the principal left and the replacement was a mismatch, that would be a cup of bitter tea.

3. The principal did leave three years later for a higher administrative post. Who the new principal was and why she was chosen is a mystery to everyone in the school. That did not surprise the teachers because their stance was: "Since when do administrators talk to and seek the opinions of teachers? That will be the day!" From day one the new principal in subtle ways, and later in not so subtle ways, made it clear that it was *her* school and she had the definite intention

---

3. I write these words at a time when the mass media are telling the public that hormone replacement medication for reducing or eliminating the hot flashes and pains many women experience during menopause had very serious negative consequences. It "worked" in the sense that it mightily reduced menopausal pains and stress. But the claim that the therapy would reduce heart attacks and cancers was not substantiated, but rather the later incidence of those diseases increased. Test scores "work" in the sense that they tell you what you think it is important to know about level of student learning. Actions are taken to raise those levels and over a period of decades those actions are fruitless, as will be President George W. Bush's policies about standards, accountability, frequent testing, and threats to close failing schools, all of this despite the evidence that beginning in elementary school students catch the virus of disinterest in school learning, a virus which middle and high school teachers know well. Schooling has not prevented the metaphorical equivalent of cancer and heart disease.

to put *her* stamp on the school. Up until her arrival the we-they dichotomy hardly existed, but now it was clear that the dichotomy was and would be ever present. There were no open confrontations. Dr. Trubowitz is as sweet, decent, bright, and interpersonally sensitive a person and educator as I have ever met, for which I thank God for big favors. He would meet with her to get a sense of her future perspective for the school, to tell her about the ideas he and his colleagues were thinking about, and to find a basis for establishing a relationship of mutual trust. He came away from every meeting with her puzzled and frustrated, finding her an enigma, someone who played her cards very close to her chest. She never expressed appreciation for what the school had become, which I regard as quite a feat of nonverbal communication. In my opinion—and this is an interpretation—she perceived the Queens people as a power block between her and teachers, thus diverting attention from her. She did not make dramatic changes but numerous cosmetic ones. What she did do was to create barriers to ideas and new programs and activities the Queens group had discussed in meetings with teachers. She never asked for the advice or opinions of the Queens people about anything. And in the many scores of meetings which I attended, and in terms of composition of the attendees they were very heterogeneous, I never saw or met anyone from the administrative hierarchy. I.S. 227 was slowly losing innovative steam. It still was an interesting place, but not the exciting one it had been. But other principals followed her and it was a case of adding insult to injury or, better yet, if you can't get your way, make sure no one else can get their way. I urge the reader to read the two books about I.S. 227 if they want to get a sense of context for what I have said. The imprint on I.S. 227 of the initial years can still be discerned today but the winds of what I call organizational craziness have eroded much of that imprint.

Now for an addendum to the story. Several years after I.S. 227 opened, Drs. Trubowitz and Longo received a call from a high-level administrator who basically said that he had heard about what had been accomplished at I.S. 227. Would they be interested in helping turn around two of the most troubled and failing high schools? He had never set foot in 227, he had not the faintest notion why I.S. 227 had become the school it was. Initially Trubowitz and Longo were intrigued and puzzled by the telephone call. Were they being asked to say goodbye to I.S. 227 because it was in good shape and there were schools that needed them far more? That made no moral, conceptual, or practical sense. They were intrigued because there was a challenging question: How could you use I.S. 227—its

rationale, its personnel, parents, community agencies supportive of
I.S. 227, and other resources—to play a role that stood a chance to
have an impact on at least one of the very troubled high schools?
They came up with the outlines of several possibilities and plans.
Each possibility took for granted that it would take several years before a recognizable degree of intended impact would or could occur,
assuming that God was on their side and organizational craziness
would not escalate. Two very optimistic conclusions, as they well
knew. But meeting challenges is a way of life for these two, the
times they learn the most. So they had a meeting with the administrator, in his office. The long and short of it is that the administrator
was not interested—could not afford to be interested—in what the
school could be in five years, he was sitting on a smoldering volcano
that was likely to erupt soon. The administrator was right in the
sense that he was on a hot seat and he had to act. I sympathize with
his plight: no one lives a life without experiencing a situation where
you had to act, you did not know what to do, and you grasped at
straws. But to understand all does not mean you forgive all. He did
not know—at least he did not act as if he knew—that the Queens
people did not have a silver bullet that would change a very troubled
school quickly. He did not know that creating and sustaining a new
school was a different cup of tea than changing a large troubled one;
you do not associate the former with the imagery of a bed of roses
but you associate the other with prolonged civil strife. The administrator had no conception of learning and its contexts, by which I
mean several things. *Learning always involves unlearning and learning.*
The road of learning has its ups and downs and their major source is a way
of thinking and acting that in some way prevents you from a different way
that you (or someone else) want or need to acquire. The source may be
personal, cognitive, emotional, motivational, or all of these, and if
that source is not identified, the individual has a hard time of it and
his or her lack of progress causes him or others to come to faulty
conclusions. The person can say, "I am dumb" and others may say he
is rigid, resistant, or stupid. That is why in what I have described as a
context of productive learning it is the obligation of the teacher to
create a context of mutual trust and safety that increases the possibility (there are no guarantees) that one can identify and deal with
what the student is having difficulty unlearning. The administrator,
who was once a teacher, never thought of learning in this way or
was helped to grasp and act accordingly. His conception of learning
was narrow and self-defeating and he probably concluded that the
problem and the solution were *in the student,* the teacher blameless.

It is, therefore, not surprising that when he was confronted with two semiexplosive schools where numerous past change efforts had had no effect and about which he had little direct knowledge, he was for a quick-fix approach which he had thought Drs. Trubowitz and Longo represented. In so doing he exposed his own failure to unlearn and learn. To have as your goal to noncosmetically change a large, troubled school heretofore intractable to change requires you to confront the inevitable tensions between learning and unlearning. When you are clear about the features of contexts of productive and unproductive learning, they are as applicable to how you think and act to efforts to change an entire school as they are to a single classroom. The failure to grasp this conception of learning goes a long way to explaining why the educational reforms of the past half-century have, generally speaking, to be judged as a failure.

4. The final example was a school change project in Tucson. The schools were in the poorest Latino neighborhood. It was spearheaded by Dr. Paul Heckman. The first book about the project was published in 1995 with the title *The Courage to Change*. The final assessment will be in a second book that should be published in the next year or so. I shall not even try to summarize the project because I would be repeating everything I have said about I.S. 227 in point 3. But I shall note one feature of the Tucson project missing in 227. I should tell the reader that over a period of six years I visited the Tucson schools at least twice a year, each visit of no fewer than three days. The missing feature was in the person of Elaine Rice, who was the administrator of the large school district in which the project was carried out. She made it her business not only to know about the schools but also to spend time in them. Like Dr. Heckman, she considered the ultimate test of a school change effort to be the degree to which the contexts of classroom learning were stimulating, aroused interest, and were productive of personal and intellectual growth. It did not take long after the project started for the highest-level administrators to express concerns of one kind or another of the value of the project. Those expressions of concern were made to Dr. Rice, never directly to Dr. Heckman. Matters got worse as time went on because one of the projects was to encourage parents— some of whom spoke little or no English—to exert pressure to get the school system and/or the city officials to expend as much money on these barrio schools as they did on other nonminority schools. There were many small and large issues about which these immigrant parents could never imagine they might have influence. School administrators and teachers much prefer docile, passive

parents to complaining ones. Elaine Rice, who is black, totally agreed with Dr. Heckman's position on parental involvement. She is a street-smart diplomat with guts, highly respected and liked by everyone above or below her in status or power. She knew that there were influential people in the system who would not have been saddened if the project disappeared. The point here is that the real and even dramatic changes that occurred in the first four years might well have been less if Dr. Rice had not been an articulate defender of the project and given line, chapters, and verse to justify her defense. In my experience at least, the Tucson project is the only one among the many I came to know where there was someone in the upper reaches of the administrative hierarchy who truly knew the rationale and activities of a change effort in their jurisdiction. Dr. Rice and Dr. Heckman did not have to be told what features distinguished between contexts of productive and unproductive learning.

Up until fifteen years ago you would be hard put to find a school of education which had a *special* program in educational leadership. Today it is unusual for a school of education that prepares school administrators not to have a leadership program. Perhaps the major reason for the change in title was (a) increasing dissatisfaction by the public and political officialdom that American schools had not improved educational outcomes despite increased expenditures, (b) that what passed for leadership was in reality a collection of bureaucrats who were essentially uncreative managers, not leaders for change, and (c) one reason for this state of affairs was that preparatory programs for school administrators were not doing a good job in selecting and training administrators who were leaders. If you examine the description or syllabi for these newly titled programs, you may be struck, as I have been, by the obvious influence of theories, research, and lauded practices to which students in schools of business are exposed. And if anything characterizes what the private sector says it is all about, it is creative leadership. And if they say that, they can point to a long list of private-sector CEOs who wrote books about how they transformed their companies to become significantly more efficient, creative, and profitable. If educational leadership programs reflect a private-sector influence, it would not be the first time in the history of American education where that influence was plain to see, and frequently acknowledged. I see nothing inherently wrong in this new influence. Having been a member of a faculty group asked to design and justify a graduate training program in the private sector, I was impressed with several of the features of the leadership program which were considered essential.

But there are two major features of private-sector companies that education cannot gloss over. The first is that no one is in doubt that they have a nonhuman product; to make that product requires people for its manufacture and sale but in a competitive market the product and its quality are bedrock facts of life. The second is that the bottom line for judging success or failure is no less clear: whether that bottom line is written in black or red ink. In the case of schooling there is not and has not been consensus about what the product is or should be. Of course the product is human but what are its defining features obligating you to assess degrees of success or failures, to use red or black ink? For example, let us imagine a school system where its administration has been commendably clear about the defining features of its human products. Whether you agree or disagree with those defining features is irrelevant here. What is relevant is the degree to which the goals of those defining features have been reached or not. Let us take the case where the evaluation of those features indicates that they are discouragingly short of expectations. How can the administrators explain, as they must, such dispiriting outcomes? Clearly, the explanation will not be a simple one—at least one hopes that the school administrators knew and know there are no simple explanations. However, there is one assumption school administrators make when they state a policy, especially if it is one to improve outcomes, and that is that the policy will be carried out in classrooms in ways reflective of the letter and spirit of the policy. The fact is that school administrators do not have that degree of *direct knowledge* of what happens in classrooms to pass judgment on the assumption. Certainly the superintendent has no direct knowledge, and depending on the size of the school system neither do the layers of administrators below the superintendent. What about the principal of the individual school? There are no data to answer the question of the degree of direct knowledge the principal has of what goes on in classrooms. Based on my experience and what teachers have told me, the amount of direct knowledge is small and for a variety of reasons teachers prefer that it be small. If the amount of time a principal is in classrooms to judge the degree of relationship between policy and classroom practice is small in the elementary school, it is virtually zero in the much larger middle or high school. I am saying more than there is a disconnect between administrative and classroom practice. Ironically, although school administrators may have little or no direct knowledge of what goes on in classrooms, it is not at all unusual that when expectations are not realized, they will in private conversations frequently blame the victim: teachers. It is like explaining students' and teachers' inadequacies by their genes; it explains everything and, therefore, nothing. What are the obligations of leadership? You can fill a modest-sized building with the books and articles on leadership and I have no intention even to attempt a summary of that literature. However, there is a recent book by Eliot Cohen (2002) that on the surface has absolutely nothing to do with education but which is illuminatingly relevant to what I have said in this chapter as well as what I have said earlier about what we mean by learning.

The title of Cohen's book is *Supreme Command*. The subtitle is *Soldiers, Statesmen and Leadership in Wartime*. I read this book because every review of it praised it most highly; and, of course, the civil-military relationship has been, is, and will always be a major set of problems for countries that are or aspire to be democracies. Here is an excerpt:

The Normal Theory of Civil-Military Relations

We can call this consensus the "normal" theory of civil-military relations, which runs something like this. Officers are professionals, much like highly trained surgeons: the statesman is in the position of a patient requiring urgent care. He may freely decide whether or not to have an operation, he may choose one doctor over another, and he may even make a decision among different surgical options, although that is more rare. He may not, or at least ought not supervise a surgical procedure, select the doctor's scalpel, or rearrange the operating room to his liking. Even the patient who has medical training is well-advised not to attempt to do so, and indeed, his doctor will almost surely resent a colleague-patient's efforts along such lines. The result should be a limited degree of civilian control over military matters. To ask too many questions (let alone to give orders) about tactics, particular pieces of hardware, the design of a campaign, measures of success, or to press too closely for the promotion or dismissal of anything other than the most senior officers is meddling and interference, which is inappropriate and downright dangerous.

The difficulty is that the great war statesmen do just those improper things—and, what is more, it is because they do so that they succeed. This book looks at four indubitably great and successful war leaders, Abraham Lincoln, Georges Clemenceau, Winston Churchill, and David Ben-Gurion. The period of their tenure spans a substantial but not overwhelming period of time and different kinds of democratic policies. These four politicians have enough in common to bear comparison, yet differ enough to exhibit various features of the problem of civil-military relations in wartime. Given the dangers of thinking through these problems exclusively from an American perspective, it makes sense that only one of them should come from the pages of American history. (p. 4)

As I read the chapters about these men I was forcibly struck by Cohen's descriptions and discussion of one feature common to the four leaders, a feature dramatically relevant (to me at least) to what I was writing in this chapter. The feature has several parts.

1. Each leader was crystal clear about what the outcomes of the war should be and articulated his message to the citizenry.

2. He devised means, formal and informal, that enabled him to know in detail what was going on in different regions of combat. And "what was going on" meant among other things whether what his generals thought and the actions they took were consistent with intended outcomes.

3. Consistency was not judged solely by what generals said but also by what was learned informally and often secretly from military personnel in areas of action. It was not that these four leaders did not respect or trust military leaders but that each took it for granted that generals, like the rest of humanity, have predictable frailties of one kind or another—temperament, personality, judgment, self-regard, sensitivities, fear of failure, imagination, response to criticism, courage, etc.—frailties that are exacerbated by the chaos and pressures of war. Put it this way, none of the four civil leaders regarded humans as perfected outcomes of evolution or divine intent. Cohen describes instances when Lincoln instructed his *formal and informal sources* of information to send him telegraphic messages every ten minutes about the course of a particularly crucial battle!

4. These civil leaders visited scenes of battle not only to get a firsthand feel for what was going on but to contribute to the morale of those who were in the line of fire. The morale of those in the trenches was no less important than that of generals and their officers.

5. When these civil leaders changed generals, as they did, it was not an impulsive act but rather one based on a variety of sources of information as well as principles.

Earlier in this chapter I said that school administrators' most frequent complaint was that their duties and pressures, especially in the case of superintendents, prevented them from doing anything resembling equal justice to all of their major responsibilities and kept them from knowing what is going on in classrooms. Keeping in mind that the four civil leaders Cohen discusses were in office during a war in which the military had suffered disastrous defeats or, as in the case of Ben-Gurion, was a leader of a tiny country with a small, very ill-equipped army facing large armies of five large surrounding countries, these leaders made it their business to seek sources and ways to obtain information and a myriad of details relevant to what was going on where the action was. And they did this not because of unusual curiosity or because they did not value those people but rather because they knew that for a variety of reasons some could screw up, misinterpret, ignore or launder their mistakes, hesitate or procrastinate, and could have the tendency to regard the war as *their* war. In each case the civil leader trusted his own judgment about the conduct of the war as much as or more than he did the judgment of his generals. You could say that the stance of these leaders was cynical, arrogant, dangerous. Dangerous it was and they knew it, but they also knew they needed means of getting information that would allow them independently to judge whether the war was being conducted in ways appropriate to national policy and purposes.

You could also say that Cohen chose to discuss four very, very unusual leaders and that puts obvious constraints on drawing conclusions about leaders in general, e.g., in education, the military, in the private sector. However, you cannot reply to that criticism as it applies to schools and school systems until you answer this question: Is there a purpose to schooling more important than ensuring that what happens in classrooms is an appropriate implementation of the policies formulated by school administrators? *That question has to be asked regardless of whether as an outsider you agree or disagree with those policies.* Those who formulate policies expect that the classroom will reflect the spirit and letter of the policies. If you agree with the above purpose— which is to say that it has top priority—then school administrators should never be in the position where they defend their lack of direct experience of the classrooms because they do not have sufficient time or because of other pressures or constraints to which they are subject. So why is that defense so frequent? Some readers may be surprised, some will say it is outrageous, that a good part of the answer is that school policies and mission statements say next to nothing about learning and teaching. I have read more policy and mission statements than I care to remember. What you get are clichés, slogans, e.g., "Each child is respected as a unique person," "We will help each child realize his or her potential," "No child will be left behind," "Students will learn to respect diversity in a democratic society," "We will not set low expectations for our students," etc. I regard these examples as well-intentioned statements of values and goals with which nobody will disagree for the same reason that everyone is in favor of motherhood. What criteria will be employed to determine whether the intent of a policy can be said to be appropriately in evidence? Are any or all contexts of learning equally appropriate? On what basis can one assume that all teachers understand and implement a policy (even a curriculum) in ways the statements *implicitly* require? As a group, teachers vary, and one cannot expect that in their classrooms they can or should appear as clones of each other. Each teacher is, like each student, unique just as he or she was unique in their childhood classrooms. That is all the more reason that direct experience of teachers teaching, the context of learning they create, is as necessary as it is difficult, and requires clarity about criteria. How much direct experience is required will vary from teacher to teacher. But many school administrators have little or no direct experience, and as you go up the administrative hierarchy the amount of direct experience is zero. I am sure there are exceptions but they are just that: exceptions.

But Cohen's book raises a question that gets to the heart of the matter. School superintendents, like presidents, have "generals" who are their eyes and ears about how policies are having their intended effects in the classroom. Let us assume that superintendents respect and trust their generals. Can they afford to go on the assumption that they do not—some would say should not—need to seek ways to obtain information about what is going on in classrooms that is *independent* of what the generals say and report? That sounds as if I am contradicting myself in that I said earlier the superintendent respected and trusted his generals and now I am describing him or her as a spy, a one-person FBI. It would be a contradiction if the superintendent's understanding of human behavior was so superficial that she did not know that her generals are imperfect observers and reporters, or, to be more charitable, to assume that their imperfections are within what she deems to be acceptable limits. It would be a contradiction only if by action and words the superintendent never made clear that it was her responsibility to obtain information from whatever source possible, information which has to be judged in light of information from other sources. Generals have responsibilities that do not trump those of the leader. But the verb *trump* is appropriate only if the relationship between leader and generals is like a high-stakes game of cards in which you tell the other players nothing—indeed you try to mislead them—because your goal is to win, to elevate your sense of competence. If that relationship is one in which the players do not feel safe to put their cards out on the table, it is an efficient way to produce and sustain problems. *When that kind of relationship is seen in terms of the*

differences between contexts of productive and unproductive learning, it is
clearly an unproductive context. The significance of the differences between the
two kinds of context is not peculiar to the classroom.

I will now relate an experience which illustrates some of what I
have just said. When the Yale Psycho-Educational Clinic was created,
New Haven had a new superintendent of schools, Dr. Larry Paquin,
who accepted the mandate to try to improve the clearly dysfunctional,
inadequate, failing school system. He understood the culture of
schools and school systems: he was a candid, self-confident person
who had a low threshold for suffering fools gladly. At least that was
his reputation. In my first meeting with him I concluded his reputation was well earned. It was at this meeting that he said he would like
to use our services in two inner-city schools in need of change, both
schools being in walking distance from the clinic. In the spring of that
school year I wrote him to ask if he wanted us to continue the following year. He said he would be back to me in two or three weeks. In
that interval, and unknown to me, he met for somewhat more than
two hours with the teachers of the two elementary schools. What follows is what I learned from teachers who volunteered the substance
and tenor of the meeting, which is how I found out that a meeting
took place. I shall integrate what they told me and relate it as if it
were coming from one teacher.

> We didn't know what the purpose of the meeting was. We didn't ex-
> pect good news. We knew he did not have high regard for what we
> were doing. But none of us ever imagined that a superintendent, at
> least among the ones we had, would come to a meeting in one of
> the two schools. We expected the worst: maybe closing the schools,
> wholesale transfer of teachers and students, new principals. He
> started off by saying that the Yale Psycho-Educational Clinic had
> been in our two schools for almost a year and was now asking if he
> wanted to continue the arrangement for another year. He said he
> wanted our opinion and advice. And then he went on to say in his
> no-nonsense way that he did not know whether we liked the clinic
> people or praised them for their good intentions. What he wanted us
> to describe in concrete terms was if, when, and how the clinic was or
> was not helpful. "I value good intentions but I value them only if it
> has payoff for teachers and kids in the classroom."
>
> Someone got the ball rolling but the rolling stopped because Dr.
> Paquin stopped her and said, "You are too general and you are not
> describing an instance which tells me what the problem was, what
> the clinic staff member did or did not do, and whether or why it had
> any effect on you or that kid." That went on for over two hours. He
> should have been a prosecuting attorney or a detective who is only

interested in evidence. It was an exhausting, stimulating experience. It was a first for all of us. Imagine, this was the first time any administrator, let alone a superintendent, had ever spent that much time with us because he regarded what we had to offer to be important to a decision.

He called me to say that he wanted us to stay on for the following year. (Dr. Paquin went on to become superintendent in Baltimore, where a few years later he died of cancer.) Neither after his departure nor in any of the not-so-few school systems to which I consulted or got to know, did I ever hear of an instance of an administrator who did what Dr. Paquin did and why. Was Dr. Paquin a busy, pressured superintendent? You can bet your bottom dollar he was. He could have made the decision on his own and quickly. *He could not rely on his generals because in the scores of days we were in the two schools—averaging a minimum of three days a week—I (in one of those schools) never met an administrator and no administrator was curious enough to arrange a meeting with me.*

What I have said in this chapter will be criticized in different ways by different groups. Teachers will say, "You are right on target in recognizing that school administrators, all of whom were once teachers, have forgotten how difficult a task a classroom teacher has. When test scores are lower than they are supposed to be, we are the ones who are blamed, implicitly or explicitly, and new policies are proclaimed which we have to implement whether we agree or not with those policies. No one tells us in any concrete way why what we are doing is wrong, and the new policies also lack specificity or concreteness. We get marching orders, really commands, we are expected to obey. You say, and so do school administrators, that teachers don't want principals and those above them to come into our classrooms to pass judgment on what we do. You make it sound as if we think we know what is right, that we don't want anyone telling us that we have something to unlearn and learn. Maybe there is a kernel of truth in that—as you say, no one likes to change—but what you do not understand is that when you say that most classrooms are not contexts of productive learning it is true in spades in teacher–administrator learning contexts. They are not set to be sympathetic to and understanding of us and we of them. We do not feel safe or trustful of them or they of us. We live in two different worlds, light-years away from each other. Where you are both unfair and dead wrong is that you do not see the implications of your conception of learning for teachers, as if teachers don't know that the process of learning engenders many factors in a student which affect, positively or negatively, his or her performance. May we point out to you that we are not psychologists trained to be diagnosticians and therapists? We are specialists in teaching and we cannot be expected to be more than that. We cannot even be that because we are under tremendous time pressure to cover a prescribed curriculum with classes that have an average of about twenty-five students. You seem to understand that but you end up blaming teachers for not having more stimulating classrooms. Your sympathy is not appreciated."

The above argument concedes two points. The first, bluntly put, is that as a group teachers are not psychologically sophisticated. That does not mean they should be psychologists before they become teachers. What it does mean is that those who seek to become teachers will vary in their psychological sophistication, that because you want to become a teacher is not reason enough to be selected for a preparatory program. Preparatory programs and the educational research community have for all practical purposes ignored the issue of selection (Sarason 1999). When I say that, I am not criticizing those who are now teachers and whom I regard as victims. Simply to say that teachers should take more psychology courses misses the point. You may be a historian, a world-renowned one, but that does not mean you will teach history well to middle and high school students. A colleague of mine, Dr. Kenneth Wilson, who is a Nobel Laureate in physics, put it to me this way: "If I went to the Juilliard School of Music and said I wanted to learn to play the violin, they would walk me to the door and politely tell me to return when I could demonstrate that I *might* have some talent which *might* suggest a career as a musician. I could then go to several teacher training programs in the city and apply for admission so that I could teach physics and science in a high school. I have no doubt they would accept me." Dr. Wilson agreed with me that he would be a disaster as a teacher.

The second point that is conceded is that most classrooms are boring and unstimulating. But I have always—and I think *always* is the appropriate word—explicitly said that teachers teach the way they have been prepared to teach. I have not criticized teachers as if they have willed the situation I have observed and described countless times. Even so, I understand why they would see me as an insensitive critic. They are locked up in a system which over time extinguishes whatever capacity they may have had for self-scrutiny, an incapacity that extends both to a school system and preparatory programs. I am not locked up in that system and given my interests in education I felt obliged to write about what I think I have learned. I claim no market on the whole truth but as the decades have rolled on and educational reform has not had its intended results, I feel justified in saying that I have grasped part of the truth. My past predictions, based as they have been on what I have said in this and previous books, have been 100 percent correct. You could say the predictions were right but for the wrong reasons. I know that. I also know that, given my age, I will not be around when the results of current and future reform efforts are judged. Posterity is the cruelest of critics.

What about the criticisms administrators direct to what I have said? I have already indicated that they regard me as someone who is ignorant about myriads of responsibilities and pressures they confront and to expect that they have time directly to experience the contexts of learning in classrooms exposes my ignorance. However, as I have learned over the years, what administrators will say publicly is not what many of them have told me privately, and very understandably so. Briefly, here is what they say.

1. Although their job descriptions emphasize leadership qualities and responsibilities, in reality they have little power to effect any noncosmetic change. It is easy to proclaim a policy for a change but if and how the policy is implemented depends, for example, on whether the superintendent and/or the board of education is supportive and, in addition, whether principals, teachers, and the union agree to and understand the policy and implement it appropriately. Change by fiat is self-defeating. The situation is made more complicated and difficult if the change involves the collaboration of other administrators.

2. Superintendents come and go and so does the composition of the board of education. Also principals come and go. And, you must not forget, it is a myth that the political system does not, formally or informally, seek and have ways to influence policies of educational change. If you are an administrator in an urban school, you learn early on that the external political system interacts with the school system's internal politics. We do not talk about that but we are playing in a political game, usually a struggle. You and the public may say we are leaders but we are not. "You, Dr. Sarason, wrote a book about the culture of the school but you said next to nothing about internal and external politics. Of course we are concerned about classroom contexts of learning but we do not have the resources of time and personnel to do a good job of ensuring that the classroom changes in accord with the policies. So, when you criticize us for not being leaders, for not having direct experience with the teachers and students in classrooms, you are being insensitive, unfair, and misleading."

3. An educator obtains certification for an administrative post and then leaves the classroom for one or all of several reasons. First, he or

she has found teaching intellectually and personally confining, however satisfying and challenging teaching may have been; the teacher has no power to change the system in ways he or she considers important. Second, climbing the administrative ladder is associated with the power to effect change. Salaries are higher, he or she is accorded more respect. For some the power motive may be stronger than the fantasy that one can improve the system; for others the opportunity to make a contribution to reform is stronger than the allure of power. Third, in a career of classroom teaching your tomorrows will not be radically different from today: you will be spending most of your days with very young people. As an administrator you do not spend all of your time in your office. You are interacting in different sites with diverse adults who may or may not be part of the school system. Your tomorrows are not all that predictable and that is a plus. Challenge and diversity are what you need, they give you kicks.

Administrators are reluctant to talk about the motivations which propelled them to start climbing the hierarchy of status, power, responsibility. We do not expect a politician seeking elective office to say other than things need to change, he or she knows what those changes need to be, and he or she is motivated only by the desire to make this a better world. He or she presents a picture of selflessness, as if personal needs and ambitions are sacrificed for the good of the public welfare; to reveal those needs and ambitions will not sit well with the public. It is no different in the case of school administrators.

I cannot claim that I have spoken to more than a couple of dozen administrators in private conversation where they on their own told me what I have said above. We were by no means friends; indeed, except in one case I never saw them again. For reasons not clear then or now they began to reveal themselves because they saw me as unsympathetic and ignorant. When I say reveal themselves I do not mean that they were blaming themselves. Rather it was an attempt to set me straight about aspects of the school culture glossed over or ignored in my writings. Those conversations—most of which took place at professional conventions I had been invited to address—were separated by months, years, even decades. I didn't put their significances together until I finished writing my 2002 book, *Educational Reform. A Self-Scrutinizing Memoir*. When you subject yourself to self-scrutiny, you realize at least two things: Your remembered past is a selective sample of what you experienced, and there were things you wish you had learned—you could have learned—but you missed the boat. I was ready to put together occurrences separated in time but conveying similar messages. No one occurrence hits you in the face, so to speak. What those conversations with school administrators did was to allow me to see other experiences I had in my immersion in the school culture in a new light, by which I mean I saw relationships of which I had been only dimly aware.

Administrators, teachers, and students are kissing cousins (and do not know it, of course). When children begin schooling they are wide-eyed, curious, eager, ready to start to become "grown up," to enter a new world of learning, knowledge, and skills. By the time they are in high school the bloom is off the rose of that new world of learning. The school is not the sole explanation, of course, but it is an important and crucial part of it. The beginning teacher is no less wide-eyed and curious, although anxious about how well he or she will meet the challenges ahead. For a variety of reasons some of them will find the classroom, the school, the system and its culture disappointing and disillusioning, and will abandon teaching as a career. There will be those who develop a sense of competence and satisfaction and will remain on even though they come to see that what they can do for their students is limited by the traditions, organization, and pressures they must accommodate. Policies change, criteria for teacher and student performance and evaluation change, the expectations and role of parents change. The only thing that does not change is the powerlessness of the teacher to change anything beyond the confines of his or her classroom, and even directives from on high to improve test scores is a constraining influence on what a teacher does. Teachers do not feel as respected as they should be, and resent being seen by the public and the administrative hierarchy as the major obstacle to improving schools. All they can count on is self-respect but over time that is often not enough to see their future as at best a balancing of the positives and the negatives and at worst a passive succumbing to an unrewarding future which ends with a much-desired retirement. It is not that dreams become nightmares but rather that dreams remain dreams. Who cares? Who understands what teachers are confronted with in today's schools? Who knows that many teachers feel guilty that they have not the support, time, or know-how to help students more than they do? These are hard questions with which to live and it should not be occasion for surprise that they are a major source of burnout and routinization in many teachers.

In light of what I have said earlier about administrators and why over time their zeal, optimism, and sense of accomplishment diminish, we round out an account in which the three major actors or groups do come to regard life in schools as far less rewarding than they had anticipated. I know that is a disappointing generalization. I also know that there are exceptions which remain exceptions, which is why parents seek them when they are dissatisfied with their child's school.

And it also explains why administrators seek to move to other schools where presumably the grass is greener. And it is no different with teachers for whom greener means more respect, more collegiality, a more enlivening environment. In my experience not all exceptions deserve that label. But a number of them—several in inner-city areas—do deserve that label because they have taken seriously the differences between contexts of productive and unproductive learning. They are exceptions in a school system; despite the fact that the system of which they are a part has for all practical purposes no explicit criteria for contexts of productive learning, or even what it means by learning which, therefore is like an inkblot interpreted differently by different people.

I hope the reader now understands why this chapter is the longest in this book. We expect a superintendent and his closest associates to be educational leaders who formulate policies, to take actions the aim of which is to ensure that teachers understand those policies, to gain their support at the same time that the system provides means to support teachers for whom a policy may not be clear in regard to implementation in the classroom. However, there is one important step I deliberately omitted because I consider it the litmus test of the adequacy of the administrator's conception of productive learning. The step is that when a change in policy that is intended to affect learning in the classrooms is *contemplated*, not yet locked in concrete, it should be discussed with teachers for the explicitly expressed purpose of providing them an opportunity to voice their ideas, reactions, suggestions. There is a difference between listening to and *learning* from what they say. This is not an instance when administrators can adopt a stance of benevolent paternalism or noblesse oblige. It is an instance where the administrator can hear or intuit the problems the adoption of the policy will encounter. The omission of this step comes close to being universal in school systems. That omission in part explains why reform efforts fail as they do, why teachers regard administrators as people who have forgotten what it is like to be teachers who huddle at the bottom of a mountain on top of which their "rulers" spend their days dreaming up programs the mindless drones below will implement once the programs are announced together with marching orders. It takes parents time to learn that their child does not thank them for giving them marching orders.

Why is it that when you read the annual reports of foundations which support educational reform, you are not in doubt that they are in favor of training better-qualified teachers? And during political campaigns, every office seeker will say he or she recognizes the need for better-qualified teachers. And these statements convey to the public that if better-qualified teachers are produced, educational outcomes will follow; a cause has been identified and we have to deal better with it. Question: Why is it I have *never* heard any groups say we need better-qualified administrator-leaders? And why is it that with rare exceptions—I assume they are rare for I have not seen or heard them—no one describes what they mean by qualified, let alone better-qualified, classroom contexts of learning?

Whose responsibility is it to judge whether a classroom context of learning is a productive or unproductive one? But that responsibility requires that administrators have a relatively clear conception of the learning process and take it seriously so that they have developed means, formal and informal, to judge whether others in the system also take it seriously. I have been around a long time, I have been in hundreds of schools, I have talked and listened to thousands of teachers and administrators. Some readers will find it hard to agree with my assertion that there is hardly any discussion, let alone analysis, of what they mean by learning. When a famous psychologist was asked what intelligence is, he said intelligence is what intelligence tests measure. In the land of the blind the one-eyed astigmatic man with glaucoma is king. In regard to what educators say about what they mean by learning we find ourselves in a modern version of the biblical Tower of Babel, with the difference that in this modern Tower of Babel the occupants believe that when they say "learning," it means what others mean and, therefore, they understand each other.

In the next chapter I shall discuss a book by a world-celebrated economist who applied his way of thinking to education. Unfortunately, despite his many intellectual gifts and his recognition that schools appeared to be intractable to reform, Professor Milton Friedman did not start with the basic question about what he means by learning and, therefore, undercuts his suggestions for improving educational outcomes.

Chapter Eleven

What Is Missing in a Voucher Policy?

Winston Churchill quipped that democracy is the worst form of government except for all the others. His quip was based on an iron law of human affairs: There is no free lunch. All forms of national political-economic management have their pluses and minuses. In a democratic-capitalist society, more than in any other form, the ratio of positives to negatives is far more conducive to human welfare (broadly conceived) than all other forms because (a) it encourages, supports, and protects individual liberty, (b) it provides the freedom to choose courses of action as long as those actions do not restrict similar actions by others, and (c) it fosters competition in free markets, which is a spur to people's creativity and entrepreneurial spirit. That is to say, the free market frees the mind of the individual to imagine, create, and realize concrete material rewards and the sense of personal accomplishment. There are, so to speak, winners and losers—that is and will always be the case in any political-economic arrangement—but the historical record indicates that democratic capitalism best protects the freedom of the individual to make choices, not to decrease the capacity to make choices or, worst of all, to succumb to forms of political-economic arrangements in which individual liberty and choice hardly exist. The twentieth century was the bloodiest in human history. One way to describe that century is as a clash between democratic-capitalistic countries and autocratic, fascist, and communist ones. And at the beginning of the twenty-first century it appears that the clash will include autocratic, theocratic countries whose conceptions of individual liberty and choice are on a collision course with democratic-capitalist countries.

What are the political-economic arrangements that can protect life, liberty, and the pursuit of happiness? The framers of our constitution were not in doubt about how to answer that question. One part of the answer was that the colonies needed and wanted a government that did not arrogate to itself autocratic, unilateral power to restrict individual liberty and the freedom to choose how people will live their personal and working lives. The protection of *the individual and individuality* against arrogant and intrusive government was front and center. The second part of the answer was arrived at after much debate and is captured in the saying that that government is best which governs the least. The framers sought and devised a government with built-in restrictions against unwarranted exercise of power. What we today have difficulty grasping is that the colonies had been governed by a monarchy and parliament more than two thousand miles away. It took weeks to make the voyage and a piddling number of colonists ever made the trip. It was a form of absentee ownership fraught with predictable sources of conflict, insensitivities, misunderstandings, and ultimately revolution. The lesson was clear: If those who govern you do not and cannot know you, the needs and liberties of the governed are at best endangered and at worst extinguished. Similarly, the thirteen colonies lived in what to them was a vast land and some of the founding fathers looked forward to increasing that expanse to the Mississippi River! Going from one town or city to another was a long journey that could take many days. The colonists were not about to create a national government separated by long distances from the governed whose outlooks, needs, and opinions could not impact on that government. That added fuel to the heated issue of states' rights. States were closer to the people than a distant central government and therefore more knowledgeable about and responsive to their citizens. That explains why the issue of slavery was such a bone of contention at the Constitutional Convention. The compromise on that issue was because the northern states' representatives realized that without such a compromise there simply would not be a United States. If the slavery issue illustrates the fear of a strong national government, it was but a reinforcement of the view held by all that citizens had ever to be on guard against the tendency of government to enlarge its powers in ways inimical to individual freedom, liberty, and decision making.

The word *education* is not in the constitution. That was not an oversight. It was literally inconceivable to the framers that national government should have anything to do with education. Education was a parental and local responsibility because the two in tandem best knew their children and, in addition, could ensure that the substance and goals of education were in keeping with their views. Distant government meant regulations based on ignorance of parental and local customs and values.

The above is the sketchiest of sketches of why the constitution has the substance it does. I will relate the sketch to the issues surrounding school vouchers but for that discussion to be meaningful I need first to return to what I have said earlier about learning.

I have said that the most basic problem in schooling is clarifying and demonstrating with credible evidence the distinguishing features of contexts of productive and unproductive learning. Until and unless that is done we can expect little from efforts of educational reform. *That was what the Constitutional Convention was in principle all about.* The founders were not in doubt about the features of an unproductive form of government. Their problem was how to create and structure a government that would be productive and sustaining of certain inalienable rights of all its citizens. No one had to tell them that the word *democracy* did not refer to a thing but to a process involving elected officials and the electorate, a relationship in which the former were chosen by and the servant of the latter. The electorate was the ultimate source of power and its overarching responsibility was to exercise that power so as to prevent their governors from straying from stated values and purposes. How to understand and take into account such a complicated process so that the abuse of power both by officialdom and the electorate would be kept in check? It was not only a design problem but a bedrock psychological one. They faced squarely what to them was obvious: people were very complicated organisms who could be partisan and nonpartisan, selfless and selfish, reasonable and irrational, calm and excitable, moral and immoral, flexible and dogmatic, devoted to the truth and capable of ignoring it, independent thinkers or people who were easily swayed by the opinions of others, etc. The electorate, no more or less than officialdom, were capable of both great and ignoble motivations and actions. To design a governance structure as if people were not such complicated organisms was folly. The constitution is incomprehensible apart from the framers' understanding of human behavior. Even when the convention ended after four months of meetings during a steamy Philadelphia summer, the framers were by no means sanguine that what they came up with would be long lived. Their wisdom in the realm of human affairs and psychology is illustrated by their request to the diverse and flourishing Philadelphia publishing media to refrain from reporting anything about the convention's deliberations. Why? Because the participants knew the challenge and difficulties they would encounter, the fears and passions regional and slavery issues would arouse, and, therefore, the importance of participants to feel free to voice frankly their ideas and opinions, to adopt stances and change them as discussion went on, and to avoid external pressures stimulated by accounts and leaks which gave a distorted picture of the proceedings; it was essential that the participants feel safe with and trustful of each other to understand that problems are complex, that what you said today you may retract or amend tomorrow. *The media of the time agreed to and did honor the request.* I still find that hard to believe.

The convention was a context of productive learning. The participants learned a lot from, with, and about each other. They knew they had embarked on uncharted seas. They had chosen a reluctant George Washington to be the captain because he was not enamored of power and because he (like all good teachers) would respect and understand them and keep them on course. If he was the captain, he was also in their service. Although they were a heterogeneous group on any variable of human temperament and behavior, they knew that the test of the governance they would design would be if its basic values and goals were understood, honored, and implemented in daily living. And the value undergirding the design was individual freedom to think, make choices, and act in ways that give meaning to living, however different that may be from what others think and do. The design for governance is for the purpose of protecting individual liberty from encroachments, subversions, and the siren songs of those who seek to aggrandize power by diluting or eliminating the freedom of others. Would people born to freedom have the wisdom and courage to protect it from all comers, including their own government? The framers were not sure. They hoped and prayed.

I said earlier that the colonists knew well the characteristics of an unproductive context of governance. They had revolted against such a context. They were not pie-in-the-sky theorists, although that is precisely how their former rulers regarded them. Question: What do we know about unproductive classroom contexts of unproductive learning? Who is rebelling, why, and in what ways? I have endeavored earlier in this book to address those questions, in part at least, and in more detail in earlier books. Let me list in bare-bones fashion some (and only some) of the characteristics of a classroom context of *unproductive learning, for the purpose of asking the reader to consider how those characteristics are in principle identical to those motivating the rebelling colonists.*

1. Parents have no role or the power to participate in any noncosmetic way in a school's organization or educational decisions.

2. Point 1 is also applicable to teachers who feel and know that they have no role in the corridors of power, a form of taxation without representation.

3. School administrators have some formally delegated powers the exercise of which they feel is drastically constrained by distant policy makers in the state capital, state legislatives and executives, Washington, unions, and university preparatory programs which are laws unto themselves.

4. Students feel like and are the most powerless group in the arena of schooling: what they will learn, when they will learn it, the ways they will learn it are the prerogatives of others. They are expected to conform. They may be told that they have to learn to think for themselves, to be independent and critical thinkers. It has no meaning for them in terms of life in the classroom.

5. Students ask very few questions, no one seeks their opinions on anything, they do not feel safe to criticize their teachers or the rules of living for the classroom or school. They are citizens of the school but have no rights. They do not feel that anyone recognizes or is interested in the fact that they think and feel, dream, have interests and curiosity, a sense of what is fair or unfair, a desire to explore and understand self, others, and the fascinating, challenging, puzzling, world outside of school.

6. Though students start schooling with eagerness, curiosity, and a strong desire to learn, by the time they are graduated from high school they have lost a great deal of interest in or respect for schooling and learning. They have become apathetic, but scratch the surface and there is resentment, disillusionment about schooling and formal learning. By the time they are graduated many students have explored diverse ways of getting kicks out of life, ways that are alarming to parents, educators, and those of previous generations. Many students never graduate, especially in urban areas. Most explanations of those who drop out center on maladaptive characteristics of the dropout. Someone said that for some of these students the act of dropping out is realistic and wise, because the individual has experienced school as a place that speaks not at all to his or her needs and interests, so why continue to waste time?

Federal, state, and local officials, colleges and universities, educators (teachers) administrators, parents, students—these are the players with a vested interest in and responsibility for schooling. Aside from parents and their children, they hardly know or talk to each other, let alone seek to understand each other, to seek to learn from each other. They do not like and respect each other. They blame each other for poor educational outcomes. Each has a different explanation and reform proposal for the current state of affairs. None is a villain with malevolent intent.

They do agree about two things. The first is that in the sixty years after World War II a staggering amount of money has been spent on efforts to improve schooling and people are puzzled about why these efforts have failed. If and when a book is written that carefully describes and analyzes the substance and consequences of these reforms, the book will weigh five or more pounds and will contribute to an increase in the incidence of depressive disorders. The second is that if the current state of affairs continues, it will have untoward effects on the character and stability of the country. I have never met anybody in any walk of life, high or low, who did not agree with these two points. The six points I listed earlier were not for the purpose of explanation but a description of a context, a system, guaranteed to be unproductive for the players in the system. It is a system with many parts and people, especially educators who privately have no hope or ideas but are compelled publicly to say they have found the silver bullet that will make things better. Reports appear in the mass media about a school here and a school there that have been "turned around," where test scores have risen, where the educational thermometer gives a basis for hope. Then come the reports of state and national mass testing using kindred thermometers indicating that the exceptions have remained exceptions which no one can explain. Like Shakespeare's Hamlet who surmises that something is wrong in Denmark, one should pardon those who conclude that something is very wrong in the educational arena. In the 1930s John Gunther wrote a book in which he discussed the social-political health of European countries. The chapter on Austria came after the one on Hitler's Germany. It begins with the saying, "In Germany the situation is serious but not hopeless. In Austria the situation is hopeless but not serious." It turned out, of course, that Gunther was wrong about both countries.

Many people today regard educational reform as a hopeless endeavor but not a serious one because somehow or other we will muddle through without paying too high a societal price. I sincerely hope they are right but I am not betting on it. For sixty years I have lived through, observed, participated in educational reform efforts. My previous book *Educational Reform. A Self-Scrutinizing Memoir* (2002) details at length my mistakes of omission and commission, misplaced emphases, and my unwillingness or inability directly to confront an issue which hit me with full force when from 1945 to 1960 my research on test anxiety in elementary school children required that I observe several hundred classrooms (Sarason et al. 1960). Concretely, I was appalled by how routinized, unstimulating, and boring the classroom context of learning was, and how passive, conforming, and intellectually uncurious students seemed to be despite the fact that the IQs and test scores of the students were average or above. The classroom atmospheres were peaceful, business-like, utterly without humor or laughter or even occasional signs of strong emotion or excitement. I interviewed samples of parents of the students. The picture they painted of their children was in substance the difference between a still life and a Breughel depiction of villagers in a town square.

After I wrote the last sentence above I received a telephone call from a friend, Dr. Robert Felner of the University of Rhode Island. He has for a long time conducted reform efforts to foster changes in teacher-student and teacher-teacher ways of relating. He asked me what I was up to those days and I told him the gist of a book I was writing about what people meant by learning. His reply was, "If teachers were told by their physicians that they had been in practice for a long time and proudly said that they treated the ills of patients in the same way as when they had started to practice, most teachers would look for a new physician. What I encounter is that when I suggest that there are alternate, more productive ways of structuring relationships, they respond in ways and tones that convey the message that they have learned, mastered their craft, and see no reason to change. I don't tell them to change but only to *consider*, mull over what I have said. It is as if they truly believe that from the time they started to teach until now—which on average would be an interval of five or ten years or more—nothing has been learned or written by anyone anywhere that would persuade them they should change what they think or do. They have learned and they have no need to learn more."

So let us turn to the rationale for vouchers which would give a direct subsidy to parents to allow them to send their children to any school—public, private, religious—anywhere they choose. The element of choice is unrestricted. In recent years some school systems have allowed parents to choose to send their children to any school in the system. With a voucher, parents can use the subsidy toward tuition in a neighboring town or city. In this discussion I shall not be concerned with size of subsidy, availability of openings in schools parents choose, transportation costs and difficulties, or what in general might be called practical considerations. My focus will be on how the rationale for vouchers is expected to improve the outcomes of the learning process and context. Let us start with the following obituary.

School Vouchers

Passed away on Capitol Hill June 12, 2001. Born in 1956 to Milton Friedman, noted libertarian. Defeated by voters more than ten times in the United States. Most recently, suffered overwhelming defeats at the hands of voters in California and Michigan despite generous financial support from wealthy donors. After the election of voucher supporter George W. Bush in 2000, relocated to Washington, D.C. Expected to find greener pastures on Capitol Hill with the support of Bush. Ultimately, however, the popular sentiment against vouchers prevented even Bush from saving vouchers. Defeats in numerous elections, opposition from a broad and diverse coalition of Americans, and voluminous polls, studies, and other research left vouchers in critical condition. Died with a handful of fervent but out-of-the-mainstream supporters on hand. Survived by several elements of the Bush tax plan which aim to sneak a new style of education through privatization through the back door to replace the deceased. Voucher advocates refuse to accept the death of vouchers, spending millions on advertisements, holding pro-voucher conferences, publishing papers and "studies" and meeting with the President to devise schemes to push voucher-like programs. No memorial services are planned.

(Vouchers obituary provided courtesy of the California Alliance for Public Schools, a coalition of community organizations whose mission is to protect and promote public schools.)

In light of recent court rulings, the way in which the Bush II administration is expressly implementing the No Child Left Behind legislation, the privatizing of some schools in Philadelphia and elsewhere, the obituary may well be premature. Where in my opinion the writers of the obituary are very mistaken is that although it is certainly true that most people would like to promote and protect the public schools, many of them are aware that (a) there is a lot wrong with public schools, especially urban ones, (b) efforts to improve them have failed, and (c) there must be ways and answers short of something like vouchers. That is to say, their support is implicitly conditional and based on hope and prayer that public schools in the future will be discernibly better than they are now and were in the past. To someone like me who long before vouchers came on the scene predicted and explained why schools would not improve, why they at best would remain what they are or would get worse, writing the obituary for vouchers is premature. The obituary could only be written by people who interpret a vote the way test scores are interpreted: as if they have but one significance, as if the way people think and vote today will be a carbon copy of their thinking and voting next week. When do people rebel and take radical action? Until a decade or so before the American Revolution, George III had no reason to believe that the colonists would not continue to be loyal to the crown. He either ignored or was insensitive to indications of the nature and depth of colonists' grievances until grievances led to overt actions. He made the mistake of assuming that loyalty was unconditional. A more recent example was the assumption by those administering school systems that teachers' grievances and poor pay would not lead them to join labor unions and take part in militant action to change power relationships. Would teachers ever strike? For ages such "revolutionary" action was literally inconceivable by officialdom, teachers, and the general public. Beginning in the early 1950s, there were already signs that what was literally inconceivable might not be inconceivable. *In a few years the inconceivable became a reality.* The assumption that vouchers are dead, cremated, and in a vase in a museum of stupid, antisocial ideas may very well end up as an example of Santayana's axiom that those who ignore history are doomed to repeat it. Polls indicate that a very high percentage of people are in favor of school choice within a single school system. And a somewhat lower percentage are in principle in favor of vouchers, especially among racial and ethnic minorities. When you take this into account together with the rise of charter schools, the steady increase of home schooling, and the increase in the number of enrollments in private schools, you have to conclude that the number of people who are dissatisfied with public schools is very far from piddling.

No one more than Milton Friedman has given intellectual, conceptual, and moral credibility to a policy for vouchers (Friedman 1963). He is no ideologue, dogmatist, or closet racist who does not appreciate the origins of and need for the public schools, or who does not see that they had no recognizable accomplishments for much of their history. He is aware of and condemns any form of discrimination. His advocacy of vouchers is based on his belief that democratic capitalism is by far the best form of political-economic societal organization because it holds out the opportunity for people to demonstrate their inventiveness, creativity, and entrepreneurship, and to promote and sustain the public welfare and the bedrock importance of individual freedom. Professor Friedman does not say that democratic capitalism is without imperfections and inequities but rather that better than any alternatives it fosters opportunities for people to realize their potentials by virtue of the gift of individual freedom, a gift that comes with the constraint that your actions do not diminish the individual freedom of others. He is an optimist about people's desire and capacity to make their own decisions, act on them, and take responsibility for the consequences. He is a realistic pessimist about people in that he knows they also have the capacity to be aggrandizers, to engage in illegal acts, and to trample on the freedom of others. In human history, as well as in many countries today, most people have no individual freedom; freedom is for their governmental rulers. The masses are conforming, dispensable ciphers, poor and struggling for existence; justice and growth for themselves and their offspring are not in their future. For Professor Friedman, government should be the servant of the people and not vice versa. Unfortunately, governments have the seemingly inevitable tendency to extend their reach and power, sometimes with good intentions, but with consequences that limit individual freedom and choice. That, he believes, is precisely what has happened to our educational system as it has grown. People are locked into the system to which they must conform. Parents have neither voice nor power, the rulers of the system have both, at the same time that the system is failing and many of its students are unprepared to use their abilities to make choices that will enable them to complete in the marketplace of opportunities. Professor Friedman expects schools to regard vouchers as threats rather than a spur to compete and improve. He is an advocate of the free market but he also knows that the free market as we know it has never been, cannot be, and should not be totally free. There is a role for government.

There are two things missing in Professor Friedman's advocacy. The first is that before a public policy intended to have widespread, indeed revolutionary effects is adopted, should there not be a handful of pilot studies carried out and analyzed in as rigorous a scientific way as possible so that we are not in doubt about what implementation problems were encountered and the credibility of the policy's outcome measures? It has long been a feature in education that innovations are either not subjected to any prior trial before wholesale application or the evaluation is thrown out of a court of evidence. We do not allow a drug to be marketed for use until there is credible evidence that it does what its makers say it does, that its side effects are far outweighed by its positive effects.

Vouchers are intended to affect children and parents, the schools they leave, and even the schools which accept their vouchers. For example, to how many schools did a parent apply before finding one that would accept the child? What information did she have about those schools and why did schools A, B, or C say they could or would not accept the child? Did the child want to leave his previous school? Did he encounter any difficulties when he became a student in his new school? What does the new school report—say, every three months—about the child's adjustment and performance? Should we not try to determine what the child has to say about his new school and new classmates and teachers? Or are we to regard the child as a puppet empty of feelings that may or may not be associated with his behavior or performance in the new school? I could ask many more questions because their answers may help us understand the *predictable* variations in measures of outcome at the end of the first or second year. Is there anyone who expects there will be no variation? Should we not collect whatever data we can that would tell us what steps we have to take that will increase the chances that the voucher policy will have its intended outcomes? Or do we go by the seat of our pants depending on personal anecdotes or data so sloppily collected as to be worthless as a test of the policy? I regard not asking these and other questions as tantamount to playing around with the lives of children and robbing ourselves of the opportunity of improving the implementation of a policy with goals with which I agree.

Take another example. Assume that Mary, Frank, and John are in different but very similar schools, failing schools. They are similar in age, grade, IQ, and achievement test scores. Their parents use vouchers and transfer them to the same new school. (It could, of course, be three different schools but let us keep it simple.) After one year their academic achievement level has increased somewhat, not dramatically, but still less than other students in their grade. Since you do not collect test scores for the hell of it, you make judgments about the possible significances (plural) of the test scores. You can use other data in seeking to understand their academic performance and you do. Question: What if for *each* of the three children you had data on a child in their previous classroom and school who had the same IQ and test scores but who had remained in that inadequate school rather than using a voucher? Would you, should you, want to know how these students are similar or different after, say, one or two years?

If you selected ten knowledgeable researchers and had them meet for one week of ten-hour days to come up with a research design to test the degree to which the voucher policy is achieving its purposes and, therefore, how it can be better changed and implemented, the one thing they could tell you ahead of time is that they would be confronting a devilishly complicated and daunting problem and that whatever they came up with would cost a great deal of money to implement.

I am not calling into question the freedom of a parent to place their child in a school of their choice. However, when a policy is intended to affect the lives of parents and students and it is explicitly intended to impact on schools as they now are, should we not feel obligated initially to determine whether negative side effects of such a policy are credibly outweighed by its positive effects? If education is to operate in a free market, what do we know about that market? I shall assume that no reader will deny that people are not angels. That is no argument against Professor Friedman's rationale and justification of a democratic-capitalist society; he knows that the market is not literally free, that there is a governmental role to oversee and regulate the market to prevent and penalize individuals and companies whose activities threaten the credibility of the market because when the public loses confidence in the market the entire society is at risk. That is why we have antitrust laws, a Securities and Exchange Commission, a Federal Drug Administration, antipollution agencies, and so on. All of these instrumentalities were a reaction against a free market unable or unwilling to patrol itself. The benefits of competition and individual freedom are real and many but they come with a price: the "no free lunch" axiom in this instance is that competition can be a source of practices and the withholding of information inimical to the public health and welfare, not only to individuals here and there. The history of the tobacco companies is, of course, a case in point: all tobacco companies withheld information crucial to the health of millions of people. Does anyone—liberal, libertarian, conservative—say that the tobacco companies should be free to withhold such information? I must emphasize that I am not arguing against competition and the concept of the free markets but against ideas and practices promoted on the basis of no supporting information, or of inadequate or misleading information, or the withholding of information that indisputably will affect many people in untoward ways. The most damning aspect of the tobacco story is that the companies not only had damaging data, but for decades also ignored and derogated data from the research community.

Several things in the post–World War II era characterize the many efforts to reform the public schools. First, and as never before, there has been an increasing dissatisfaction with the quality and outcomes of schooling. Second, reform efforts have failed to have their intended effects. Third, the reform efforts have been largely stimulated by individuals and agencies external to the educational community. Fourth, there is a lack of evidence that the educational community can reform itself. This is why someone like Professor Friedman can rightly say that the public schools are essentially a monopoly with all of a monopoly's predictable adverse consequences. From the standpoint of the bedrock importance Professor Friedman (and I) attach to individual freedom and choice, the great bulk of people do not have the freedom to place their child in a school of their choice.

I have two criticisms of his advocacy of vouchers. The first is that Professor Friedman is far too sophisticated not to know that applying the economic-political-psychological rationale for vouchers to the public schools poses many problems of implementation which can cause a worthy idea to be rejected. There is no one way of implementing and evaluating vouchers, but there is one moral and scientific obligation which must be observed: You do it in a way that is not subject to the criticisms of sloppy analysis and reporting, selective bias in choosing students, and unwarranted generalizations. Education has had a surfeit of such efforts and we do not need another. It is no criticism of Professor Friedman to say that he has not told us how he or we might do it. His task was to make a case for seriously considering a voucher policy, and he has done that well. But he has a following which is passionate and militant (and well connected and influential) and he has not cautioned them that a policy of vouchers comes with the obligation to discriminate between credible evidence and subjective opinion, between assumption and demonstrated fact. As I have discussed elsewhere (Sarason 2002a) we should not imitate the charter school movement. We do not have and will not have credible evidence about why most charter schools fall short of expectations or why a not much smaller number have presumably fallen far short of their mark, or were aborted very early in their existence.

The second criticism is as serious as the first, indeed I would say that in some ultimate sense it is more serious, because a voucher policy confronts you with the question: If there is a free market in education, what are the sellers selling and the buyers buying?

For what will the sellers be competing? Let us assume they will compete to achieve reasonable profit. What is the product they will be selling? At worst they will say they will provide an education as good as a public school and at best a much better one, and they will also say that in regard to other schools who seek voucher students. But what do these competing schools mean by education? What goals do these schools implicitly and explicitly convey when they say they are in the education business? How are those goals different from those public school educators who say that education has multiple goals all of which directly and indirectly involve formal and informal contexts of individual and social learning? The two will not be radically different in their statement of goals. And so we have to ask why the sellers will do a better job. From my standpoint the only defensible answer is that they have a conception of learning that is far more productive for the development and future of students than the unproductive aspects of learning contexts so prevalent in the public schools. For example, I assume they will not say that their goal will be for students to meet academic standards as they are judged by test scores, period. I assume they will say that meeting academic standards is very important (and indeed it is) but also that they will be on the road to becoming critical, independent thinkers who willingly embrace learning because of its applicability to understanding the world they live in, the questions and puzzles it presents, the choices they will have to make as they mature, and the responsibilities they have to assume for learning. Learning will not be experienced as a chore, a compulsory activity foisted on them by uncomprehending adults insensitive to how students see and interpret the world, past and present. They will learn that learning is not always easy but has a payoff. They will say they go beyond test scores to the quality of student' thinking, which may or may not be reflected in test scores. They respect individuality and exploiting it is what they do best, one kid at a time. They say that is why they're not a large school with large classes; that is why they charge the tuition they do. Getting to know someone to the point where you both trust and feel safe with each other takes time and time is money.

Some people will say that the answer I hope for is empty rhetoric devoid of a road map telling us how the stated ideal goals will be achieved. That criticism both concedes the argument and defines the problem. It concedes the argument because it does approve of its substantive purposes. The critic is not opposed to the goal of students becoming independent, critical thinkers who feel free to explore issues and raise questions which others may see as an unwelcome departure from the norm. Nor is the critic opposed to the importance placed on respect for and the embrace of learning which enlarges the student's understanding of self, others, and the world in which he or she lives. And when pressed, the critic will agree that the accumulation of knowledge, like the accumulation of money, cannot be judged if we are ignorant of how it was accumulated and how it is used. What turns off the critic about the answer is that he has not been provided with a road map describing the steps by which you go from generalizations to concrete actions by which stated goals are reached. He could say, "If education operated in a free market, you have nothing but generalizations to sell that no one in his right mind would invest in or buy outright. The only thing you can hope for is that someone in that market will not only provide the road map but also have evidence that it works, if not perfectly, then with a degree that others will seek to improve so that therefore, over time you will outsell competitors." In other words, stop dreaming, don't tell us what might be or should be, show us what works and why it is a better mousetrap.

What if I asked this critic, who says he agrees in principle with much of what I have said, about its emphasis on freedom to think independently and critically and to explore, "If I said there is one instance in which the educational rationale I have discussed has been tried, and there is credible evidence that it discernibly approximated its goals, would you to any degree change your mind?" The critic might say that one approximation is but one approximation, an encouragement to go on and demonstrate that it was not an unreplicable fluke. If I then said that there has been more than one demonstration, again with credible results, in public schools serving poor people and minorities whose academic development has been deplorable, what might they say? (I could remind him that before the Wright brothers kept an airplane in the air for less than a minute they and many others had experienced failure after failure. That one flight at Kitty Hawk was unconvincing to or not even believable to many other people when they heard or read about it.) Well, the critic can then ask, "If these small number of instances have taken place in public schools, why have they not, for all practical purposes, spread throughout our public schools?" Since I know that my critic is a free market advocate I do not ask him to read what I have written but to read how Milton Friedman has provided an answer to his question. He reads what Professor Friedman wrote and comes back to me and says, "The two of you certainly agree that the public schools are by their monopolistic nature allergic to change and innovation. Only the free market can save education."

He is half right. I have had to conclude that as presently constituted, with the reform efforts currently being proclaimed and implemented, the public schools cannot and will not take seriously the distinguishing differences between contexts of productive and unproductive learning. But I see no reason to believe that a voucher policy will stimulate the creation of private schools that take these differences in context seriously and, therefore, will stimulate the public school to compete by taking those differences seriously. *(One of the arguments for charter schools was that they would be a spur for public schools to compete and change. It has not happened and will not happen.)* There is nothing in Professor Friedman's writing that says anything about the substance, quality, and purposes of the product to be sold. If in an educational free market nothing is said to help the consumer make a more informed choice *consistent with their values and goals,* what does that say about a voucher policy? Do we not know ahead of time what some of the predictable problems may be and that unpredictable problems will appear? Should we not try to determine ahead of time how we might dilute the force of predictable problems by conducting carefully carried out pilot studies, or do we just plunge ahead? Have we learned nothing from sixty-plus years of efforts to reform education that is relevant to the success of a voucher policy?

Why do we have a Securities and Exchange Commission that requires, among other things, that companies make public the data about their financial transactions, health, and honesty? The first part of the answer is that the public demanded it because the crash of the stock market in 1929 exposed shenanigans that had devastating effects on millions of people. And over the decades those requirements changed and increased as companies found new ways of hiding activities from public scrutiny. The free market is a spur to competition and creativity but that creativity can also be a spur to nefarious practices. What is called human nature has not changed and in the history of free markets there is a long, depressing chapter on people's capacity to cheat, deceive, and mislead. If you believe, as I do, that over time the benefits of the free market outweigh its perverse effects—in keeping with Churchill's quip that democracy is the worst form of government except for all other forms—it is no basis to proceed with a voucher policy without consideration of how one should think about this question: In an educational free market what *educational* data are we justified in requiring of old or new schools who become players in that market? Let us not gloss over that it is only in recent decades that the public schools have been required by states and the federal government to make public educational data that a public disenchanted with those schools should be provided. The public schools were and are a monopoly and monopolies are not noted for their self-revealing inclinations and their welcome to competition. So, for example, public school personnel were among the most vociferous lobbyists against charter school legislation. The question I have asked in no way suggests that schools created to serve students with vouchers should be told who, how, and what they should teach but rather to provide consumers with data they should have when they exercise their right to choose. When you read the annual financial report of a corporation do you not wish you had a cadre of statisticians and economists to tell you not what it says but what it means? The meanings of educational data are frequently not obvious and for many consumers, numbers are just that: numbers. I am surprised that someone as extraordinarily sophisticated as Professor Friedman is about economic markets in general and free markets in particular says nothing about this issue, just as the administrators of public schools said and did nothing. If I can understand why as an economist he says little about what he means by learning, I cannot understand why as an economist he says nothing about the question I posed above.

Finally, I want to make a point obvious as it has not been taken seriously in discussions of why reform efforts have failed. It is an issue that will inevitably—and I use that word advisedly—confront voucher programs in their judgments about their accomplishments. Simply put: of all the major factors that can have positive or negative or mixed effects on outcomes, none is more fateful than the classroom teacher who is the vehicle, the instrument, the conduit through which *any* educational goal comes to have its intended effects on how students think and perform. And why discussions about how to improve that human conduit have been misguided and fruitless was clearly explained by a psychologist more than a century ago. Reading William James' *Talk to Teachers* (1902) brought together in my mind a cascade of memories from the hours I had spent observing classrooms. That accounts for why I wrote *Teaching as a Performing Art* (1999). Teaching is not and cannot be a science, although science can be helpful in offering ideas and data that are psychologically absorbed, transformed in ways characteristic of a teacher's individual style or what James calls "genius." Dewey expressed the same idea when he said that knowledge is impersonal but it is only when knowledge in some way becomes related to something in your personal experience with the sense that you possess and own it, that knowledge becomes knowing.

As I point out in my book, recognizing that teaching is a performing art has enormous implications for how you select individuals who wish to become teachers and how once you have selected them you nurture those of their characteristics that lead you to believe that they would make good teachers. The Julliard School and kindred schools of music do not admit students because they very much want to become performing artists; by means of auditions they are looking for signs that the applicants have or may have the personal ingredients to become a performing artist. This is almost the polar opposite of the practices of teacher preparatory programs.

I have never heard or read of anyone in or out of the educational arena who voices even a hint of disagreement with the statement that we have no cause to be satisfied with the quality of teaching, a statement which some people regard as charitable in the extreme. A few years ago the refrain was "We need more qualified teachers." In the last year or so the refrain is "We need *better* qualified teachers." What is meant by *better* and *qualified* is never defined. All that has happened is that teachers are obliged to take more courses to firm up their grasp of subject matter, as if the correlation between the level of knowledge of subject matter and quality and effectiveness of teaching is high, which is clearly not the case. No one is against a deep understanding of subject matter. What gets almost totally lost by those who should know better is the recognition and implications of the obvious fact that teaching is a performing art.

The point of all this is that all reform efforts are handicapped from the get-go because teacher preparatory programs do not consider teaching a performing art and do not select or train their students with that as a guiding goal. And if and when vouchers as a policy are adopted and new schools are created to meet the demand, their accomplishments will be diminished for the same reasons the reform efforts of public schools have been so paltry. It is not enough for a voucher policy to be justified only on economic or treasured political values. They are necessary but not sufficient unless it can be demonstrated that students experience the learning context as personally meaningful and intellectually rewarding now and for their futures. The achievement of that goal depends on the teacher, about whom voucher advocates have nothing to say. From Professor Friedman's writings on education I conclude that besides being a creative, fertile thinker he is reasonable, nondogmatic, and knows that implementation of a voucher policy will encounter problems. Unfortunately, he does not recognize problems that I consider crucial, predictable, and as potentially lethal to a voucher policy as they have been to reform efforts to improve learning in the public schools. I would heartily support carefully described and evaluated pilot studies from which we may get answers, if only partial, which justify proceeding further.

Chapter Twelve

What Can People Become?

Regardless of what you consider the goals of education, what you believe is good teaching, what indices of learning you think are appropriate, or what kind of substance and organization of a curriculum you think is consistent with goals and purposes, there is one question you have asked and answered, albeit the answer you give may be accompanied by the belief that the answer is indisputably true, on one extreme, or range to the other extreme that you really do not feel that you can answer the question because it implicates a host of interrelated factors for which neither you nor anybody else has persuasively employed an answer. The question is, What are people capable of learning? Put it this way: We cannot deny that people vary considerably in how well and fast they learn this or that task or subject matter. So we ask ourselves how we explain these *individual* differences? You can ask that same question about *group* differences. Why, for example, *as a group* is the average score of blacks on intelligence and achievement tests lower than that of whites? Anyone familiar with the history of the nature-nurture controversy knows the strong passions these controversies aroused when they erupted, for the very good reason that explanations confirm or refute, in whole or in part, your belief in what people are and can become and, therefore, what practical actions you advocate or disdain. The passions are such that the participants and the general public cannot recognize that from an ethical-moral standpoint it makes no difference what your explanation of group differences is because no one disputes the obvious fact that by no means do all white people get scores higher than all black people. So we are still left with the obligation to explain individual differences. I consider it unethical and immoral to use group differences, especially since there is obvious overlap between the groups, as a basis for how you will be set to see, relate to, and seek to influence the next member of the groups about whom you will be making judgments. Anyone who needs confirmation of the dynamics of the self-fulfilling prophecy should read Dr. Rhona Weinstein's recent book on how the self-fulfilling prophecy works in schools (2003). Let me give you three examples of the point I am trying to make here because you do not need to know the research literature, it is that obvious.

The first is what I have called the quarterback problem. Up until two or three decades ago there were no black quarterbacks on professional football teams. From football's earliest beginnings up until today the nature and complexity of offensive strategies of the game require not only physical skills but also cognitive skills of a high order. And no position more than the quarterback rivals the cognitive skills a person should possess: prodigious memory, ability to "read" and exploit the opponent's defensive strategies, ability to keep track of the game clock at crucial points, foresight, and staying alert to exercise judgment to employ plays that will surprise the enemy. I venture the opinion that if you could compare the cognitive skills a quarterback should or is expected to possess with those of a chess player contemplating moves, you would be struck with how similar they are. If you watch pro football games on TV and a celebrated and cerebral John Madden displays on the screen a diagram explaining why a particular play succeeded or failed, that diagram resembles a chessboard.

It was an open secret that coaches (all white) and owners (all white) did not believe blacks could be good quarterbacks because the cognitive demands of that position were not likely to be found in blacks, who may pass muster in college football but not on the professional level. They could be linemen, where bulk, brawn, and speed were all important, but these attributes were not crucial for the most important position on the team. That argument has been settled, of course. But that is not why I used this example.

Let us imagine a scenario in which someone devises a way to measure and compare professional black and white quarterbacks on the level and quality of their cognitive attributes by combining the measures into a total score so that we can say whether on average the groups of white and black quarterbacks are or are not equally good. And let us also imagine that he finds a statistical difference favoring whites. Not a huge difference but still a statistically significant one.

What significances can be deduced from such a finding? It is not relevant to my purposes here to answer the question in any detail because to me what is most significant is that the study demonstrated that there are many blacks who could do something many people thought unlikely or even impossible. Thirty years from now a replication of the study might find no differences or differences favoring blacks. It could also find that the differences favoring whites have increased; I would not advise anyone to bet on it. So why, then, would I rejoice at the results of the first study? Because it is grist for the mill of my belief that we know far less than we think we know about how contexts determine what people can become, which of them have enabling or disabling effects. Yes, I know it is "only" a belief which I cannot prove but it is a belief that explains why I regard the need to distinguish between the features of productive and unproductive learning to be the most important problem in education, and why the too-few studies which took those differences seriously are so important to me.

The second example is nothing less than human history. One perspective from which you can describe that history is the struggle for individual freedom as we know, define, and experience it today in perhaps a score of countries represented in the United Nations. For millennia, individual freedom was not an issue because rulers considered it obvious that their masses were unthinking, immature, ignorant, stupid globs to whom a divine providence had given rulers to control, direct, and protect them. The masses may have bemoaned their predetermined fate but they accepted it. Who were they to claim, receive, and enjoy the gift of civic responsibility and freedom? At the 1787 Constitutional Convention the founding fathers, who well knew the history of the struggle for freedom, were very concerned about whether the people of the new nation would have the wisdom and courage to do justice to the freedoms accorded them. They were crystal clear about what they believed freedom would enable people to become but they had their doubts. The events of the twentieth century would not have erased their doubts or even lessened them. The obvious point is that the concept of individual freedom is relatively new in human history and that it is an indulgence of hubris to assume that we have learned all we need to know in order to answer the question of what people can become. When you read what the founding fathers, especially Jefferson, said about the necessity of education as a way of protecting freedom, it is more insightful and stimulating than what their counterparts say today because their goal was to achieve an education that would be judged by more than graduation rates and test scores. If there was a way of telling the founding fathers the percentage of people who vote in elections, they would turn over in their graves. (I know you can't blame that solely on education.) If you observed the modal American classroom for, say, a week and you were then asked, "What did you observe that was relevant to a student's experience and understanding of individual freedom?" your answer would be very brief. John Dewey said that schooling is not a preparation for life, it is life. Dewey did not have a felicitous writing style, as William James did, but that sentence of his packs more relevance for schooling than any other sentence written since, whether by educators or anyone else.

What bearing does a voucher policy have for the question of what people are capable of becoming? Such a policy has more than one goal in the short or long term, but certainly one of those goals is the expectation that it will increase the chances that children will demonstrate that their capabilities are greater than their previous schooling had suggested; they could climb higher on the ladder of accomplishment. Professor Friedman rightly refers to the success of the GI Bill for returning World War II veterans, a voucher program that was probably the most ambitious such policy ever. Here are some of the features of that bill.[1]

1. If a returning veteran could not find work, he could receive twenty dollars a week for fifty-two weeks. (In today's dollar that would be at least eight or more times larger.)

2. Regardless of previous education or vocation, a veteran, for purposes of more education or retraining, could enroll in any state-accredited institution which would accept him. The choice was totally that of the veteran and in no way fettered by state or federal government.

3. The federal government would pay the tuition, fees, and a monthly living allowance. If the veteran was married and had children that allowance would be larger.

---

1. In several of my books I have said that it is scandalous that the consequences of that bill were never systematically studied. The recent book by Bennett (1996) is the first meticulous description and discussion of the legislative history of the bill, the political-philosophical stances of its proponents and opponents, and why the Bonus March on Washington in 1932 by disgruntled World War I veterans, plus the Great Depression of the 1930s, were very much in the picture. Bennett's book is a must for anyone opposed to or in favor of a voucher policy today.

4. If the veteran wanted to purchase a house, even without a down payment, the government would guarantee the mortgage in case of default. (This was one of the major factors of the building boom and the rise of suburbia.)

Bennett cites many anecdotes and small studies testifying to what no one has ever disputed: the GI Bill not only transformed the lives of veterans, most of whom never expected they would ever be able to go to college, but also the larger society as well. The country as we know it today is unexplainable apart from the role of the GI Bill. The historian Stephen Ambrose has said that it was the single most important legislation of the twentieth century. One should not gloss over the fact that opponents of the bill feared that poorly educated, intellectually mediocre (or worse) veterans would enter colleges and universities and, therefore, a measure of ability should be employed as a screening device. President Conant of Harvard and President Hutchins of the University of Chicago initially opposed the bill on that score not only because it would be a failing experience for many veterans but because it would also adversely affect the ability of those institutions to devote their resources and time to the education of able students. Bennett presents arguments by other opponents of this bill who regarded the mass of veterans as intellectually and socially ill equipped to make career- and, therefore, life-determining choices.

Bennett discusses an account by Keister of twelve veterans who had been graduated in the high school class of 1944 in the factory town of Turtle Creek in Pennsylvania, and fifty years later had a class reunion. He starts with Les Faulk.

Faulk was one of twelve Turtle Creek High School graduates that Edwin Keister Jr. interviewed for an article in *Smithsonian Magazine* in 1994, a class that was a microcosm of hundreds of thousands of others. The young man who left high school in 1944 expecting to become no more than a steel mill stoker or an armature winder instead spent thirty-eight years as a teacher and an elementary school principal. Les Faulk had not only gone to college, he also had acquired both a bachelor's and a master's degree and several credits toward his doctorate, even though the name on his high school diploma was "Falcocchio." That name—and his decision to change it—was significant. In those days, being the son of an Italian immigrant family with a "foreign" name could be almost as much a barrier to getting into college as a black skin. "College," as Faulk recalled fifty years later, "was for teachers' kids and the preacher's kids. For the rest of us, with names like Tarantini and Trkula, it was a distant dream."

Faulk and his classmates in Mrs. Whittum's American history class had been urged to believe that that dream, no matter how distant, could come true for them. But the hopes held out in school didn't stand up very well to the living and working conditions Faulk and his classmates grew up in. Turtle Creek was a factory town where half the male students dropped out of high school. Only 5 percent went on to any kind of postsecondary education, even barber or secretarial school, the latter being one of the few avenues to white-collar work then pursued by men as well as women. The war and the GI Bill changed everything. Faulk, like millions of other young Americans sent off to war, grew up fast in a foxhole. That alone might have made it difficult to accept what Turtle Creek had to offer when he came back home, even with a job awaiting him as an apprentice bricklayer, a job arranged by his father. That wasn't the reason he quit after one day, though, throwing away an opportunity for a skilled, well-paid, and prestigious job at the time. He had heard of the GI Bill, and he had made a decision. "I went to the poolroom and told my old boss, 'I'm going to college.' He said, 'I read that only one vet in 20 who enters college will finish.' I said, 'I'm going to be that one.'" The government had turned him into a soldier who had helped beat the best the German army had to offer; now the same government thought he had the makings of a college graduate. Who was he to argue?

Faulk wasn't alone. Among the eleven other graduates of Turtle Creek High School who joined him at the fiftieth reunion of the Class of '44 were an aerospace engineer, a federal judge, a microchip engineer, a professor of law who is also a research scientist, and an engineer specializing in military survival techniques. The title of one classic book about the war, *Catch-22*, has entered the language as a shorthand expression for the insanity of war; the title of another book by the same author, Joseph Heller, sums up what occurred to those who came back, *Something Happened*.

I began teaching in the university in 1945. I had friends who were teaching in colleges and universities around the country. I had also come to know older faculty at Yale and elsewhere who had been teaching before World War II. They all had stories to tell identical to Keister's. In later years we would get together and shmooze about the past; as one of them said, "The ten years after the GI Bill are an instance of the good old days truly being good."

How to explain the consequences of that legislation? What is their relevance for today's proposal for school vouchers? There is no simple explanation and Bennett does not offer one. But among the diverse factors that an explanation must consider is one that Bennett almost practically-lyrically discusses, which is directly relevant to what I have said in these pages. That factor is wrapped up in the phrase *wanting to learn*, a wanting in veterans that was an intense fire that could not be extinguished. Their stance could be put this way: "Tell me what I have to learn and do to become what I want to become, which before the war I could only dream about, the stuff of fantasy; I will make the dreams come true." The title of Bennett's book is *When Dreams Come True*, a title that does justice to the veteran's phenomenology. It was not easy for many of them but they did not complain about long days reading and studying in their room and the library, or about large classes and instructors whose teaching style left much to be desired, or about the length of time it would take them to become what they wanted to become. They were not alone, they were surrounded by other veterans seizing the opportunity, intent on making their dreams of becoming come true. Please note that I am not saying they were happy but rather that they were serious and goal oriented as no other cohort of students has ever been. They had a picture of a future, dramatically different from their pasts, and the present was essential to making that future real.

Of all the factors always present in the learning process I consider the strength of wanting to learn to be the most fateful. That is why, beginning years ago, I would pose this question to groups of parents and educators: "When your child is graduated from high school, what is the one characteristic you hope your child has? There is, of course, more than one characteristic you consider important but is there one you consider as of overarching importance?" People have difficulty answering the question. When I give my answer, their agreement has been nearly unanimous: I want my child to *want* to learn more because she knows she needs to know more, not because parents or someone else requires it but because that is what makes life interesting.

The transforming effects of the GI Bill cannot be attributed solely to the single fact that it was clearly a voucher policy, period. It was a voucher policy for a cohort of adults who were shaped by the Great Depression, who participated in a war, to whom a grateful society was expressing its gratitude. It was a society aware of its failure to respond appropriately to World War I veterans and it was a society fearful of the economic and social consequences of a flood of returning World War II veterans. Those favoring the bill never expected that several millions of veterans would take advantage of it and, therefore, mightily increase the costs of it. They vastly underestimated how many veterans would seize the opportunity to make dreams come true. (By the time of the Korean and Vietnam wars the benefits of the bill had been scaled down for reasons Bennett discusses.)

This GI bill was a voucher policy for and under the control of veterans; they would make the choices. A policy for school vouchers is for a parent who wants what they hope will be a better education for their child. The strength of "parental wanting" cannot be assumed to be matched by the strength of the wanting of their children. Indeed, the advocates for school vouchers make clear that vouchers will make it possible for poor parents to take their children from failing or inadequate schools to more effective ones, and in an undetermined number of instances their children neither liked nor were learning in those original schools. *That is reason enough for a school voucher policy. But that does not mean that the strength of wanting to learn will magically increase in children who are removed from a failing or inadequate school.* Students are not puppets. They, like the rest of us, do not always take kindly to being put in a new setting whose rules, traditions, and members are totally strange. So much depends on how well those members identify and take appropriate steps to dilute the child's insecurities and fears. This, of course, is especially important for a child of color. This is but another way of saying that if the adult members of the setting have little or no understanding of the context of productive learning, the child's wanting to learn may be decreased. Anyone who has had the clinical responsibility to treat children experiencing conflict with a new stepmother or stepfather will grasp the import of what I am trying to convey. (My clinical experience has been largely with children. My colleagues who worked with adults remind me that what I have said is no less true of the stepmothers and stepfathers who seek help in understanding why they are having difficulties with their "new" children.)

What are we entitled to learn from a voucher policy using public funds? As one in favor of a voucher policy, am I being unreasonable to ask if the implementation of such a policy will be accompanied by a clear and careful evaluation process that includes but goes beyond tables of test scores and can be a source of ideas for how to improve the effectiveness of a voucher policy? Who will pay for such a research program, which should not be done on the cheap? Have we learned nothing from corporate scandals of recent years when the "inside story" was one thing and what the public was told (too late) was quite another thing? Leave criminal acts aside, what about sheer ineptitude of the kind which so many public schools are accused of monopolizing? Evaluation is not regulation, its purpose is to provide information to consumers of education. There are companies whose sole purpose is to test and compare new products for their good and bad, healthy and unhealthy, features and present their findings to the public. Professor Friedman is no ideologue incapable of acknowledging that the free market comes with a price. His position rightly is that on balance the free market's virtues are greater than its vices, and that will be the case with school vouchers. But does it make me a doomer and a gloomer to suggest that in the case of a policy of school vouchers which may come to affect many children, we should feel morally obligated to evaluate (not, I must emphasize, regulate) such a policy, which can give us credible evidence indicating that on balance its negative features are outweighed by the positive? I have been in the educational arena too long to unreflectively put school vouchers on the top of the hit parade of educational reforms.

Postscript

Mr. Rogers' Neighborhood

I finished writing this book a couple of days after the death of Fred McFeely Rogers on February 28, 2003. For thirty-three years he was Mister Rogers in the TV children's program *Mister Rogers' Neighborhood*. The obituary in the *New York Times* began on the first page and occupied a full inside page, an allotment of space usually given to people of national or international renown. On and off the screen he was a soft-spoken, relaxed person, the polar opposite of what is conventionally meant by the label *entertainer*. There was not a hint of condescension in the way he talked to his young viewers, most of whom were below the age of six, not a whiff of an adult talking down to them. And what did he talk about? Damn near everything: anger, jealousy, self-esteem, divorce, illness, curiosity, self-control, etc. He wrote songs like the following:

> What do you do with the mad that you feel
> When you feel so mad you could bite?
> When the whole wide world seems oh, so wrong
> And nothing you do seems very right?
> What do you do? Do you punch a bag?
> Do you pound some clay or some dough?
> Do you round up friends for a game of tag?
> Or see how fast you can go?
> It's great to be able to stop
> When you've planned a thing that's wrong.

Mr. Rogers had all of the characteristics of a teacher who understood how to create and sustain a context of productive learning. Early in the 1990s C-SPAN televised an address he gave at the National Press Club in Washington. He did something during his address which I have to assume reflected his understanding that words alone take second place to *seeing* such a context. He related to his audience that five years earlier he had been in Washington, and he went down to the hotel's dining room for breakfast. He sat down, looked around him, and saw a couple with a child waving at him. He walked to their table and saw that their six-year-old son was handicapped and in a wheelchair: He had no use of his legs, limited use of his arms, but he was alert and bright. They were avid viewers of *Mister Rogers' Neighborhood*, and they were from Wisconsin. They talked. Mr. Rogers and the family began a correspondence. When Jeff was eleven, Mr. Rogers invited him to come to Pittsburgh and appear on his program. Jeff came in on his electric-motored wheelchair. The conversation that followed was a model of sensitivity, spontaneity, humor, and self-revelation. I venture to say that no person, child or adult, who saw the episode felt any pity for Jeff but rather admiration and respect for his gutsiness, liveliness, and something akin to aplomb. He was having a ball! He was talking to Mr. Rogers! You could talk about anything to Mr. Rogers because Mr. Rogers understood, he listened, you could trust him.

It is too simple to say that Mr. Rogers understood how children think and feel about themselves and their world. Understanding is one thing, a very necessary one, but unless it is wedded or embedded in a personal style that engenders the feeling of trust or safety, the chances that you will learn from and be able to help a child are reduced. Jeff *wanted* to be with and talk to Mr. Rogers. The video with Jeff reminded me of the movie *Mr. Holland's Opus*. It is about a beginning teacher in a high school. The first half of the film depicts a context of unproductive learning; the second half depicts a productive context of learning. It is the second half that reminded me of Mr. Rogers with Jeff: Mr. Holland learned how and why he had to listen and hear what his students were saying through their words and body language. He unlearned all that he had been told about teaching.

Finally, Mr. Rogers' video reminded me of the two cases I described in Chapter 2 of this book. How did Jeff's parents rear him to become a bright, alert, engaging human being? The only answer that makes sense to me is that they created the conditions wherein he could learn, grow, flourish. They looked and went beyond his incapacities. They are special people for the same reasons Mr. Rogers was special, and by *special* I do not mean that few people could do what they did: there are far more than a few people who have done or are doing or could learn to do what they did. They are special in the sense that they had a conception of what children needed and wanted that obliged them to use themselves in ways consistent with that conception. It was not a conception given them by their genes. In ways about which we know too little they were exposed to and absorbed a conception of learning compatible with their own experience as learners.

Teaching is not a science, it is an art fusing ideas, obligations, the personal and interpersonal. The chemistry of that fusion determines whether or how subject matter matters to the student.

Bibliography

Aiken, W. A. (1942). *The Story of the Eight Year Study with Conclusions and Recommendations*. New York: HarperCollins.

Bennett, M. J. (1996). *When Dreams Come True*. Washington, D.C.: Brassey.

Bensman, D. (2000). *Central Park East and Its Graduates*. New York: Teachers Press.

Brody, J. (2002). "No Proof of Value." Health Section, New York Times.

Cohen, E. A. (2002). *Supreme Command*. New York: The Free Press.

Dewey, J. (1960). *The Quest for Certainty*. New York: Putnam.

Flexner, A. (1960). *Medical Education in the United States and Canada*. Washington, D.C.: The Carnegie Foundation for the Advancement of Teaching. (Originally published in 1910).

Friedman, M. (1962). *Capitalism and Freedom*. Chicago: University of Chicago Press.

Goodlad, J. (1984). *A Place Called School*. New York: McGraw-Hill.

Heckman, P., et al. (1995). *The Courage to Change*. Newbury Park, CA: Corwin Press.

Hulbert, A. (2003). *Raising America. Experts, Parents, and a Century of Advice about Children*. New York: Knopf.

Johnson, A. L. (1947). *A Treatise on Language*. Berkeley: University of California Press. (Originally published in 1836).

Kamii, C. and R. D. DeVries. (1978). *Physical Knowledge in Preschool Education. Implications of Piaget's Theory*. Englewood Cliffs, NJ: Prentice-Hall.

Keister, E. (1994). "The G.I. Bill May Have Been the Best Deal Made by Uncle Sam." *Smithsonian* Magazine, November.

Koch, K. (1970). *Wishes, Lies, and Dreams. Teaching Children to Write Poetry.* New York: Chelsea House.

————. (1977). *I Never Told Anybody. Teaching Poetry Writing in a Nursing Home.* New York: Random House.

Levine, E. (2001). *One Kid at a Time. Big Issues from a Small School.* New York: Teachers College Press.

Ravitch, D. (2000). *Left Back. A Century of Failed School Reform.* New York: Simon and Schuster.

Sarason, S. B. (1976). "The Unfortunate Fate of Alfred Binet and School Psychology." *Teachers College Record*, Vol. 77, 579–592.

————. (1977a). *The Challenge of Art to Psychology.* New Haven: Yale University Press.

————. (1977b). *Work, Aging, and Social Change.* New York: The Free Press.

————. (1985). *Psychology and Mental Retardation—Perspectives in Change.* Austin, TX: Pro-Ed.

————. (1988). *The Making of an American Psychologist.* San Francisco, CA: Jossey-Bass.

————. (1993a). *The Case for Change. Rethinking the Preparation of Educators.* San Francisco, CA: Jossey-Bass.

————. (1993b). *Letters to a Serious Education President.* Newbury Park, CA: Corwin Press.

————. (1994). *Psychoanalysis, General Custer, and the Verdicts of History.* (Chapter 11). San Francisco, CA: Jossey-Bass.

————. (1995). *Parental Involvement and the Political Principle.* San Francisco, CA: Jossey-Bass.

————. (1996a). *Barometers of Social Change.* San Francisco, CA: Jossey-Bass.

————. (1996b). *Revisiting the Culture of the School and the Problem of Change.* New York: Teachers College Press.

————. (1998). *Charter Schools. Another Flawed Educational Effort?* New York: Teachers College Press.

————. (1999). *Teaching as a Performing Art.* New York: Teachers College Press.

————. (2001). *American Psychology and Schools. A Critique.* New York: Teachers College Press.

————. (2002a). *Charter Schools and Vouchers.* Portsmouth, NH: Heinemann.

————. (2002b). *Educational Reform. A Self-Scrutinizing Memoir.* New York: Teachers College Press.

Sarason, S. B., et al. (1960). *Anxiety in Elementary School Children*. New York: John Wiley.

Sarason, S. B. and E. Lorentz. (1989). *The Challenge of the Resource Exchange Rationale*. Cambridge, MA: Brookline Press. (Originally published in 1979.)

————. (1998). *Crossing Boundaries*. San Francisco, CA: Jossey-Bass.

Shirley, D. (1997). *Community Organizing for Urban School Reform*. Austin, TX: University of Texas Press.

Steinberg, L. B., et al. (1996). *Beyond the Classroom*. New York: Simon and Schuster.

Susskind, D. (1969). Questioning and Curiosity in the Elementary School Classroom. Ph.D. Dissertation, Yale University.

Todd, C. L. and R. Sonkin. (1977). *Alexander Bryan Johnson: Philosophical Banker*. Syracuse, NY: Syracuse University Press.

Trubowitz, S., et al. (1984). *When a College Collaborates with a School*. Institute for Responsive Education: Boston University.

Trubowitz, S. and P. Longo. (1997). *How It Works. Inside a School–College Collaboration*. New York: Teachers College Press.

Weinstein, R. (2003). *Reaching Higher*. Cambridge, MA: Harvard University Press.

Wertheimer, M. (1945). *Productive Thinking*. New York: Harpers.